This book by Pierre Macherey is his first dealing with literature and theory since his seminal *A Theory of Literary Production*. Continuing the project of Althusserian theory, Macherey engages in a series of close exegeses of classical texts in French literature and philosophy, from the late eighteenth century down to the 1970s, that explore the historically variable but thematically similar ways in which literary texts represent philosophical *topoi* in an unmediated manner, Macherey shows the conceptual sophistication — and broad intellectual influence — that literary art has displayed in the modern period. At once a theoretical meditation of great originality and a historical work of scrupulous scholarship, *The Object of Literature* will entrench Pierre Macherey's already considerable reputation as one of the most significant contemporary theoreticians of literature.

The object of literature

❖❖❖

General editors

RICHARD MACKSEY, *The Johns Hopkins University*

and MICHAEL SPRINKER, *State University of New York at Stony Brook*

The Cambridge *Literature, Culture, Theory* series is dedicated to theoretical studies in the human sciences that have literature and culture as their object of enquiry. Acknowledging the contemporary expansion of cultural studies and the redefinitions of literature that this has entailed, the series includes not only original works of literary theory but also monographs and essay collections on topics and seminal figures from the long history of theoretical speculation on the arts and human communication generally. The concept of theory embraced in the series is broad, including not only the classical disciplines of poetics and rhetoric, but also those of aesthetics, linguistics, psychoanalysis, semiotics, and other cognate sciences that have inflected the systematic study of literature during the past half century.

The object of literature

❖❖❖

PIERRE MACHEREY

University of Lille-III

Translated from the French by David Macey

CAMBRIDGE
UNIVERSITY PRESS

Published by the Press Syndicate of the University of Cambridge
The Pitt Building, Trumpington Street, Cambridge, CB2 1RP
40 West 20th Street, New York, NY 10011-4211, USA
10 Stamford Road, Oakleigh, Melbourne 3166, Australia

Originally published in French as *A quoi pense la littérature* by Presses Universitaires de France
1990 and © Presses Universitaires de France

First published in English by Cambridge University Press 1995 as *The object of literature*

English translation © Cambridge University Press 1995

Printed in Great Britain at the University Press, Cambridge

A catalogue record for this book is available from the British Library

Library of Congress cataloguing in publication data

Macherey, Pierre
[A quoi pense la littérature? English]
The object of literature / Pierre Macherey.
p. cm. – (Literature, culture, theory: 14)
Includes bibliographical references and index.
ISBN 0 521 41955 7 (hardback)
ISBN 0 521 47678 x (paperback)
1. French literature – History and criticism – Theory, etc. 2. Literature – Philosophy. I.
Title. II. Series.
PQ45.M313 1995
840.9–dc20 94-15012 CIP

ISBN 0 521 41955 7 hardback
ISBN 0 521 47678 x paperback

Hardback edition
at paperback
price

Contents

Contents

MICHAEL SPRINKER

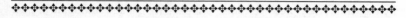

Foreword

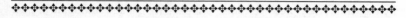

An English-speaking audience may be pardoned for wondering what ever became of Pierre Macherey. After the translation in the mid-1970s of his youthful *Pour une théorie de la production littéraire*, little of his work appeared in English. A few articles in coterie journals like *The Minnesota Review*, *Diacritics*, and *Sub-stance*, but no other books. The same audience might also, with this new translation before them, take away the impression that Macherey's work has primarily been in literature all along, even if the author is quite clearly identified here as a philosophy teacher at the University of Lille. Yet those who have followed the trajectory of Althusserianism – an ambiguous desig-nation whose use here I shall attempt to justify later on – know only that Macherey was one of the contributors to the original *Lire 'le Capital'* (1965), but that he has written much more in philosophy than in literature. Even a brief listing of some of his major writings in French discloses the true focus of his work since the mid-1960s: *Hegel ou Spinoza* (1979); with Jean-Pierre Lefebvre, *Hegel et la société* (1984); *Comte, la philosophie et les sciences* (1989); *Avec Spinoza* (1992). Macherey was trained in, and has in fact principally written about, philosophy, both the classical tradition and its reverberations in modern France (he has published notable essays on Lacan, Foucault, Deleuze and Canguilhem).

And yet, as the present collection, composed of essays written during the 1980s, illustrates, Macherey's early interest in literature as a site for theoretical investigation has scarcely waned. *The Object of Literature* returns to the question posed, but scarcely answered, by *A Theory of Literary Production*: what is the object to be studied, analysed, explained in a yet-to-be constructed science of literature? In an influential essay on Macherey's earlier writings, Terry Eagleton summarized the original Machereyan project in literature thus:

For Macherey, the literary object is determinate, and so can be the object of rational study. It is the effect of a specific labour, the product of a writer who

ix

does not fabricate the materials with which he works ... Those materials are not neutral, and so spontaneously assimilable to a unity imposed upon them by the writer; they preserve, rather, a specific weight and autonomy of their own ... The necessity of the text — which is precisely what renders it *readable*, yields us a determinate object of analysis — inheres ... in the fact that the text *produces itself* — unfolds and activates its multiple lines of meaning without conformity to 'intention', pre-given normative model or external reality. The task of criticism is to discover in each text the laws of that self-production, or (what amounts to the same thing) the conditions of a work's possibility ... [1]

This Macherey has often been charged (by among others Eagleton himself) with being a formalist,[2] while in a somewhat later incarnation, he is said to have succumbed to the opposite errors of functionalism and reductionism.[3] Doubtless, both sets of indictments will re-surface in response to the present volume. Warrant for each can be found. For example, the formalist Macherey appears virtually without adornment in the following passage from the essay on Céline:

We must abandon the attempt to look behind literature's statements for the other discourse of which it is the distorted and deformed expression, and which constitutes its authentic meaning. For if literature does deal with truth, the truth in question has no value other than that conferred upon it by literature. It is the truth of its style. Literature establishes a real stylistics of depth rather than a metaphysics, and stylistics is in itself a partial substitute for philosophy. (p. 132 below)

Or consider the following lapidary observation from the programmatic essay that brings the book to a close: 'In the final instance, all literary texts have as their object — and this seems to be their real "philosophy" — the non-adhesion of language to language to language, the gap that constantly divides what we say from what we say about it and what we think about it' (p. 234 below). From Roman Jackobson to Roland Barthes, the specificity of literary language has been the mark of that 'literariness' which Macherey has elsewhere

1   Terry Eagleton, 'Macherey and Marxist Literary Theory', *The Minnesota Review* (Fall 1975); rpt. in Eagleton, *Against the Grain: Selected Essays* (London: Verso, 1986), pp. 11, 13.

2   See ibid., p. 18; and also Terry Eagleton, *Criticism and Ideology* (London: NLB, 1976), pp. 83–4.

3   See Eagleton, 'Macherey and Marxist Literary Theory', p. 20. Eagleton bases this interpretation on two articles: Etienne Balibar and Pierre Macherey, 'On Literature as an Ideological Form', originally published in French as the introduction to Renée Balibar, *Le Français fictifs* (Paris: Hachette, 1974); and Macherey, 'On Reflection', *Sub-stance* 15 (1976), 6–20.

been at such great pains to deny is even a proper category for articulating literature's objectivity.

But consider the following formulation:

the objectivity of literature is its necessary place within the determinate processes and reproduction of the contradictory linguistic practices of the common tongue, in which the effectivity of the ideology of bourgeois education is realised.

This siting of the problem abolishes the old idealist question, 'What is literature?', which is not a question about its universal essence, human and artistic. It abolishes it because it shows us directly the material function of literature, inserted within a process which literature cannot determine even though it is indispensable to it.[4]

Plainly it is possible to construe Macherey's pronouncements on literary language in other than a formalist manner, viz., in the materialist spirit in which, one surmises, he intended them. There is indeed such a thing as 'literary language', distinct from and in a sense derivative of ordinary language. Its existence issues less from the intrinsic properties of literary texts, than from a system of social stratification that trains certain readers to identify (and identify with) literature, while consigning others to the lower ranks of mere users of the *lingua franca*. *Pace* Eagleton, there is no inherent contradiction between the ostensible formalism of the early (and also the most recent) Macherey and the sociological criticism Macherey produced in the mid-1970s. The task of formal analysis is to expose the contradictions in a text's linguistic practices that sociological investigation demonstrates to be constitutive of literature as an ideological apparatus.

Compatible, then, with these two earlier Machereys, *The Object of Literature* nonetheless stages the literary problematic somewhat differently. It brings together in a single speculative project the philosophical and the literary. These essays all concern the ways in which literature and philosophy, representation and concepts, are intimately entwined in a range of texts from Sade and Mme de Staël to Queneau and Foucault. The relationship between these two domains is conveniently summarized in the following passage from the essay on Hugo:

4 Balibar and Macherey, 'On Literature as an Ideological Form', trans. Ian McLeod et al., *Oxford Literary Review* 3,1 (1978); rpt. in Robert Young, ed., *Untying the Text: A Post-Structuralist Reader* (London: Routledge and Kegan Paul, 1981), p. 86.

By comparing texts borrowed from Marx or Tocqueville with texts written by Sue or Hugo, and by demonstrating that comparable schemas of representation are at work in them, we are not attempting to deny the originality of their content by arguing that, ultimately, everything is mere literature; the point is to call attention to that content by showing how fictional texts can, in their own way, not only convey but produce forms of speculation which are directly expressive of a determinate historical reality. They allow us both to understand it and to imagine it. (p. 109 below)

The concept of literature scouted here is in line both with the so-called 'formalist Macherey', and with the much-vilified passage from Althusser's 'Letter on Art' that almost certainly inspired it.[5] Literature is not history (or science or philosophy), but it stands in a quite particular relation to the historical materials out of which it produces its specific mode of existence.

What is the nature of that relation? Macherey remains an utterly impenitent Althusserian on this point, which he puts most directly near the end of the present book:

The problematical thought which runs through all literary texts is rather like the philosophical consciousness of a historical period. The role of literaure is to say what a period thinks of itself. The age of literature, from Sade to Céline, does not project an ideological message which demands to be believed on the basis of the actual evidence. If taken literally, the message seems to be patently inconsistent and incoherent. It projects an outline sketch of its own limits, and that sketch is inseparable from the introduction of a relativist perspective. What, from this point of view, is the philosophical contribution of literature? It makes it possible to relocate all the discourses of philosophy, in its accredited forms, within the historical element which makes them the results of chance and circumstances, the products of a pathetic and magnificent throw of the dice. (p. 234 below)

No one trained in the history of philosophy is likely to miss the way in which a certain Hegelianism has been turned on its head in this passage. According to Macherey, it is not philosophy that paints its grey at the end of an epoch, but literature that exhibits the self-consciousness of an age. In a much-cited – if seldom understood – passage, Hegel opined that art 'is and remains for us a thing of the

---

5   See Louis Althusser, 'A Letter on Art in Reply to André Daspre', in Althusser, *Lenin and Philosophy and Other Essays*, trans. Ben Brewster (New York: Monthly Review Press, 1971), pp. 221–4. The passage has been criticized by Eagleton in *Criticism and Ideology*. For a more sympathetic reading, see Michael Sprinker, *Imaginary Relations* (London: Verso, 1987), pp. 271–4.

past'.[6] Macherey takes up Hegel's point, while giving it a characteristically Althusserian twist. Art is a thing of the past in the same
way that historical science can be said to expose to view the
ideological (and other social) structures of a social form on its way to
extinction. The literature of the bourgeois epoch – in Macherey's
view there has never been any other – brings that epoch's ideological
contradictions into plain view. We are not so far here from Marx's
and Engels's celebration of Balzac, except that, as Macherey remarks
elsewhere, it is not only generic realism that is capable of laying bare
the contradictions of capitalist society: 'the idea of reflection correctly
understood teaches us that a product can very well be objective, i.e.,
determined by material reality, without being exact, i.e., conforming
to this reality or to our idea of reality: Kafka is no less objective than
Thomas Mann, even if he is differently so ...'[7]

If there ever was a functionalist Macherey – a description I hope to
have shown is open to challenge – he would appear to have been
given his quietus in the essays translated here. The ambiguities and
incoherences (for at least some of which Althusser himself was surely
responsible) that admittedly adhere to the term 'Althusserian' cannot,
for all that, disguise the fact that the research programme launched by
For Marx and *Reading 'Capital'* has been continued in many works by
his students and admirers.[8] That programme, which insisted, among
other things, on the necessity for any science to produce its object of
investigation, has been rejoined in *The Object of Literature*, with results
that will ultimately be judged not only by this book alone, but by the
future that it stimulates. If we may hazard a prediction, this project is
unlikely to be without issue.

6 G. W. F. Hegel, *Aesthetics: Lectures on Fine Art*, trans. T. M. Knox (Oxford:
   Clarendon Press, 1975), p. 11.
7 Macherey, 'The Problem of Reflection', p. 15.
8 For a preliminary assessment of Althusser's legacies in the human sciences,
   written twenty years on from Althusser's major interventions, see Gregory
   Elliott, *Althusser: The Detour of Theory* (London: Verso, 1987), pp. 330–5.

Bibliographical note

Chapters 4, 5 and 8 are based upon articles originally published as
'Corinne philosophe', *Europe* 193–4 (January 1987), 'Culture nationale
et culture cosmopolite chez Mme de Staël', in *Transferts* (Paris:
Editions Recherche sur les civilisations, 1988); 'Queneau scribe et
lecteur de Kojève', *Europe* 650–1 (June–July 1983); 'Raymond la
sagesse' in *Queneau aujourd'hui* (Paris: Editions Clancier-Guénaud,
1985); 'Figures de l'homme en bas', *Hermès* 2 (1988, Editions du
CNRS); 'Le Métro magique de Céline', *Siècle* 2 (Autumn 1986).

Chapters 3, 6 and 9 are based on papers read to the Groupe de
Recherche sur l'Histoire du Matérialisme, Université de Paris I.

❖❖

What is literature thinking about?

❖❖

Literature and philosophy entwined

Philosophie dürfte man eigentlich nur dichten: 'Philosophy ought really to be written only as a *poetic composition*.'[1] Heidegger could have written that sentence, and perhaps he did write it. It appears in a collection of fragmentary notes drafted by Wittgenstein, and if we read it in a critical perspective or look, so to speak, beneath the surface, it has an ironic ring to it. In another of these notes, Wittgenstein playfully recalls the example of Pascal admiring 'the beauty of a theorem in number theory; it's as though he were admiring a beautiful natural phenomenon'.[2] The truth is so beautiful, and it is still more beautiful to be recognized as true! In what appears to be the same vein, Wittgenstein also points out 'the queer resemblance between a philosophical investigation (perhaps especially in mathematics) and an aesthetic one', and adds, presumably in order to distance himself from the trustingly naive attitude that he elsewhere ascribes to Pascal, 'E.g. what is bad about this garment, how it should be, etc.'[3] Writing philosophy as a poetic composition would reduce philosophy to solving the problem of 'how it should be', and that problem is 'aesthetically' subordinated to judgements of taste.

To pursue this type of approach further, we might say that philosophy is mere literature, or that the truth about philosophy will ultimately be found in literature. It will be a silent truth that is relegated to the margins of its text. This is the thesis argued by Derrida: 'Metaphysics has erased within itself the fabulous scene that has produced it, the scene that nevertheless remains active and stirring, inscribed in white ink, an invisible design covered over in the

---

1 Ludwig Wittgenstein, *Culture and Value*, tr. Peter Winch (Oxford: Blackwell, 1980), 24e. The comment is dated 1933–34.   2 Ibid., 41e.
3 Ibid., 25e.

palimpsest.'[4] We might also say that the philosophical element in philosophy, or in other words its critical reflection on its own discourse, is in the last analysis a matter for literature, which in some sense defines the limits to which philosophy returns, as though to a secret origin where the speculative pretensions of pure and absolute thought founder.

To see literature as the repressed of philosophy is to invert the traditional hermeneutic position which sees literature as the site of an essential revelation, and which therefore assumes philosophy to be the unthought, or not-yet-thought, element in literature. This is a way of exorcising, by recalling its fictional nature, the myth that literature is filled with a meaning-content that has only to be grasped or unveiled for it to blossom, as though in the bright morning of its primal truth. It is also an admission that literary texts are so rarely traversed by allusive thought that it seems to be absent from them, to have been erased. To what extent can such thought figure in the discourse of literature as something incidental that can remain unnoticed without causing any major problems? Or does it necessarily contribute to the weaving of its texture? What form of thought is contained in literary texts, and can it be extracted from them? For if we recognize the truth of philosophy in literature, we must also find some truth, in the philosophical sense of the term, in literary writings.

'The clash between philosophy and literature does not need to be resolved. On the contrary, only if we think of it as permanent and new does it guarantee us that the sclerosis of words will not close over us like a sheet of ice.'[5] The debate between literature and philosophy seems always to have been circular. According to Diogenes Laërtius, the Pythagoreans accused the philosopher-poet Empedocles of having divulged the secrets of their sect by using poetic forms borrowed from Homer to make them public. Yet in his life of Plato, where he reports that, according to Alkimos, Plato derived 'much assistance' from the comic poet Epicharmus, Diogenes Laërtius himself cites these lines from Epicharmus: 'Another man will come, who'll strip my reasons/Of their poetic dress, and, clothing them/In other garments and with purple broidery/Will show them off; and being invincible/Will make

---

4 Jacques Derrida, 'White Mythology: Metaphor in the Text of Philosophy', in *Margins of Philosophy*, tr. Alan Bass (University of Chicago Press, 1982), p. 213.

5 Italo Calvino, 'Philosophy and Literature' in *The Literature Machine* (London: Picador, 1989), p. 40. This essay first appeared in *The Times Literary Supplement*, 28 September 1967 (special issue entitled 'Crosscurrents').

all rivals bow the knee to him.'[6] In the great debate between the exoteric and the esoteric, between the revealed and the hidden, philosophy and literature are caught up in a circular argument, rather as though one were constantly giving the other the initial impetus that set it in motion, and vice versa. By tracing the figure of 'Socrates as musician', Plato himself plunges *mythos* and *logos* into the same primal element.[7]

Literature and philosophy are inextricably entwined [*mêlées*].[8] Or at least they were until history established a sort of official division between the two. That occurred at the end of the eighteenth century, when the term 'literature' began to be used in its modern sense.[9] Diderot witnessed the turning point, which saw the disentanglement of literature and philosophy, and gave a nostalgic account of it, rather as though he himself were standing on a ledge that had been cut off by the break:

The wise man was once a philosopher, a poet and a musician. Those talents degenerated when they were divorced from one another; the sphere of philosophy became narrower; ideas deserted poetry; songs lost their force and energy; and, deprived of these organs, wisdom could no longer speak to the peoples with the same charm.[10]

---

6 Diogenes Laërtius, *The Lives and Opinions of Eminent Philosophers*, tr. C. D. Yonge (London: George Bell & Son, 1905), pp. 360, 119.

7 Plato, *Phaedo*, 60d-61c in *The Last Days of Socrates*, tr. Hugh Tredennick (Harmondsworth: Penguin, 1959).

8 *Littérature et philosophie mêlées* is the title of a collection published by Victor Hugo in 1834. Philippe Lacoue-Labarthe and Jean-Luc Nancy adopt it as the general title of an issue of *Poétique* (No. 21, 1975) devoted to that very connection.

9 The moment occurred between 1760, when Lessing began to publish his journal *Briefe die neueste Literatur betreffend*, and 1800, which saw the appearance of Mme de Staël's *De la littérature considérée dans ses rapports avec les institutions sociales*. On this point, see Escarpit, 'La Définition du terme littérature', Communication au IIIe Congrès de l'Association internationale de Littérature comparée, Utrecht, 1961.

10 Denis Diderot, *Entretiens sur le fils naturel* (1757), 'Troisième Entretien', in *Oeuvres complètes* (Paris: Club français du livre, 1970), vol. 3, p. 198. Elsewhere ('Refutation suivie de l'ouvrage d'Helvetius intitulé *L'Homme*', *Oeuvres complètes* (Paris: Club français du livre, 1971), vol. 11, p. 533), Diderot's conception of genius seems to lead him to advance the thesis of the primacy of poetry over philosophy: 'Poetry presupposes an intellectual exaltation which is almost like divine inspiration. Profound ideas come into the mind of the poet, and he knows nothing of their principles or implications. The astonished philosopher, for whom they would be the fruits of long meditation, cries out: "What inspired so much wisdom in that madman?"'

Kant, who stood on the other side of the same divide, legitimized the division it had introduced by locating it within a radical evolution in thought that precluded any return to an earlier state: 'There is no ... elegant [*schöne*] science, but only a fine [*schöne*] art ... A beautiful science – a science which, as such, is to be beautiful, is a nonentity. For if, treating it as a science, we were to ask for reasons and proofs, we would be put off with elegant phrases [*bons mots*].'[11] It would therefore be preferable for the truth to be ugly. By rejecting the classical identification of truth with beauty, Kant established between them 'a limit that cannot be transcended' and argued that to submit speculative discourse to a judgement of taste would be to weaken its rational content: 'Genius reaches a point at which art must make a halt, as there is a limit imposed upon it which cannot be transcended. This limit has in all probability been long since attained.'[12] Here, Kant seems to be anticipating the Hegelian conception of the death of art: once art reaches the limit imposed on its pretensions, all it can do is step aside and leave the field open for other forms of intellectual production that are irreducible to its criteria. Ultimately, this idea results in an aestheticism of the type professed by Croce, for whom the aesthetic phenomenon represents, by virtue of its pre-rational character, an immediate intuition free of any dependence on ideological or theoretical allegiances: the creative act expresses itself directly in the pure totality of the work of art, where, in the absence of any distinction between form and content, the reign of intuition and emotion is absolute. Freed from any rational concerns, art can then assert its independence from ethics, politics and philosophy, which inevitably exploit it for their own ends.

The conditions in which this schema of separation was traced demonstrate that the encounter which constitutes Literature and Philosophy as autonomous essences confined to the respective fields

---

11   Immanuel Kant, *The Critique of Judgement* ...44, tr. James Creed Meredith (Oxford: Clarendon Press, 1991), p. 165. This idea, which seems to be echoed by the comments from Wittgenstein that were cited above, may have provided the starting point for Kant's speculations. It was outlined in an earlier text, added to the *Observations on the Feeling of the Beautiful and the Sublime* of 1764 where Kant remarks: 'Taste can be an obstacle to understanding. I have to read and reread Rousseau until the beauty of his style is no longer disturbing; only then can I grasp it rationally.' (French translation R. Kempf (Paris: Vrin, 1953), p. 65.) All these passages from Kant, and those that follow, are cited in Jean-Luc Nancy's study 'Logodaedalus', *Poétique* 21 (1975).

12   Kant, *Critique of Judgement*, §47 p. 170.

that both define them and establish their limits, is a product of history. Its production corresponds to a very particular moment in the development of philosophical and literary work, to a precise moment when both become subject to independent and contrasting rules. That moment sees the simultaneous emergence of two 'modern' paradigms par excellence: the realm of Literature and speculation about the end of Philosophy.[13]

Could the moment of that division have passed? That is what we are not allowed to say, unless we prophesy, which is another way of remaining modern. But it must be possible to look again at the distinction it establishes, and to strip it of the essentially determinant character it has had for almost two hundred years. Disentangling what, in a certain number of texts, belongs to the philosophical and what belongs to the literary then becomes a matter of unpicking, in order to reveal how it was woven, the complex web in which the threads cross, entwine and interweave to form the differentiated network in which they combine without merging as they trace configurations of singular, enigmatic and hybrid meanings. In a way, I am proposing here to defend literature's speculative vocation by arguing that it has an authentic value as an intellectual experience; in that sense, we can speak of a 'literary philosophy'. At the same time, we avoid having to choose between a 'literature' which is either empty or full of 'philosophy', and a 'philosophy' which is either full or empty of 'literature'. For whilst, as I have suggested, literature as such exists only by virtue of a philosophical concept, that concept does not exhaust the complex reality of literary texts.

Rereading works that are considered to belong to the domain of literature in the light of philosophy must not become a way of making them admit to having a hidden meaning that sums up their speculative purpose; it is a way of revealing the pluralistic constitution that necessarily makes them amenable to differentiated modes of approach. For there is no more a pure literary discourse than there is a pure philosophical discourse; there are only mixed discourses wherein language games that are independent in their systems of reference and their principles interact on various levels. It is also impossible to

---

13 This modernity is illustrated perfectly by the mythology of the absent Book (or the 'book to come') which, from the poets and theorists of the Athenaeum to Mallarmé and then Blanchot, commemorates the lost community of literature and philosophy.

establish once and for all the relationship between the poetic or the narrative, and the rational; that relationship always manifests itself in the figures of its variability. It thus becomes clear that the philosophical intervenes in literary texts at several levels that must be carefully dissociated in accordance with the means they require and the functions they fulfil.

At the most elementary level, the relationship between literature and philosophy is strictly documentary: philosophy shows through the surface of works of literature either as a cultural reference that has, to a greater or lesser extent, been worked into the text, or as a mere quotation which, thanks to the ignorance of their readers and commentators, usually goes unnoticed. At a different level, a philosophical argument can play the role of a real formal operator with respect to the literary text; this is what happens when it sketches the character of a protagonist, organizes the overall shape of a narrative, sets the scene for it, or structures the mode of its narration. The literary text can, finally, also become a support for a speculative message whose philosophical content is often reduced to the level of ideological communication. If we are to answer the question 'What is literature thinking about?' we must take into account all these orders of consideration without, at least to begin with, privileging any one of them. That is the precondition for the eventual emergence of philosophical lessons from a reading of literary texts.

Exercises in literary philosophy

Take a more or less random corpus consisting of:
 Les Cent Vingt Journées de Sodome (Sade, 1784)
 Corinne, ou de l'Italie (Mme de Staël, 1807)
 Spiridion (Sand, 1839)
 Les Misérables (Hugo, 1862)
 The Temptation of St Antony (Flaubert, 1874)
 Documents (Bataille, 1930)
 Pierrot mon ami (Queneau, 1942)
 Entretiens avec le professeur Y (Céline, 1955)
 Death and the Labyrinth: The World of Raymond Roussel (Foucault, 1963)
One is immediately struck by the disparate character of this list, which juxtaposes narrative texts like *Corinne* and *Pierrot mon ami*, texts

belonging to the genre of the literature of ideas like *Spiridion* and *The Temptation of St Antony*, and the theoretical reflections on the nature of the literary phenomenon contained in the articles published by Bataille in *Documents*, in Céline's *Entretiens avec le professeur Y* and in the study Foucault devoted to Raymond Roussel. *Les Cent Vingt Journées de Sodome* and *Les Misérables* are unclassifiable because all these categories are equally applicable to them, and because they transcend them all: they are monuments isolated in their exceptional singularity, which seems to be the incarnation of a sort of absolute.

And yet all these texts are related by the fact of their belonging to the age of Literature, which began to unfold some two hundred years ago and which is still with us today. Together, they punctuate a specifically literary space. It has its peaks and its depressions. It has its broad perspectives and its very narrow paths, even its blind alleys, and they all result from the complex system of connections which relates apparently spontaneous and obviously reflective forms of writing, as well as 'great' and 'minor' literature, by establishing dialogues between Victor Hugo and Eugène Sue, Gustave Flaubert and Jules Verne, Raymond Queneau and Pierre Véry. At the same time it also blurs the frontier that seems to divide what may be said from what cannot be named. Leaving aside genre distinctions and the evaluative criteria that conventionally divide the 'literary' from what is not recognized as such, this corpus provides, because of its non-systematic character, raw materials that can be worked independently of any essentialist prejudices. The hypothesis on whose basis it is constructed is simply that a 'historical *a priori*' supplies conditions of possibility for a variety of experiences in which literature and philosophy become entangled and disentangled without there being any doctrinal form to stabilize relations between the two, or in other words to resolve the problem that results from their encounter.

The study which we are about to make of this corpus is based upon a postulate that might be formulated thus: the texts it brings together are, insofar as they belong to the historical field of 'literature', amenable to philosophical readings in which philosophy intervenes, in a non-exclusive way, as a system of reference and an instrument of analysis. Let us be quite clear about this: the point is not to offer *a* philosophical interpretation of these works which would relate them to a common intellectual core, of which they are different manifestations. The point is to suggest *readings* in which the philosophical mode of approach to literary texts will in each case be singularly implicated, in a determinate and differentiated manner. By adopting this approach, we will attempt to avoid a direct confrontation between literature and philosophy.

How are we to describe a study which elevates the disparate to the level of a principle? We began by listing some book titles in chronological order. It is, however, obviously impossible to leave matters at that, if only because to do so would give the illusion of a continuous line of evolution. It might then be thought that Literature, like the hero of one of its fables, is devoted to the gradual exploration of the space that defines it with a view to finally occupying it in its entirety and identifying itself through a gesture of appropriation resulting from a process in which philosophical thought intervened as a mediation. Nor will we retain a mode of classification of texts based upon a typology that categorizes once and for all the modes in which what we will finally term, when the time comes to propose a transversal reading of all these works, a 'literary philosophy' takes shape.

Chronological and typological modes of exposition having been ruled out, there remains only one other possibility. That is the mode we will adopt, even though it too has its disadvantages. It is based upon a thematic grouping organized around the three statements which give the three parts of this book their titles : 'Roads to History', 'Into the Depths' and 'All Must Pass Away'. The complacency of thematic criticism has led it into bad habits that have finally completely discredited the notion of 'theme', which is no longer recognized as having any validity. It is that notion that I propose to rehabilitate by displacing its field of application and modifying its working principles. 'Theme' is to be understood in the musical sense of the term. I propose to demonstrate that seemingly quite different approaches to literature are simply ways of playing variations on given themes and exploiting their various possibilities in a totally open-ended way.

Thus, Mme de Staël, George Sand and Raymond Queneau all, in their different ways, follow 'roads to history' by turning literature into a sort of machine for exploring the paths of human evolution, usually by adopting an anthropological point of view. By following a trajectory that takes them into the depths, Victor Hugo, Georges Bataille and Louis-Ferdinand Céline give literary writing an ontological dimension in the specific form of what might be called a negative ontology. In their reflections on the stylistic problems bound up with the experience of narrative, the Marquis de Sade, Gustave Flaubert and

Michel Foucault outline, finally, the principles of a rhetoric which is equivalent to a general analysis of thought. It is as though one could find, thanks to a reading of these literary texts, elements of a logic, a physics and an ethics, to adopt the categories we have inherited from classical philosophy. Such might be the foundations for a literary philosophy: we will come back to them in the final chapter.

The following studies are 'exercises', as defined by Czerny rather than Saint Ignatius of Loyola. Rather than constituting successive moments in a three-point argument, the three parts of this study develop the themes on which they are based, and should resemble a sonata or symphony in which the interplay between the resonances and echoes both establishes a mysterious correspondence between the movements and brings out their individuality. By linking Mme de Staël and Raymond Queneau, Victor Hugo and Louis-Ferdinand Céline and, more indirectly, Georges Bataille and Gustave Flaubert or George Sand and the Marquis de Sade, we may be able to outline the general features of a form of thought which is neither philosophical nor literary because it is both, and to evoke it in the same way that the structure of successive 'movements' can be evocative. It is dispersed and concentrated, diluted and condensed in texts whose fabrics and margins were woven by the speculative issues that historically conditioned their production and their reception. From this point of view, it should indeed be possible to give a philosophical interpretation of literature; but that interpretation must proceed in the way that one performs a musical score.

Let us listen, then, to literature talking about philosophy.

PART I

Roads to history

A cosmopolitan imaginary: the literary thought of Mme de Staël

Mme de Staël's seemingly disparate *oeuvre* constantly revolves around a problem that haunts her: what role does culture play in the constitution of a people and its national identity? To put it in more abstract terms: how is it possible to synthesize collective ways of thinking relating to a system of ideal representations that might be termed a collective 'theory', and a political state or a collective practice? In order to answer that question, Mme de Staël introduces a mediating element which has, so to speak, the function of schematizing the imagination; to that end, she forges a concept of 'literature'. She was one of the first to use that term in its modern sense in her *De la littérature considérée dans ses rapports avec les institutions sociales*, which was published in 1800. She therefore treats as a literary problem a basic question which she developed in two directions. She both elaborated general considerations on national literatures, and used forms of literary narration to produce literary texts that allowed her to embody her thoughts in concrete figures. *Delphine* and *De la littérature*, *Corinne* and *De l'Allemagne* complement and echo one another, and establish a dialogue between speculation and fiction.

From this point of view, the new image of literature, which was forged in the very last years of the eighteenth century and which is still alive today, seems from the outset to be inseparable from authentically philosophical concerns: it is the application of thought, of 'knowledge', to a configuration which is also new. Mme de Staël's multiform *oeuvre* articulates several discourses or several levels of discourse with a sinuous rigour, and illustrates that essential relationship; more specifically, it occupies a space which, because it lies between literature and philosophy, both separates and unites them.

National culture and universal culture

Mme de Staël encountered the problem of culture or, more accurately, of cultures and of communication, both as an abstract question concerning the transition from particular to universal, and as a concrete question pertaining to the effective realization of a modern aesthetic capable of linking the two. The other members of her circle in Coppet, and especially A. Schlegel and Sismondi, undertook, in the same context, parallel investigations into the same general theme of national literatures.

Their reflections take on their full meaning if we relate them to the mental revolution that was taking place at the time. Ways of looking at the major forms of human activity – speech, life, labour – were undergoing a complete transformation. To adopt the analysis of that mutation given by Michel Foucault in *The Order of Things*, we can say that whereas these activities had previously been seen in abstract terms, with their manifestations being organized into systems subject to uniform organizational rules, as though they were pure representations bound up with a basic demand for universalization, they were now beginning to be related concretely to their objective and subjective presuppositions, in the twofold sense of an empirical starting point and a transcendental origin. The latter constituted their basis or place of origin. At the same time, the conditions for their rationalization were being modified completely. In order to understand and master these manifestations, it was no longer enough to relate them, in a purely analytic fashion, to the surface of a table whose preestablished order imposed its internal homogeneity on their differences. They began to be seen as elements in synthetic processes, and to be inserted into networks with multiple references. As a result, it became possible to compare mutually irreducible structures which could, because of the very difference that individualized them and gave them their identity, be the object of a comparative evaluation. The common system of general grammar, for example, took no heed of the specificity of the national languages and subjected them to uniform analytic rules as it reconstructed a universal model of expression applicable to thought and language alike. It was now giving way to the concrete study of various linguistic systems. This presupposed abandoning attempts to force them into a single organizational framework by overlooking or erasing their individual features.

This new problematic applied to all domains of cultural production, and it also explains the constitution of an aesthetic of singularities which, unlike the models inherited from classicism, rejected the principle of imitation. Classicism subjects artistic creation to evaluative criteria that have been established once and for all, which are always and everywhere identical, and whose truthfulness is therefore not open to debate.[1] The famous 'rules', which are supposedly valid for all places and all times, are in fact localized in time and space; the generalization of their field of application obscures the fact that they have specific origins. To adopt another mode of argument, it was becoming necessary to reject the imperialism of French taste, as embodied in a linguistic monopoly exercised to the detriment of the other peoples of Europe, and as represented in *Corinne* by the ludicrous figure of the comte d'Erfeuil. Mme de Staël has him say: 'Surely you would not, beautiful foreigner, wish us to admit into France Teutonic barbarism, the *Night-Thoughts* of the Englishman Young, and the

1 These new preoccupations are illustrated by the following passage from the beginning of *De la littérature du midi de l'Europe* (vol. 1, pp. 8–9) by Sismondi – a member of the Coppet group. It was published in 1813 and reproduces the content of lectures given in Geneva a year earlier. 'To dwell upon the state of our literature alone is to remain in a state of semi-consciousness. Those who shaped that literature had within them an inspiration that has been quenched; they found in their hearts rules of which they were not even aware; they produced masterpieces, but masterpieces are not to be confused with models, for models exist only for those who are willing to lower themselves to the wretched craft of imitation ... Other great men have existed in other languages; they were the glory of other literatures; they too moved souls deeply and produced all the effects we are accustomed to expect from eloquence and poetry. Let us study their style; let us judge them not in accordance with our rules, but in accordance with the rules they followed; let us learn to distinguish between the human spirit and the national spirit, and let us rise high enough to be able to distinguish between rules that stem from the essence of beauty and are common to all languages, and rules that are derived from great examples, sanctioned by habit and maintained by convention, but which, for other peoples, are replaced by other rules based upon other conventions, sanctioned by other examples and justified by a different but no less intellectual analysis. We therefore believe that it would be both useful and profitable to review modern literature that is produced outside France, to examine how it first originated in the various nations of Europe, the spirit that inspired it and the various masterpieces it has produced.' Taking into account national characteristics does not, then, represent a challenge to either the unity of the human mind or the idea of the essence of the Beautiful. National characteristics arise from different points of view, but it is possible for them to communicate, provided that the distinction between the two is maintained.

concetti of the Italians and the Spanish? What would become of the taste and elegance of French style after such adulteration?'[2] Exclusivism, disguised here as the universalism of one style and one taste, is really no more than a national characteristic which dare not speak its name because it deliberately refuses to recognize itself for what it is.

Corinne, the 'beautiful foreigner', therefore argues the case for a poetics of dispersal: 'I find it difficult to think it desirable that the entire world should lose all national colour, all sentimental and intellectual individuality.'[3] The foreign must cease to be considered barbarous in the name of a fragile stereotype, and must, on the contrary, be recognized in its native or natural characteristics. It must be related to the specific conditions that render it both necessary and inimitable. National cultures must therefore first be identified and the spirit of each literature must be defined on the basis of the particular features that individualize it. Literary forms should not be classified horizontally, as though in a table, or as though they all obeyed the same abstract regulatory principles; they should be vertically related to their primary determinations, or in other words to the national or popular characteristics that make them different. Does this mean that there is a parallel between Mme de Staël's analysis and the speculations which, following Herder's example, the new German intellectuals had, at this very time, begun to develop around the notion of a *Volksgeist*? If that were the case, she would have merely exchanged one cultural model for another: the French for the German. As we shall see, she in fact adopts a very different approach by rising, as she attempts to do in her interpretation of the French Revolution, above the debate between universals and particulars, and by refusing to choose one as opposed to the other.

The creative activities of peoples are of course restricted to and by their frontiers, but the fact that they are restricted does not result in an absolute divorce between the cultural configurations it differentiates; on the contrary it makes possible a permanent exchange, and that exchange is based less upon the specific contributions of each national spirit than upon its failings and lacunae. We see here the first outline of more general considerations on the notion of 'limit'. Differentiating between types of national cultures does not preclude the establishment of correlations between them, and those correlations then make it

2 Mme de Staël, *Corinne*, in *Oeuvres complètes* (Paris: Firmin Didot, 1886, reprinted, Geneva: Slatkine Reprints, 1967), vol. 1, p. 710.   3 Ibid., p. 709.

possible to evaluate them in comparative terms. When reduced to its basic axes, Mme de Staël's conception is based upon the combined application of two differentiating criteria: ancient/modern and southern/northern. The stakes of the first dichotomy are specifically historical and allow the reintroduction into the interpretation of cultural phenomena of the principle of perfectibility inherited from the philosophy of the Enlightenment, to which Mme de Staël is deeply attached. According to this criterion, history is subject to a developmental law which both governs and totalizes its effects. The second dichotomy, whose criteria are geographical, derives, in contrast, from the view that individuation particularizes historical elements. If the two orders of determination are combined, national cultures can be inscribed within a schema looking roughly like this:

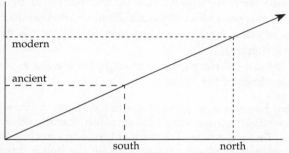

This means that cultural polymorphism can be reconciled with a developmental model subsumed within the framework of a philosophy of universal history. It is not dissimilar to the Hegelian concept, which makes an analogous synthesis between the geographical and the historical. In Mme de Staël's case, we find the hypothesis that southern literatures are essentially archaic – and here we see the establishment of the paradigm that sees the Greeks as children and which will still be functioning fifty years later in a famous text by Marx. Conversely, she asserts that northern literatures and, more generally, cultures, have innovative virtues and appear to be better adapted to the present stage of historical evolution.[4]

---

4 Cf. Mme de Staël, *De la littérature considérée dans ses rapports avec les institutions sociales*, in *Oeuvres complètes* (Paris: Firmin Didot, 1836, reprinted, Geneva: Slatkine Reprints, 1967), vol. 1, p. 236: 'When we study history, it seems to me that we acquire the conviction that all major events lead towards the same goal of a world civilization. We see that, in every century, new peoples have been introduced to the benefits of social order and that war, despite all its disasters, has

Whilst the mutual irreducibility of forms of sensibility — Homer and Ossian, for instance — has to be recognized, they cannot escape the dynamics of their comparison, which plays one off against the other precisely because they are mutually irreducible. All cultural times and spaces are therefore, as in Hegel, traversed by the same spirit. It does not, however, move through them as though they were a transparent, abstract and non-differentiated milieu that ensures its uniform diffusion. On the contrary, they subject it to an internal principle of variation which organizes their diversity dynamically and which is the precondition for the evolution that leads from one place or time to the next. This is why it is not legitimate to confine national cultures within their spatial and temporal frontiers, or simply to register their specific characteristics in such a way as to perpetuate the differences between them; those differences must also be interpreted in terms of the progressive movement that organizes different cultures into successive moments within a single series that is oriented towards the present and by the present.

Mme de Staël therefore gives primacy to the literatures of the north rather than those of the south:

Melancholic poetry is more in keeping with philosophy. Sadness penetrates much deeper into the character and destiny of man than any other humour of the soul ... The imagination of the men of the north soars beyond the land whose confines they inhabit; it soars through the clouds that limit their horizons and seems to represent the obscure transition from life to death.[5]

Being the immediate expression of a sensual and untamed imaginary, the fantastic literature of the south can look pedestrian, precisely

often extended the empire of enlightenment. The Romans civilised the world they subjugated. Initially, enlightenment had to come from one point of light, from a small country; only a few centuries later, a warrior people could unite under the same laws a part of the world so as to civilize it by conquering it. Although they brought about the temporary extinction of the literature and the arts that once flourished in the South, the nations of the North nonetheless acquired some of the knowledge of the defeated; and the inhabitants of more than half of Europe, who had until then been strangers to civilized society, shared in its advantages. Time therefore reveals to us a purpose in a sequence of events which appeared to be the result of mere chance, and we see thought, which always remains the same, welling up out of the depths of events and centuries.' Just as Sismondi insisted upon the unity of the human mind (see the text cited in note 1 above), this text, which prefigures in astonishing fashion the broad lines of Hegel's philosophy of history, insists upon the idea of a universal culture.
5 Ibid., p. 253.

because it is so spontaneous, whereas the misty dreams of the men of the north appeal to an ideal that is loftier than the immediate realities and elementary passions they inspire. Chthonian culture/uranian culture; *diesseits/jenseits*; profane world/sacred world: the interpretative model that is being established here will go on functioning throughout the first half of the nineteenth century. The revelations of the new peoples of the north – and they are new because there is something essentially modern about their very antiquity – are the product of the ascending movement which gradually frees the spirit from its primitive roots and reveals its new transcendence. Hence the undeniable cultural superiority of those peoples and the message they transmit: 'Philosophical ideas seem to have a spontaneous affinity for sombre images. Far from being conducive, like that of the north, to meditation and inspiring, so to speak, that which reflection must prove, the poetry of the south, that voluptuous poetry, almost precludes ideas of a certain order.'[6] This assessment is based upon a sense of history.

Does this mean that a new model – and when she wrote the lines cited above, Mme de Staël was thinking of England rather than Germany – must replace the old and that the paradigm inherited from Graeco-Roman antiquity, which is so limpidly clear in its naive grace, must give way to the more sophisticated, albeit obscure, paradigm, transmitted by the cold cultures of northern Europe? If that were the case, the aesthetics of the present day would be a new classicism, or a new exclusivism which merely displaces the principle of imitation by giving it a new content and leaving its form intact. The attempt to make cultures communicate with one another through the limits that differentiate them would have to be abandoned. Mme de Staël outlines the solution to this problem in the preface to her novel *Delphine*, which appeared in 1802:

One can only imitate authors whose works are accomplished; and there is nothing illustrious about imitation; but writers whose rather bizarre genius has not fully polished all the riches they possess can be advantageously stolen by men of taste and talent; gold from the mine can serve all nations; gold which has been minted as coin can only be used by a single nation.[7]

6 Ibid., p. 254.
7 Mme de Staël, *Delphine*, in *Oeuvres complètes* (Paris: Firmin Didot, 1836, reprinted, Geneva; Slatkine Reprints, 1967), vol. 1, p. 336.

Individualized cultural configurations cannot exchange finished products whose intrinsic value makes them immediately convertible; they can exchange raw materials that have yet to be worked, that allow themselves to be reappropriated in order to be transformed. If peoples who are rooted in the traditions that are the heritage of their geographical and historical situation do have something to say to one another in the here and now, and if something resembling a cultural relationship between them is possible, it is only by virtue of their having escaped the twofold exclusivism of abstract universalism and concrete particularism, and they can only do that on the basis of a mutual recognition of the limits that both keep them apart and unite them by establishing the conditions for mutual communication.

Beautiful foreigners: a rhetoric of the composite

The implications of the conception we have just evoked are not only theoretical, so closely does this conception correspond in practice to the concrete situation of Mme de Staël and her group. Living in a marginal position on the frontiers that divided political, poetic and intellectual Europe, and being both foreign to and familiar with forms of expression from several nations, they could monitor the major cultural border crossings of the day. Mme de Staël lived her ideas to the extent that they derived from her very life, or in other words from the situation imposed upon her by her birth and circumstances. She used the complementary but competing forms of the novel and theoretical speculation to analyse her situation, and her actual adventures were imbued with the same forms. She created Corinne in the image of the 'beautiful foreigner', which was also her own image. English by extraction, abandoned at birth, Corinne became, in mysterious circumstances, Italian by adoption. Corinne is more Italian than any real Italian despite the clandestinity forced on her by the need to live in disguise, a borrowed form which is still further accentuated by the fact that the story of this Anglo-Italian, who combines the characteristics of north and south, is written in the French language for a French-speaking audience. Because she is a cosmopolitan being, this foreigner is 'beautiful', and therefore interesting from the point of view of the narrative imaginary: having stepped outside all forms of culture – and she never identifies totally with any one form – she reveals the gap that divides them, but she is also the mediator they need if they are to communicate.

In the early years of the nineteenth century (*Corinne* appeared in 1807), it was possible to see such a figure as the true heroine of modern times. Her inner foreignness, which defines her essence, allows her to play, with respect to the various manifestations of the national spirit, the role of someone who both reveals and interprets. She *plays* that role: the phrase has to be taken literally since the point is that she displays, as though on a stage, traits that identify characters. In an attempt to ward off boredom, a lot of acting went on in Coppet, and Mme de Staël herself appeared in a wide variety of guises: Greek, French, Christian, mother, mistress, slave, queen ... In a key passage in *Corinne* the English Corinne appears in *Romeo and Juliet* before an Italian audience from whom her real identity remains concealed. She acts in a play about Italian passions which was written in her own language by an English playwright, and which has, for the purposes of this performance, been retranscribed into the original language of its plot. This twofold interplay of mirror-images and equivocations also reveals, thanks to its ambiguities, the preconditions for authentic cultural communication, which Mme de Staël likens to 'a divided, reflected, variegated ray'.[8] *Corinne* is therefore a celebration of a cosmopolitan culture which can transmit across frontiers the characteristic values of quite alien sensibilities: those values complement one another, mingle without merging and project their virtues outwards without renouncing the particular identity that constitutes them, and without corrupting it.

A system is thus established. It is a shattered aesthetic of the disparate. At the same time, a new culture is born after having undergone the ordeal of a linguistic, ideological and poetic migration. It facilitates comparisons and exchanges between elements that were originally quite foreign to one another by bringing them together on the basis of their reciprocal foreignness. For if cultures are foreign to

---

8 Cf.ibid., p. 716. 'Shakespeare, more so than any foreign writer, understood both the national character of Italy, and that fecundity of mind which finds a thousand ways to vary the expression of the same feelings, that oriental eloquence which uses images from the whole of nature to paint what is happening in the heart. Ossian paints in one hue, and constantly uses the same sound to pluck at the heart's most sensitive chord; but the multiple colours used by Shakespeare in *Romeo and Juliet* do not give his style a cold affectation; it is the divided, reflected and variegated beam that produces these colours, and one can always feel the light and the fire from whence they come. When translated into Italian, the play *Romeo and Juliet* seems to be restored to its mother tongue.'

one another, it is primarily because they are foreign to themselves in the sense that an inner foreignness lies at the heart of any particular form of expression. Just as it constitutes that form, foreignness also provides a secret link with the other forms of expression with which it is differentially associated. We are dealing here with an infinitely open cosmopolitanism. The universality that founds it is a negative universality in the sense that one can speak of negative theology; we can get no permanent purchase on it and it can be glimpsed only in its perpetual migration, that being the sole visible form of its permanence. The particular features of a culture are revealed by the absences and gaps which leave it incomplete in its own order, but they also indicate the contributions, which will of necessity come from the outside, it needs to develop and become complete.

Delphine and Corinne, who are the central characters in Mme de Staël's great novels, crystalize these theoretical preoccupations by embodying them in concrete characteristics. These heroines are fantastic, not by accident but of necessity, because their instability illuminates all their actions with the light of the 'divided, reflected and variegated beam' we mentioned earlier.[9] Being composite individuals, they evoke a whole poetic system: the system that replaces convention with nature.[10] Nature, or indifference to differences, allows

9 Mme de Staël has someone say (ibid., p. 370) of Delphine: 'I did not believe it possible for one person to combine so many different graces, which should, it would seem, belong to very different ways of being. Always the appropriate expression, a movement that is always natural, gaiety of mind and melancholy of feeling, elation and simplicity, passion and energy! An adorable mixture of genius and candour, of gentleness and strength! She possesses in equal degrees all that could inspire admiration in the deepest thinkers, all that could put the most ordinary minds at their ease, if they have any goodness, if they enjoy encountering that touching quality in its simplest and most noble forms, its most attractive and naive forms.' And of Corinne (*Corinne, Oeuvres complètes* vol. 1, p. 702): 'You are an incredible creature: you feel things deeply, yet you have frivolous tastes. You are independent because of the pride of your soul and yet a slave to the need for amusement, capable of loving one man, but needing all men. You are a magician, alternatively disturbing and reassuring; you are sublime, but you suddenly vanish from a region where you are alone to merge with the crowd. Corinne, Corinne, one cannot stop oneself from both dreading you and loving you.'

10 Corrine responds to the comments cited in the previous note (ibid., p. 703): 'What it pleases you to call the magic in me is unconstrained nature, which sometimes displays different feelings and contrasting thoughts without making any attempt to reconcile them, for their reconciliation, when it exists, is almost always artificial, and most true characteristics are illogical.'

Mme de Staël's heroines to exploit all differences concurrently, without worrying about their apparent incompatibility. And this sovereign talent for improvisation allows them to slip into any situation, to act out the most diverse roles by bringing out the very features that make them different.[11] Artificial and spontaneous, swept away in an unbroken sequence of metamorphoses, unpredictable and unexpected because they never are where we think they are, Delphine and Corinne are constitutionally 'beautiful foreigners', always ready to abandon their face of the moment, which they temporarily adopted, as though it were a costume, and to adopt another, to which they will attach no greater importance in any lasting sense.

The way their characters are portrayed sketches a representation of an ideal which has more than a psychological value pertaining to the existence of individual personalities. It also expresses the general principles of a thought characterized by unanimity, an implicit philosophy that can meet the demands of a conciliatory cultural politics. It is left to Corinne's lover to bring out the secret meaning of her presence and her power: 'One of the reasons why you are so incomparably graceful is that you combine all the charms that make up the different nations.'[12] The diversity of her naturalness expresses her links with all the cultural forms whose 'divided, reflected and variegated' beam shines through her. One could also demonstrate how, in the domain of morality, Mme de Staël tries in analogous manner to combine masculine and feminine characteristics without attenuating their contrasting features. In politics, she attempts to 'reconcile the freedom of republics and the tranquillity of mon-

11 Delphine captivates her audience by dancing a Scottish reel: 'Never before have grace and beauty produced a more extraordinary impression on such a large assembly; nothing we had seen could give any idea of the charms of this foreign dance: it is a quite Asiatic mixture of indolence and vivacity, of melancholy and gaiety. Sometimes, when the tune became gentle, Delphine would walk a few steps with her head hung down and her arms folded, as though some memory or some regret had suddenly intruded upon the festivities; soon, however, she would return to her lively, graceful dance, and would wrap herself in a calico shawl which, as it outlined her waist and hung down like her long hair, made her whole person a ravishing figure' (*Delphine, Oeuvres complètes*, vol. 1, p. 377). Corinne (*Corinne, Oeuvres complètes*, vol 1, p. 806) displays a similar versatility when, during a stay in Venice, she plays the role of Semiramis in Gozzi's *La Fille de l'air*: 'Brought up in a cave like a savage, as cunning as an enchantress, as imperious as a queen, she combined natural vivacity with premeditated grace, warlike courage with the frivolity of a woman, and ambition with heedlessness.'
12 Ibid., p. 701.

archies'.[13] In philosophy, she attempts, as we shall see, to synthesize the new values of sensibility and enthusiasm and the progressive, rational approach characteristic of Enlightenment thought, without sacrificing one reference point to the other.

Kant revised and corrected

In making her characters so versatile, Mme de Staël is 'staging' her own style of thought, which is defined by an attempt to embrace opposites without reducing them.[14] When he expounds abstract ideas, Oswald, the male protagonist of *Corinne*, makes it clear that he is attracted to the changeableness which, in his view, typifies the grace of his mistress, even though an uninformed observer would dismiss it as inconsistency:

Dogmas which offend my reason also chill my enthusiasm. No doubt the world as it exists is a mystery which we can neither deny nor understand, and he who refuses to believe what he cannot understand would therefore be mad indeed; but the contradictory is always the creation of man. The mystery given to us by God is beyond our mental understanding [*lumières de l'esprit*], but it is not opposed to it. A German philosopher said: 'I know of only two beautiful things in the world: the starry sky above our heads and the feeling of duty in our hearts.' All the wonders of creation are indeed contained in those words.[15]

We can recognize in these words the shadow cast by a specific philosophy, namely that of Kant, who, it is being intimated, is the thinker of universal reconciliation who has succeeded in overcoming the heart/reason dichotomy.

The sudden and localized appearance in a novel of philosophically derived themes is always problematic. The transposition on which it depends seems to be a distortion that gives rise to an apparently bloodless speculative content. As the above quotation shows, Mme de Staël is to that extent no exception to the rule. Yet when in the course

---

13 Mme de Staël, 'De l'influence des passions sur le bonheur des individus et des sociétés' (1796), 'Introduction', *Oeuvres complètes*, vol. 1, p. 108.

14 Chateaubriand evokes this instability in a letter to Fontane published in the *Mercure de France* of January 1801, in which he describes Mme de Staël's *De la littérature*: 'Sometimes Mme de Staël seems to be a Christian; a moment later, philosophy gains the upper hand. At times, inspired by her natural sensibility, she gives free rein to her soul, but all at once the argumentative spirit is aroused and stems the outpourings of the heart ... This book is a singular mixture of truths and errors.' The expression 'singular' is well chosen.

15 *Corinne, Oeuvres complètes* vol. 1, p. 747.

of a narrative she refers, in a necessarily allusive way, to philosophical ideas, she at least does so logically, if not rigorously, thanks to her constant attempt to base communication between cultures on a synthesis of universals and particulars. When she studies philosophers, not for their own sake but in order to make them serve the cause she is defending, she therefore applies to them the same art of equivocation that allows her to sustain an ambiguous relationship with their doctrines. She is attempting to draw from them a lesson that seems to be essential, without becoming confined within the limitations of any one system. In this domain, her guide was presumably Gérando who, long before Cousin and perhaps more skilfully, promoted a theoretical 'eclecticism' that allowed him to flit between the strangest forms of thought and to slip into their interstices and lacunae without taking up a permanent abode in any of them.[16]

When Mme de Staël met Fichte during her travels in Germany, she granted him a quarter of an hour in which to give her a coherent idea of his system and even advised him to forget about his metaphysics, which was of no interest to her, and to begin with an exposition of his ethical doctrine. In the chapter of *De l'Allemagne* which she devotes to Kant, she remarks, after having summarized the content of the three *Critiques* in some ten pages:

I certainly do not flatter myself with being able to summarize in a few pages a system which has preoccupied all the great minds of Germany for twenty years, but I do hope that I have said enough about it to outline the general spirit of Kant's philosophy and to be able to explain in the following chapters the influence it has exercised over literature, the arts and science.[17]

This does indeed seem to testify to the extreme superficiality with which a mind categorized as 'literary' approaches the discourse of philosophers. We must, however, go beyond this negative conclusion; by adopting the twin criteria of clarity and profundity, Mme de Staël is in fact attempting to speak both to the heart, which reduces all ideas to general themes by simplifying them, and to the intellect, which respects their complexity by arguing them. Once again, we see her preoccupation with making extremes meet.

Hence the need, when one speaks of philosophy in literature, to transpose or translate, or in other words to adapt, in the sense that one can speak of an actor slipping into a role in order to give it a new

16 See his *Histoire comparée des systèmes philosophiques* of 1804.
17 Mme de Staël, *De l'Allemagne, Oeuvres complètes*, vol. 2, p. 186.

meaning. In the passages she devotes to Kant, Mme de Staël might be said to be 'acting out' his philosophy in order to reveal what is at stake in it, in exactly the same way that Corinne interprets a play by Shakespeare. She is a shrewd and self-possessed actress who both completely identifies with the character she is playing and looks at it from the outside. She can slip into her role without fully identifying with it. If we wish to grasp the meaning of a philosophy, we must not, according to Mme de Staël, be taken in by the particular mode of expression that constrains it.[18] Now whilst the German philosophers of the period, and the German philosophers alone, did have a universal philosophy, they were not, in her view, able to formulate it in a universal way. They rendered their thought impenetrable by identifying themselves with it so completely that they broke the links that would otherwise have connected it to different intellectual developments. It was because they refused to become foreigners to themselves that they produced the effect of radical alterity that made them obscure for the rest of the world.[19] Hence the need to think both with them and against them.

We can now understand why Mme de Staël's discussion of the content of doctrines is so shallow; she is merely trying to extract general lessons by summarizing them. This is particularly true of Kant's philosophy, which she tried to make accessible to a general public at a time when it seemed extremely rebarbative. In order to do so, she had to rework completely its internal organization and to take considerable liberties with what Kant called the architectonic of his system. The general idea behind her interpretation might be summarized thus: although he appears to be a specialized thinker whose originality derives directly from specific intellectual categories and procedures, Kant is a philosopher of unanimity, and his principal role has been that of a conciliator and synthesizer who has expanded the intellectual domain by bringing together activities which were previously thought to be mutually exclusive. It follows that we can

18 'Kant's style is very difficult when he is speaking about his theory and the application of his theory. In his treatises on metaphysics, he treats words as though they were numbers and gives them the value he wishes, regardless of the value given them by usage. This, it seems to me, is a great mistake because the reader's attention is exhausted by the attempt to understand the language even before he gets to the ideas, and what he knows is never a rung on a ladder that helps him to reach what he does not know' (ibid.).

19 Ibid., p. 195. The passage in question is cited below.

say: 'Kant, who seemed destined to conclude every great intellectual alliance, makes the soul a single centre where all the faculties are in harmony with one another.'[20] Astonishing as it may seem, Mme de Staël turns Kant not only into an eclectic philosophy, but into the prime spokesman for the doctrine of eclecticism.[21]

According to Mme de Staël, Kant is therefore the philosopher of experience *and* reason; he did not give a predominant role to either, but by delineating their fields of action, he was able to temper their mutual interventions. In that sense, when Emile Bréhier writes that 'Mme de Staël borrowed the material for the chapter on Kant in her *De l'Allemagne* from Villers', he misses the real point.[22] In the important study of Kant he published in 1801, Charles de Villers did indeed, in polemical fashion, try to promote the idea that Kant was a pure theorist of the innate faculties of reason who came close to psychologism, and thus turned him into a weapon to be used against the philosophies of experience inherited from the eighteenth century. As has already been suggested, it was, rather, Gérando who inspired Mme de Staël's reading of Kant. In his essay on *La Génération des connaissances humaines* of 1804, Gérando explained that Kant 'occupies, so to speak, the middle ground' between the Descartes-Malebranche-Leibniz trinity and the Bacon-Locke-Condillac trinity; the same theme was taken up and expanded in chapter 10 of his *Histoire comparée des systèmes philosophiques* of 1804.[23] The attention of Gérando and Mme

20 Ibid., p. 186.
21 Cf. ibid., p. 189: 'Kant made a strict distinction between the realm of the soul and the realm of sensations; this philosophical dualism was tiresome for minds who like to take refuge in absolute ideas. From the time of the Greeks to our day the axiom that "All is one" has often been repeated, and philosophers have always attempted to find, either in the soul or in nature, a single principle that can explain the world. I would be so bold as to say, however, that one of the rightful claims Kant's philosophy makes upon the trust of enlightened men is that it has asserted what we feel: both the soul and external nature exist, and they act mutually upon one another in accordance with certain laws. I do not know why it is assumed that there is more philosophical dignity in the idea of a single principle, either material or intellectual. The existence of either one or two principles does not make the universe easier to understand, and we have more emotional sympathy for systems that recognize the distinction between the physical and the moral.'
22 Emile Bréhier, *Histoire de la philosophie* (Paris: PUF, collection 'Quadrige', 1981), vol. 3, p. 567.
23 For Gérando's theoretical orientations, we can rely upon the judgement of Maine de Biran, who knew his work well: 'He is very concerned with ethics and is fully preoccupied with the fine plan he has drawn up: reconciling the disciples

de Staël was particularly caught by the fact that Kant refused to choose between materialism and idealism, whereas Villers saw him as the champion of idealism *par excellence*. They were, that is, struck by the fact that he had integrated two contrasting perspectives into a single system in which they ceased to appear incompatible. From the point of view of the rigorous history of philosophy, as practised today, this reading was far from arbitrary: did not Kant indeed elaborate an antagonistic – or 'tragic', as Lucien Goldmann puts it – concept of the human essence when he described it as standing 'between two roads',[24] because it is doubly determined by nature and by reason? Mme de Staël was attracted to this conception precisely because it was antidogmatic and allowed her to wrest Kantian philosophy from the circle of partisan interpretations which, at the time when it began to be introduced into France, had restricted its impact.

In accordance with the same principle, Mme de Staël attaches particular importance to the fact that, in his moral doctrine, Kant also overcomes the opposition between the intellect and feeling,[25] the weak point of Kantian philosophy being, in her view, that it still makes too many concessions to rigour and therefore distorts the relationship between reason and emotion. By outlining a critique of formalism, Mme de Staël therefore rallies to the position Benjamin Constant had adopted in his polemic with Kant over the question of the right to lie. And at the same time she reasserts the principle behind her own reasoning: the search for a 'marvellous point', which she also identifies with reference to Christianity, that allows the most distant perspectives to converge without losing anything of their specific singularity.[26]

of Kant and those of Condillac. He claims to have found the link between the two doctrines', letter of 18 August 1802, cited in H. Gouhier, *Les Conversions de Maine de Biran* (Paris: Vrin, 1947), p. 163.

24 Immanuel Kant, *Fundamental Principles of the Metaphysic of Morals*, tr. Thomas K. Abbott (Indianapolis and New York: Library of Liberal Arts, 1949), p. 18.

25 Cf. *De l'Allemagne, Oeuvres complètes*, vol. 2 , p. 185: 'Not only are Kant's moral principles austere and pure, as might be expected from his philosophical inflexibility; he fully reconciles the truths of the heart with those of the understanding, and takes a particular delight in making his abstract theory of the nature of the understanding confirm the simplest and strongest feelings.'

26 Cf. ibid., p. 214: 'If feeling does not support morality, how can morality command obedience? How are we to unite reason and will, and how can the will subdue the passions, if not through feeling? A German thinker has said that the Christian religion is the only philosophy, and he certainly did not express himself thus in order to dismiss philosophy; he did so because he was convinced that the

Mme de Staël can thus describe Kant as the philosopher of enthusiasm *par excellence*, and this somewhat surprising interpretation was to prevail until after 1830, when the appearance in French translation of Kant's basic texts led to its rectification.[27] We know that the notion of enthusiasm has an important place in Mme de Staël's own thought: the last three chapters of *De l'Allemagne*, which describe a particular historical culture, also have a more general import and are devoted to the topic of enthusiasm.[28] What is enthusiasm? It is an expansive mode of thought that combines intuition and reflection, and which therefore affords an escape from the sectarian spirit and its exclusivism.[29] It is also a synthesis of opposites which reconciles the universal and the particular. When she rereads Kant in the light of this notion, Mme de Staël is an original thinker rather than an accurate commentator on his philosophy. She produces thought, even though she cannot accurately reproduce a preexisting body of thought; the details of its complex organization certainly escape her. She thus creates something of significance in every domain. *Corinne* is a novel about enthusiasm, and *De l'Allemagne* expounds a theory of enthusiasm

loftiest and most profound ideas lead to the discovery of the singular harmony that exists between that religion and the nature of man. Christianity lies midway between the two classes of moralists – those who, like Kant and other still more abstract moralists, wish all moral actions to be governed by immutable principles, and those who, like Jacobi, proclaim that all morality should be abandoned to the decision of feeling – and it seems to indicate the marvellous point where the positive law does not reject the inspiration of the heart, nor inspiration the positive law.'

27 Cf. ibid., p. 186: 'In his attempt to reconcile the philosophy of experience and idealist philosophy, Kant did not subordinate one to the other; he succeeded in giving each a new degree of strength in its own right. Germany was threatened by the arid doctrine that saw all enthusiasm as error and regarded all the feelings that console our existence as prejudices. It was a great satisfaction for those philosophical and poetic men who are capable of study and exaltation, to see all the beautiful affectations of the soul being defended with the rigour of the most abstract feeling. Strength of mind cannot be negative, it cannot consist primarily in what one does not believe or understand, or in what one despises. We require a philosophy of belief, of enthusiasm, a philosophy which rationally confirms the revelations of our feelings.'

28 Ibid., chapter 10, 'Of enthusiasm'; chapter 11, 'Of the influence of enthusiasm on enlightenment'; chapter 12, 'Influence of enthusiasm on happiness'.

29 Cf. ibid., p. 250: 'Fanaticism is an exclusive passion with an opinion as its object; enthusiasm is part of a universal harmony: love of the beautiful, the elevation of the soul, and the joy of devotion, merge in a single feeling which is both grandiose and calm. Enthusiasm means "God within us". When the existence of man is expansive, there is indeed something divine about it.'

in relation to a historical culture: that Germany whose national characteristics Mme de Staël interprets in similar terms as a universalism that has been reconciled with a concrete singularity.

Germany reinvented

Mme de Staël created a mythology about Germany, and its themes dominated France for more than half a century: it took 1870 and Bismarck for the poetically attractive image of an idealistic and dreamy people sleeping in its spiritual mists to give way to the more prosaic image (which still relied, however, on the repellent aspects of the same image) of an organized and militarized nation ruled by discipline and not by the emotions. Between 1800 and 1850, travels in America, as made by Tocqueville in Chateaubriand's footsteps, and travels in Germany — and here is Cousin who follows in the footsteps of Mme de Staël — together constituted a sort of paradigm for post-revolutionary thought. From that point of view, Mme de Staël was a real innovator. It is not that she was attempting something for which there was no precedent, since she took her inspiration from Charles de Villers.[30] She did, however, find the forms and terms which made assimilable and acceptable a representation that had previously been confined to a partisan clique of *émigrés* by expanding it and giving it a synthetic value.

Mme de Staël made her grand tour of Germany in 1802–3. It might be said that it allowed her to discover the real Germany, and that she wished to share the benefits of her discovery with the general public. It would, however, be more accurate to say that she invented, rather than discovered, Germany. Her encounter with Germany was that of a visionary rather than an explorer, though the two are perhaps not mutually exclusive. The entire experience was dominated by an image corresponding to a preestablished model based on a 'theory' about Germany. The general outline of that theory had been established even before the encounter actually took place. This preconceived theory was to prove so durable as to constitute a stable and autonomous intellectual structure for nineteenth-century French thought as a whole.

30 Mme de Staël had read and digested Charles de Villers's *Lettres westphaliennes* (published in 1797), and, more important, the articles published at the same time in *Le Spectateur du Nord*, the journal published by the French *émigré* community in Hamburg. She borrowed a great deal from them.

The first text in which Mme de Staël expounds her ideas about Germany predates her tour, which in that sense merely retrospectively confirmed her in her views. Her *De la littérature considérée dans ses rapports avec les institutions nationales* appeared in 1800,[31] and in it we can already read the themes that would be taken up again and developed after 1810 in *De l'Allemagne*. They relate to the following elementary idea: the Germans are the people of the mind because they are a nation with no real political organization. We know that Marx inherited this argument; according to this view, Germany is a theoretically advanced nation, which explains the dissemination of its cultural models, but it is politically backward. This idea eventually became a cliché, but Mme de Staël left her own mark on it by relating it to her own reflections on the problems of cosmopolitanism; she deduces from the fact that Germany is not a homeland in the narrow sense of the term, that it must be a natural home for those who, like the 'beautiful foreigners' who were the concrete incarnation of her thought, have no homeland.

This analysis started out from the recognition of a fact. There was no German nation-state; hence the need for German culture to take shape in a fragmented way around an absent centre.[32] The explanations Fichte gave her for this – and she found them confused – confirmed Mme de Staël in the belief that the Germans had a philosophical bent to the precise extent that they did not have a political bent because there was no authentic national spirit to guide their thinking in that domain. Germany was a mysteriously profound country where the impossibility of concrete fellowship between individuals left the field open for a proliferation of abstract ideas which flourished in unrestrained fashion because of the prevailing anomie!

This is also why she considered the Germans to be the philosophical people *par excellence*; in Germany, philosophy filled the vacuum left by politics.[33] In a fragmented society, individuals are bound together by

31 See vol. 1, chapter 17, 'De la littérature allemande'.
32 This idea is evoked in *De la littérature*, p. 279: 'In Germany, lengthy wars and the federation of states allowed the feudal spirit to live on, and could not provide a centre around which enlightenment and interest could unite.' It reappears in precisely the same form in *De l'Allemagne* (p. 5): 'Germany was an aristocratic federation; this empire had no single centre for letters and public spiritedness; it could not act as one nation, and there was nothing to bind it together.'
33 This too is a theme that had been touched upon in *De la littérature* (p. 273), or in other words before her travels had introduced Mme de Staël to the Germans: 'In Germany, ideas are still of very great interest to everyone ... No nation is more

ideas alone, and ideas allow them to communicate in an ideal republic of minds. Now an intellectual culture of this type, which is eminently northern, is possible only where the contingencies and obligations of concrete existence have been overcome, or, so to speak, transfigured by a supernatural light that destroys their immediately positive character.[34] Hence this elementary contrast: 'In terms of the riches of the mind, the Germans are veritable property-owners: compared with them, those who rely upon their innate intelligence are mere proletarians.'[35] There is obviously a quasi-fictional element in this study of mentalities and of national characteristics, and it gives these conclusions the character of a myth, a collective myth which would soon, and for several decades to come, take on a life of its own. Indeed, Mme de Staël's cosmopolitan imaginary, which structures the whole

peculiarly suited to philosophical ideas ... so much work on the sciences and on pure metaphysics, so much research, and so much perseverance, honour the German nation! The Germans have no political homeland but they have created a philosophical and literary homeland and its glory fills them with the most noble enthusiasm.' We find exactly the same argument in *De l'Allemagne* (p. 5): 'The philosophical spirit cannot, by its very nature, be very widespread in any country. And yet there is in Germany such a penchant for reflection that the German nation can be regarded as the metaphysical nation *par excellence*. It is home to so many men capable of understanding the most abstract ideas that even the public takes an interest in the arguments used in that kind of discussion.' The Germans, who are not really united by their social state, are brought together by the ideas they share, and those ideas constitute a mental world that is distinct from the real world: 'Whilst we recognize that German philosophy is not enough to found a nation, it has to be admitted that the disciples of the new school come much closer than any of the others to having some strength of character; they dream of it, desire it and conceive of it, but they often lack it. Very few men in Germany really know how to write on politics. Most of those who dabble in politics are system-builders and they are very often unintelligible. When it comes to transcendental metaphysics, when one attempts to sound the secrets of nature, no insight, no matter how vague, is to be disdained; any premonition may provide a lead, and all approximations count for a lot. The same is not true of the affairs of the world; it is possible to understand them, and they must therefore be described with clarity. When one is discussing thoughts that know no bounds, obscurity of style is sometimes an index of breadth of mind; but obscurity in the analysis of matters of everyday life merely proves that one does not understand them' (ibid., p. 204). The allusion to Fichte is transparent.

34 The logic of this analysis led Mme de Staël to become one of the first to celebrate what would later be called German science: 'I loved that sanctuary of science and philosophy into which the noise of the world does not penetrate, where peaceful souls and studious minds seek together the means to perfect man in his solitude', *Carnets de voyage*, ed. S. Balayé (Geneva: Droz, 1971), p. 69.
35 *De l'Allemagne*, p. 160.

of her fictional output and conditions the development of her thought, also affects the way she views her new field of investigation: it gives rise to a basic image which real Germans have only to embody when she finally visits them. To the beautiful foreigner known as Mme de Staël, the Germans looked like handsome foreigners. They were foreigners to themselves, absent from their non-existent homeland. They were intense and expansive, filled with enthusiasm and devoted to their 'ideas', which were the only possible manifestations of a collective consciousness freed from the constraints of social life. Within the frontiers that defined it, the German people therefore proved to be a people without frontiers. The mind was free to roam at will. The very characteristics which made it possible to delineate the German national character were precisely those that made it illimitable.

Described in this way, the culture of the Germans was the very opposite of a model in that the message it transmitted was ambiguous, if not actually contradictory. German free-thinkers enjoyed the independence afforded them by a social environment that was powerless to constrain them, but they were by the same criteria condemned to a new form of sectarianism. Because they speculated in isolation and because the preconditions for some mutual consensus had not been met, they inevitably became intellectual rivals. They all claimed to be in possession of an exclusive truth, and therefore imprisoned that truth in a jargon manufactured for the sole purpose of confining it and preserving its specificity. The judgement delivered by *De la littérature* is harsh:

In some respects, the acquisition of learning in Germany is restricted by a self-imposed yoke, namely the sectarian spirit. It is the idle life's equivalent to the partisan spirit, and it has some of the same disadvantages. Before one joins the ranks of the sectarian supporters of one system, one applies one's whole mind to judging it; one decides for or against it through the independent exercise of one's reason. The initial choice is made freely; those that follow are not. Once you have found the basic premises acceptable, you adopt all the conclusions the master derives from his premise in order to preserve the sect. No matter how philosophical it is in its aims, a sect is never philosophical in its means. It must always inspire a sort of blind trust in order to do away with individual dissidence; for, when their reason is free, a great number of men will never give their full assent to the opinions of a single man.[36]

Mme de Staël's argument against system-building had been tried and tested in the Enlightenment period. It comes as no surprise to find,

36   Ibid., p. 277.

after the lines cited above, a note which, at a time when an important debate about Kant's doctrine was taking place in the Institut National in Paris, recalls the positions defended by Destutt de Tracy when he criticized the Kantians for their sectarian spirit rather than those argued by Villers.[37] The greatest philosopher in Germany was, after all, merely one philosopher amongst others; and by claiming that the truth was contained in his discourse alone, he was compromising both the theoretical and the practical merits of his work.

Writing ten years after *De l'Allemagne*, and at a time when she was more familiar with Germany, even though she never succeeded in penetrating the mysteries of the German language, Mme de Staël was to return to the same argument, centred this time on the problems specific to expression:

A talent for methodical and clear expression is rare in Germany; speculative studies do nothing to encourage it. In order to determine what form they should be given, one must, so to speak, stand outside one's own thoughts. Philosophy provides knowledge of man, rather than of men. Only social intercourse can teach us how our spirit relates to the spirit of others. First candour and then pride lead sincere and serious philosophers to rail against those who do not think and feel as they do. The Germans seek the truth conscientiously, but they have a very ardently sectarian attitude towards the doctrines they adopt; for in the hearts of men, everything turns to passion.[38]

The fact that the Germans are too indifferent to one another to establish any effective mutual communication explains why their thought is so abstract, and so strangely obscure as to border on the unintelligible.

Mme de Staël was, no doubt, less impressed by the Germans themselves, or Germans in person, one might say, than by the general idea of Germany she had derived from her initial speculations about the problems of national cultures. The fascination they exercised over her therefore did not lead her to accept their distinctive mentality passively or uncritically, as though it were a self-contained cultural figure to be taken or left as such. She described the Germans as showing the way to the formation of the European consciousness that was emerging from the ruins of the feudal *anciens régimes* because, far from identifying them as the bearers of an autonomous and potentially introverted system of thought, she diagnosed, in the lacunae of that

37 'All the ingenuity of Kant's mind and all that is lofty in his principles is not, I think, an adequate objection against what I have just said about the sectarian spirit' (ibid.). 38 Ibid., p. 195.

system, elements or premonitory signs of an open and authentically cosmopolitan system which could, because of its versatility, lend itself to antagonistic exchanges.[39] Her vision of Germany was completely imbued with that conception of cultural relations.

A multinational spirit

Behind all Mme de Staël's undertakings and in all the domains in which she took an interest we find, on the one hand, ideas which are inspired by a theoretical tradition inaugurated by Montesquieu and, on the other, ideas which come from Germany, where, when mediated by Herder, Möser and a few others, they would help to elaborate a new concept of national culture, defined on the basis of the concrete and primal existence of peoples. According to this view, peoples should be seen in terms of the differences that characterize them, and not in terms of the abstract and universally shared values of an ideal spirit or an ideal nature that made its influence felt regardless of conditions of time and space. This was a real theoretical mutation, and it also coincided with the transition from 'classical' to 'romantic' thought. Yet Mme de Staël worked this raw material in such a way as not only to ensure its diffusion by adapting it to an appropriate mode of expression, but also to transform it and produce a truly original body of thought: literature now becomes an integral part of philosophy, if not *a* philosophy.

This is why we find no trace in her work of a theory of national culture in any strict sense of that term, as we do in the contemporary German authors with whom one might be tempted to compare her. Her problematic in fact displaces the implications of that notion; what interests her is not the identity of cultures considered in themselves, regardless of whether or not they are divorced from the context of the

39 Cf. ibid., pp. 161–2: 'We must appeal to French good taste to combat the vigorous exaggeration of certain Germans, and to the profundity of the Germans to combat the dogmatic frivolity of certain Frenchmen. Nations must use one another as guides, and all nations would be wrong to deny themselves the mutual enlightenment they can bring to one another. There is something very singular about the difference between one people and another: the climate, the face of nature, language, government, and all the events of history – which has a still greater power than all the others – contribute to this diversity, and no man, no matter how superior, can divine what is naturally developing in the mind of one who lives in a different land and breathes a different air; all countries would therefore do well to welcome foreign thoughts; for in this domain, hospitality makes the recipient wealthy.'

material civilization to which they belonged, but the communication that can be established between different cultures. Such communication would necessarily blur their identity, or at least modify it. Mme de Staël therefore formulates an original theoretical thesis according to which there can be no cultural identity except within the complex system of relations that brings together cultures whilst maintaining the differences and contrasts between them. It is on this principle that she founds her intellectual cosmopolitanism. From this point of view, the contradiction between the universalism of the classicists and the particularism of the romantics can be overcome because it has become as illusory to assert the radical autonomy of every particular form of culture as it is to merge them all in a single ideal model by cutting them off from their roots. A culture never exists by itself or for itself. A culture is constituted and gains recognition within a global and differentiated system in which various cultures speak to one another, challenge one another and complement one another not by pooling together their respective assets, but by comparing, and to a certain extent exchanging, their lacunae and failings.

From this point of view, there can be no such thing as a people or a culture considered in itself and in its absolute singularity, or at least if such a people or culture did exist it would be beyond our understanding and, ultimately, there would be nothing to say about it. What interested Mme de Staël about the Germans was therefore not Germany as such, or Germany 'in itself', so to speak, but the common network of exchanges that could promote a dialogue between the cultural features of Germany and France in the context of a relationship which was certainly not reducible to that dialogue alone, since the other countries of Europe, and especially England and Italy, were also involved. We can now understand why, in the whole of Mme de Staël's work, we find no trace of an organicist theory of culture which could sanction isolationist practices by deferring the dialogue between nations. According to Mme de Staël, what lay at the heart of German thought was not a single idea which could be the seed, in the organic sense of that term, of its whole development and which could possibly be interpreted as a symptom of its supremacy; it was the discrepancy, the antagonism even, between the practices which conditioned it (political backwardness/advanced theory). Now it was that very discrepancy that made German thought German. It generated an internal contradiction which brought German thought into communication with other, and at first sight completely different, forms of cultural existence. In that respect, we can truly speak of the work of negativity. It thus became possible to reflect upon cultures, not in their own terms, but in terms of the disparities that, by estranging them from themselves, projected them outside their own constituency. It is as though Mme de Staël had read Germany in France and vice versa. At a moment when the era of nationalisms was beginning, the importance of such a conception was far from negligible.

3

❖❖

George Sand's *Spiridion*: a pantheist novel

❖❖

Spiridion has a special place in George Sand's highly diversified *oeuvre*. Whilst it is now one of the least read of her books, and certainly one of the least accessible, it must be remembered that at the time of its publication it confirmed its author's reputation as a mediator or intercessor who transmitted news of major intellectual developments. Renan, who read it in his early years when he was beginning to be 'converted' to rationalism, insistently declared that he was greatly indebted to it. In a different context, Alain also celebrated its importance for his own intellectual history. One might say that, in the nineteenth century, this tale of initiation played a role comparable to that which would later be played by André Breton's *Nadja*: the very particular impact of both books resulted from the way they succeeded in weaving together the speculative and the narrative.

In the sequence of its author's most significant works, *Spiridion* comes before *Lelia* and after *Consuelo*, and when it began to appear, George Sand, who had taken up writing seven years earlier, was generally regarded as a novelist of ideas. Each of her books seemed to use fiction to defend a thesis or a cause. In other words, these writings communicated ideas by telling stories. Where did these ideas come from, and in what form can they be apprehended? Did they exist prior to their insertion into a narrative? Can we speak of the 'thought of George Sand' and say that her literary works merely served to propagate it? George Sand asked herself these questions, notably in the prefaces to her major works,[1] where she outlines the following

---

1   In the preface to *Indiana*, her very first book, George Sand was already insisting on the fact that the writer is primarily a 'storyteller' or a mere fabulist and that by reporting both the facts and the corresponding intellectual attitudes, he is simply recording what he observes. This does not imply taking sides or making value-judgements. This is the classic argument used by all writers who have to face moral censure and who, if they are novelists, remain in the background and try to hide behind the truly fictional life conferred upon their characters. In the

thesis: the role of the writer is not to uphold ideas by basing them on arguments, but rather to provoke questions, the answers to which must remain in abeyance. That is why the writer's views on truth, insofar as truth depends upon general speculations of a philosophical nature, are the views of a visionary. The writer evokes the truth, or in other words suggests it without confining it within the doctrinal limits of a system; the refusal to offer definitive solutions will, it is assumed, open up infinite possibilities for thought.

One naturally wonders whether or not George Sand respected this programme in her actual practice as a novelist. Did her relationship with the abstract content of philosophical speculation remain strictly poetic? In her fictional works, does not the reference to truths of a doctrinal order occasionally become more ponderous and more insistent, and does it not therefore lose its allusive character and answer the questions it is supposed to leave in suspense? If that were the case, her plots and narrative style would be no more than external ornaments. They would be a stage-set erected in order to promote ideas which have a meaning outside their context. The context would be a mere pretext for their dissemination.[2] Is it possible to 'translate' ideas into a fictional form? Is it desirable to do so? Does that transposition make for good novels? Does it make for good philosophy? Or, to be more specific, what kind of philosophy can be included in a novel? And what kind of novel can be written with such a philosophy?

Spiridion, which I propose to analyse here, is central to all these questions. The book was originally described as the tribute of a

preface to *Indiana,* George Sand concludes, in the name of the novelist, that she must refuse to 'put on the philosopher's robe'. Speaking of *Spiridion,* she states in apparently similar terms that, 'This is only a novel, or a nightmare if you like. But I have never claimed to be writing the solution to anything. That is not my role. Perhaps my whole life will be spent seeking the truth, without my being able to formulate a single aspect of it: each to their task' (letter to Henriette de La Bigottière, late December 1842, in George Sand, *Correspondance,* Paris: Garnier, 1969, vol. 4, pp. 826–7).

2 Sand seems to admit that this is the case when she writes of *Consuelo:* 'I must tell you that George Sand is no more than a pale reflection of Pierre Leroux, a fanatical disciple of the same Ideal, but a disciple who is both reduced to silence and delighted by his words, who is always ready to cast into the fire all her works in order to write, speak, think, pray and act under his inspiration ... I am not a vulgarizer with a diligent pen and an impressionable heart who is trying to translate the master's philosophy into novels' (letter of 14 February 1844 to Ferdinand Guillou, ibid., vol. 6, p. 431).

disciple – the writer – to a master – the philosopher Pierre Leroux, to whom Sand said she owed the greater part of her inspiration.[3] In this novel, literature and philosophy merge, as we put it earlier, so much so that it was possible to believe, wrongly it seems, that part of Sand's manuscript was written by Leroux's own hand. Two successive versions of *Spiridion* appeared, in 1839 and 1842 respectively. In the meantime, Leroux's great work *De l'humanité* was published in 1840; it contained a systematic exposition of all his ideas. Are we not entitled to invert the usual argument and wonder whether Sand's narrative work might not have influenced the elaboration and exposition of Leroux's philosophical thought, of which it claimed, perhaps with false modesty, to be a mere fictional transposition?

Spiridion, a fable

Spiridion is a strange novel set in a Benedictine monastery in seventeenth- and eighteenth-century Italy. It portrays distraught visionaries who seem to live on the borderline between dreams and waking life. The fantastic setting is not unreminiscent of certain 'Gothic' novels. The narrative is unusual in that it is the only novel by Sand in which there are no female characters, though it is true that, given that it is a book about mysteries, the elision of Woman may perhaps signify her universal and secret presence.

In order to understand how the narrative is organized, and to understand the idea-effects produced by its organization, we must first of all characterize the spatial configuration of the setting from which it never moves, not in order to reconstruct the anecdotal atmosphere but to analyse the mental space within which it unfolds. The monastery in *Spiridion* and the narrow limits imposed on it by its closure serve as a microcosm of the whole history of humanity. The events that take place between the foundation of the monastery in 1690 and its destruction some one hundred years later reproduce the overall movement of humanity's spiritual evolution. The novel is also an allegory – *Spiridion*'s first readers took it to be a *roman à clef* and tried

3 *Spiridion* is dedicated 'To Monsieur Pierre Leroux, my friend and brother in terms of age; my father and master in terms of virtue and science; please accept one of my tales, not because it is a work worthy of being dedicated to you, but as a token of friendship and veneration' (*Spiridion*, Paris: Editions d'Aujourdhui, Collection 'Les Introuvables', 1976, p. 1). This edition reproduces the text of the definitive edition of 1842.

to decipher its enigmas — about the Catholic church and the Vatican.[4] That is not, however, what is essential; the really important point is that the closure imagined by Sand in its turn encloses a fundamentally ambiguous space which is traversed by a secret that destroys its external appearance. It simultaneously presents two aspects, one evil and repulsive, the other benevolent and attractive.

On the one hand, the monastery in *Spiridion* represents a structure of exclusion whose meaning is primarily negative: it represents, by summarizing it, the entire system of material and spiritual oppression to which humanity has long been subjugated by the alliance between despotism and superstition.[5] Here we find, in a particularly virulent form, the tradition of anticlerical literature, and one understands why the young Renan should have been interested in it. But this obvious and outward aspect masks another aspect which suggests a very different interpretation: the monastery whose imaginary history is reconstructed by Sand is in fact the privileged site of a revelation, and it therefore represents an irreplaceable haven for an inspired humanity that is brought together by its joint possession of a truth. It preserves a truth and hands down a tradition.[6] The monastic regime therefore

4 Gregory XVI, the author of the two encyclicals that condemned Lamennais (*Mirari nos*, 1832, and *Singulari vos*, 1834), was the reigning Pope at the time when Sand was writing her novel, and certain pages are obviously directed against him. He was probably the model for the monastery's last Prior, who is largely responsible for its final downfall; the Prior is a Benedictine from the order of the Camaldules, to which Gregory XVI himself had once belonged. Sand paints a very black picture of the order in *Leila*.

5 Sand gained personal experience of solitude while she was writing *Spiridion*. As she later related in her *Un hiver à Majorque* (in Sand, *Ecrits autobiographiques*, vol. 1, Paris: Bibliothèque de la Pléiade, 1970), which appeared in 1842, she spent a whole winter shut up in the Chartreuse de Valdemosa with Chopin and his children. The book expresses the resentment she felt against the Majorcans. It explains their backwardness in terms of their subjugation to feudalism and Catholicism and contains an indignant description of their religious buildings, which are a visible testimony to slavery and credulity. Her account of her stay in the Balearics includes a fictional episode entitled *Le Couvent de l'Inquisition*. It takes place in a ruined Dominican monastery which Sand describes as having once belonged to the Inquisition. She attributes its destruction to a popular revolt that is reminiscent of the storming of the Bastille.

6 Once again, this can be read as a memory of something that was actually experienced by the author. The fictional monastery in *Spiridion* is reminiscent of the Augustinian convent in England where the young Aurore Dupin spent part of her adolescence and where, as she explains in *Histoire de ma vie* (*Ecrits biographiques*, vol. 1), she was happy because it allowed her to escape for a while the family quarrels occasioned by the continual differences of opinion between

represents, in a positive way, a communal structure for which Sand, who was perhaps also very indirectly influenced by the practices of the Saint-Simonian cult, would always feel nostalgic.

The monastery is therefore a double space which simultaneously displays a wrong side and a right side. That is the explanation for the strange fascination it exerts.[7] Now this intrinsically conflictual space leaves its mark on the whole story that takes place within it; the events that occur are, like their setting, ambiguous. On a first reading they are related to the typical incidents of a traditional type of fantastic literature; *Spiridion* is in the tradition of the works of Radcliffe and Lewis, from which it borrows both its mysterious and frenetic atmosphere as well as elements of religious parody. The main events consist of a series of apparitions whose supernatural character is prosaically embodied in very physical objects: hidden doors which open without being touched, fleeting nocturnal visions, books in which there is something to be read even though their pages seem to be blank, paintings which weep, shadows which speak, treasure buried in graves ... all the bric à brac of the Gothic novel, which becomes ludicrous when it attempts to give the unknown and the invisible too tangible a presence. Although it is very hard to accept that these evocations are immaterial, they are merely the surface of a stage-set which in fact signifies something very different: the apparitions stand for inspirations. They express, in other words, the insistent and unavoidable presence of an idea rather than the real existence of another world and a related system of beliefs whose deceptive character will in fact be denounced at the end of the novel. That idea, which is directly evoked by the title of the novel – *Spiridion* – cannot be exorcised: it gives a hidden meaning to all that is said and done because it contains a message which will not really be revealed until the very last pages of the story.[8]

her mother and her grandmother, who had brought her up. It was there, recounts Sand, that, when she was about fifteen, she went through an intense mystical crisis from which she never fully recovered; the whole of Sand's *oeuvre* is imbued with an air of vague religiosity.

7   Father Alexis, who is one of the novel's main protagonists, expresses the contrast clearly when he states: 'All enlightenment, all progress and all that is great have emerged from the cloister; but all enlightenment, all progress and all that is great must perish there, if certain of us do not persevere in the terrible struggle that ignorance and imposture are now waging against the truth' (*Spiridion*, p. 24).

8   One episode in the novel takes this tension to the extreme by showing the extent to which, far from being parallel but separate worlds, the real and the unreal are

George Sand's Spiridion: *a pantheist novel*

Spiridion tells the story of a revelation. It expounds a new Gospel by reproducing it in the fictional form of the novel that reveals its existence. One of the most magnetically-charged places described in the narrative, to which the action — defined as the anecdotal series of episodes that makes it up — constantly returns in moments of high intensity, is the slab in the chapel that gives access to the crypt. This is the resting place of the mortal remains of Abbé Spiridion, who was buried there together with his secret. The slab is engraved with the legend *Hic est veritas*, an emblematic formula inscribed in a double network of meanings. On the one hand, it expresses the basic tenet of an orthodoxy, which is why it also appears in the official portrait of the community's founder. It depicts Spiridion holding Bossuet's *Histoire*

inextricably intertwined and communicate in extraordinary ways. When Father Alexis, who is one of the narrators, goes into retreat in a neighbouring hermitage by the sea, he has a strange and unexpected visitor. He is the most incongruous of all the apparitions that materialize in Sand's tale: 'A young Corsican, whose severe features and thoughtful gaze have always stayed in my memory. I was struck by that young man's every feature: his careless attitude, combined with great reserve, his energetic and concise words, his bright, piercing eyes, his Roman profile and a certain gracious clumsiness which seemed to suggest a self-doubt that could turn to hot-blooded daring at the slightest challenge' (*Spiridion*, p. 204). The unexpected irruption of reality into fiction heightens its fantastic character still further by detaching it from immediate appearances. The eagle alights on the novel's shores long enough to make an astounding speech, and then takes wing again. Here are some samples: 'The desire for strength is a developmental need that necessity inflicts upon all beings. Everything wants to be what it must be. Anything that does not have will-power is destined to perish, be it a man without a heart or a blade of grass deprived of the sap that feeds it. How can men not wage war, individual against individual, nation against nation? How can society not be a perpetual conflict between contrary wills and needs, when everything in nature is work, when the waves of the sea rise up against one another, when the eagle tears apart the hare, when the swallow tears apart the worm, when frost splits blocks of marble and when snow resists the sun? ... Everything wants to have its place and to fill its place to the full extent of its potential for expansion ... Let us work then, mortal creatures, let us work towards our own existence' (ibid., pp. 207–9). The reader should not, however, be misled by this aggressive appeal to the elementary *conatus* of living nature; *Spiridion* is not a novel of energy, and the hallucinatory figure of a young Bonaparte converted to a kind of Spinozism that appears in its final pages is in fact a counter-argument which is quite devoid of truth. The figure expresses a pantheistic theory of origins based upon a profusion of elemental forces; Sand is trying to invalidate that pantheism by describing it in almost unbearably extreme terms. She is attempting to replace it with a diametrically opposed image of a spiritual pantheism which finds its privileged incarnation in the future unanimity of humanity.

des variations des églises protestantes, for that was the work which gave him his original inspiration. *Hic veritas* therefore means that, because of the exclusive character that distinguishes it from the uncertain forms of error and deviancy, the truth remains within the limits established by one Book belonging to one Church. But as the story advances, the same sentence, which illuminates the entire narrative, comes to indicate the other side of the truth, its hidden side, namely heresy. This is an immediate reminder of the personal history of Lamennais, who was the great heretic of the France of the 1840s. The formula *hic veritas* therefore refers to another book: the book Spiridion finally wrote to record his message when his ecclesiastical and monastic illusions had been gradually dispelled. The book written by Sand purports to transcribe it and, like the original, it exists in two versions. Two editions of the novel appeared, in 1839 and 1842 respectively. Sand turns Spiridion's secret book into a serial, into what we might call an entire 'history' whose moments interlock to constitute a new tradition. The tradition originates in the eternal Gospel of Joachim of Floris, is passed on by John of Parma's commentary on it and then inspires Spiridion's reflections, which reproduce Leroux's theses on the religion of Humanity. Unlike a dogma, which has a constant form from the outset, a truth of this kind is inseparable from the movement that develops it: it perpetuates itself but remains incomplete and never allows itself to be used for the exposition of a doctrine. Orthodoxy and heresy are thus brought into secret communication and are related to one another by the framework of a common history. It is the debate between the two that is described by *Spiridion* which, from this point of view, alludes primarily to the personal destiny of Lamennais, of which it is a fictional transposition.

This theme is, however, the support for a more important message which will be partly revealed only in the final pages of the book. *Spiridion* describes the lives of the four monks who, between 1690 and 1790, succeeded one another in the monastery, but who kept themselves largely from its outward life because of the clandestine communion established between them by the occult tradition they perpetuate. The tradition, of which those who are not chosen initiates know nothing, replicates the official tradition it is destroying from within. From that point of view, *Spiridion* is the story of a line of descent as well as, or perhaps more so than, the story of a heresy; indeed, it is the superimposition of the two motifs that gives the fable its ultimate meaning. One could go so far as to say that the story of the four monks, as told by Sand, symbolizes the history of humanity, which is united by religion in the mystical sharing of the spiritual truth to which it owes its unity. At this level, it is not simply about Lamennais or the crisis of a conscience confronted with the constraints of dogma. It would be more accurate to say that these teachings are completely reinterpreted in the light of Leroux's theories, which are devoid of any reference to Christian orthodoxy insofar as they represent an attempt to establish a new religion in which divine transcendence no longer intervenes: the Religion of Humanity, in which humanity is united, not in the reverential contemplation and passive preservation of a primal revelation, but by the impetus given by the process of continual innovation that projects it towards its future in an essentially solidarist movement.

The real subject of *Spiridion* and its fable is the transformation – and it is not an instantaneous mutation, as it unfolds in the course of a history which must remain perpetually open – of a primitive religion that originated in a full revelation and that is now reducible to and confined within the permanent boundaries of an exclusive dogma, into a religion of ends that freely invents its tradition as its living subject develops. Its subject is Humanity considered in all its spatial and temporal extension.

In that respect, the personal history of the first of the four monks is exemplary. Spiridion founded this new and progressive tradition, but it is clear that a 'new' tradition inspired by the movement of its constant transformation is not quite a tradition. Who was Spiridion? His real name was Samuel Hebronius; of Jewish origins, he was born in Germany and lived at roughly the same time as Spinoza. The assonance between the names Spiridion and Spinoza is certainly not the result of pure chance. After having studied at the University of Heidelberg, Hebronius forswore the Jewish religion and converted to protestantism. Having read Bossuet, especially the latter's *Histoire des variations des églises protestantes*, he then became a Catholic. Baptised by Bossuet himself, he took the Christian name Peter – a sign that he had a vocation to found a church – and the surname Spiridion – which placed him under the sign of the Spirit, the Holy Ghost, who was the source of his inspiration. It was then that he founded the monastic order which gives Sand's novel its framework; the novel retraces the full history of the order from the moment of its foundation to that of its destruction. In the monastery, of which he becomes the first Prior, Spiridion devotes himself to speculative, scientific and philosophical research. As a result, he gradually finds himself moving away from Catholic dogma, so much so that he is suspected of dabbling in sorcery and satanism.[9] At the same time, he makes his secret entry into immortality through the mediation of the occult tradition which detaches him from his physical existence: for those he 'inspires', he then becomes a symbol.

Spiridion's first disciple was Fulgence, a simple and generous soul who, in the history recounted by Sand, represents the specific moment of naive mankind. He is entrusted with Spiridion's message but does not understand it. Only a few pages of the narrative are devoted to him.

Fulgence is succeeded by Alexis, whose spiritual odyssey provides most of the book's content. Sand makes him a sort of second Dr Faustus. Unlike his predecessor Fulgence, he represents the spirit of dissension, and therefore pursues Spiridion's experiments to their logical, and negative, conclusions. He begins to question not only the form of his early beliefs, but their very content, and becomes an atheist. He takes advantage of an epidemic of the plague to make a temporary escape from his cloistered imprisonment and finds the path that will take him back to men: charity helps him to rediscover the hope that was once offered by faith.

As he is dying, Alexis passes on the secret, of which he is the last guardian, to Brother Angel, who acts as a witness to the whole story and who alone is vouchsafed the final revelation of the 'Book' preserved in the tomb where the founder of the monastery is buried. The book is a manuscript by Spiridion which reproduces the writings of Joachim of Floris and John of Parma, as reinterpreted in the light of Leroux's ideas.

The important thing is the uninterrupted development that leads to the revelation of a 'spirit', namely the spirit of Spiridion. It exists only

9 The first account of Spiridion's life to figure in Sand's narrative is given by an ignorant and corrupt monk. He has no understanding at all of Spiridion's secret, and he says of him: 'The books of the philosopher Spinoza and the infernal doctrines of the philosophers of that school turned him into a pantheist, or in other words an atheist' (*Spiridion*, pp. 48–9). After his death, however, the disciples who become the successive guardians of his message refer to him amongst themselves as 'Saint Spiridion'. That formula is obviously not unreminiscent of the formula applied to Spinoza in the context of the *Pantheismusstreit*: 'Sankt Spinoza'. As to the name Spiridion itself, Sand may have come across it in Hoffmann's *Elixiere des Teufels*, which appeared in a French translation in 1829; the name is mentioned briefly towards the end.

when it is communicated, which is why the only content of the message it finally delivers is the revelation of the immanent perpetuity that promises authentic immortality. Immortality will be granted only to those who belong to the network of unanimity. An eternal palingenesy brings together all the experiences of Humanity by giving them an eternal meaning: that is the lesson of the version of the Eternal Gospel with which Sand ends her book.[10]

Between Lamennais and Leroux

Let us now try to evaluate the underlying doctrinal content of the narrative whose general outline we have traced. How are we to situate the religious thought it expounds? It is from the outset fairly complex, even confused. It results from a construction that resembles a montage. The fictional element makes the montage possible because it supplies the preconditions for its cohesion, but that cohesion is itself fictional. Its homogeneity would, however, prove problematical if we attempted to divorce its argumentative or speculative content from the narrative that binds it together and thus gives it a certain unity.

The book's disparate character can be explained primarily in terms of the conditions in which Sand wrote it between 1838 and 1839. *Spiridion* was originally written in the form of the successive episodes of a serial published in the *Revue de Paris*; they were then rewritten for publication in book form, and rewritten once more for the second edition published in 1842.[11] The *Spiridion* project was a real *work in progress* [English in the original]. Like its subject-matter, it was modified, expanded and given a new meaning as it was written and rewritten. If anything does happen in this allegedly plotless novel, it is this internal work of writing and fiction, which gradually displaces the issues at stake in it and at the same time changes their theoretical meaning.

To give an overall, and necessarily schematic, interpretation of the displacement that occurs, one might say that it moves between the thought of Lamennais and that of Leroux. In 1838, Sand was under the influence of both men. It is as though, having initially set out to write

---

10 On the tradition of the Eternal Gospel as a whole, see H. de Lubac, *La Postérité spirituelle de Joachim de Fiore* (Paris: Le Sycomore, 1981). One whole chapter is devoted to Sand's novel.

11 For a detailed analysis of the stages of the composition of Sand's book, see J. Pommier, *Spiridion ou le rêve monastique de George Sand* (Paris: Nizet, 1966).

a novel about Lamennais, Sand finally resolved to write one about Leroux. If the fictional *Spiridion* has any philosophical interest, it is to the extent that it refers not to a single speculative content which is systematically defined and which it simply sets out to illustrate, but to at least two contents which do not quite coincide. Given that they are disparate, they cannot simply be reproduced and embellished with a suitable fable. They have to be unified, and that, as we shall see, is not unproblematical.

I would not go so far as to say the twin sources of inspiration that simultaneously presided over Sand's work as a novelist were incompatible; if they were, it would be impossible to understand how they could coexist during the composition of a single work. There was in fact a point where the thought of Lamennais and that of Leroux converged, and the two were therefore in communication. Sand's book reveals the existence of that point of convergence: the idea that eternity exists only through and in the life of humanity, or in other words its history. History gives the principle of universality an effective content by supplying it with a concrete incarnation. This idea was in fact nothing more than an avatar of the Hegelianism which was secretly circulating in a muted and watered-down form throughout French thought in the first half of the nineteenth century during the intellectual reign of Victor Cousin.

We are concerned with the 1840s, and at this stage in Lamennais's thinking, the sources of this notion are to be found in Malebranche, from whom he derived the idea that all beings co-exist within an exhaustive order, which is immutable, and that there is such a thing as a scale of perfectibility. Lamennais was beginning to outline a philosophy of unanimity which uses the figures of tradition, transmission and filiation to reconcile conservatism and development, order and progress. His speculations would result in a vision of a mystical people which was, at the time when Lamennais disseminated it, regarded as a pantheist vision.[12] Leroux was simultaneously

12 Here, for example, is what Lamennais writes at the beginning of his *Esquisse d'une philosophie*, which was published in 1840: 'Humanity preserves and hands down to successive generations all the knowledge that is indispensable to man, all the truths that make up the understanding; each man bears within him the imperishable seed of the understanding, which represents their shared reason. Humanity also preserves and hands down knowledge about observed facts, about the permanent facts of the universe. This body of knowledge is known as tradition; and we can best picture it by thinking of it as the memory which allows

developing apparently similar ideas. He was elaborating a doctrine of
individuation based upon a principle of continuity borrowed from
Leibniz. It provided the basis for integral communication between
individual existences. Individual existences merged to form Humanity,
which Leroux regarded as a developing totality that constantly
perfected the forms of their integration. This was what Leroux, who
was very fond of neologisms, was to call 'communionism'.[13]

There were undeniable points of convergence between these two
conceptions and the philosophical references on which they were
based, namely Malebranche and Leibniz. Sand incorporates the points
of convergence into her novel, and it was this that led to the
accusations of pantheism.[14] The Spirit which gives Sand's novel both
its theme and its title (*Spiridion*) is, according to the final revelation, not
an individual spirit, but a collective spirit common to all men. It exists
in the form of the ties that bind them together, and it lives in
perpetuity because it can be transmitted. The only things to perish are
particular elements, which are as nothing in the light of its overall
development. The universalist perspective which is thus opened up
makes it possible both to rethink the past history of religions and of
Christianity – Sand's book applies to the person of Christ a formula
which could not fail to strike the young Renan: 'that divine man', 'that
sublime philosopher'[15] – and to elaborate the project of the religion of
the future, a religion whose Subject would, of course, be Humanity.[16]

the human race to acquire and possess an interrupted sense of its identity; for it
is one, just as every man is one , albeit in a different way, and it makes progress
by coming ever closer to the perfect unity towards which it gravitates in
accordance with a law governing all beings.' From this point of view, order
determines progress, which is merely the manifestation or authentic revelation of
order.

13 Witness the following passage from his *De l'humanité*, which was also published
in 1840 ('Doctrine', vol. 1, chapter 7): 'But what are we in essence, and what is
the essence which will manifest itself once more, and whose new manifestations
will make up our new life? I say that we are not merely a being, a force or a
virtuality, but that that being, that force and that virtuality have, as such, a
determinate nature. I say that each of us is humanity. We are humanity. Our
perfectibility is bound up with the perfectibility of humanity or is, rather, that
perfectibility of humanity.' According to Leroux, it is progress which creates
order as it advances.

14 In his *Essai sur le panthéisme dans les sociétés modernes* (1840), which brought the
quarrel over pantheism into the public domain, Abbé Maret writes ('Préface', p.
xii) of Sand: 'In *Spiridion* she dresses up forms created by her imagination and her
style in the pantheistic doctrines of M. Pierre Leroux.'

15 *Spiridion*, p. 194.   16 Ibid., p. 202.

This essential similarity should not, however, be allowed to mask a number of discordances. The respective positions of Lamennais and Leroux with regard to the basic problems of religion, and the specific question of Christianity, were not in fact absolutely identical, and could even be contrasted. Lamennais's basic idea was – or was up to 1840 – that Christianity could be regenerated by a return to its sources. His doctrine was therefore marked by an internal contradiction, and this did not escape the notice of his contemporaries, or even his supporters. Lamennais denounced abuses of dogmatism in the name of dogma, and challenged the decisions of the Pope in the name of a principle of authority. Even though his populism was to evolve in such a way as to bring him close to a sort of socialism, the underlying theme, which in fact provided the basis for his populism, was always the same. His intellectual development was always inspired by his notion of tradition. As a result, he was inevitably torn between two tendencies: Lamennais was a man haunted by doubts, and his thought is an exemplary expression of a state of spiritual crisis. For Sand, who was irresistibly attracted to him and then profoundly disappointed by him, he represented, because of his inability to establish a syncretic religious philosophy, the paradigmatic figure of impotence and despair.[17] In terms of the spiritual trajectory that would finally lead to the truth, Leroux, unlike this negative testimony to failure, represented the radiant image of reconciliation and certainty. He had the authority to establish a new faith which would completely free itself from the presuppositions of earlier religions, whose irresistible decline had been proclaimed. We can therefore say that Sand's novel reproduces the personal odyssey that led its author from the question asked by Lamennais – and he was certainly a man who asked questions – to the answer given by Leroux, whom she saw as the apostle of resolution. From that point of view, it is as though these two references alluded respectively to the negative and positive aspects of the same doctrinal content.[18]

17 It will be recalled that Auguste Comte himself did not touch upon the theme of the religion of Humanity until after 1850.
18 Sainte-Beuve may have been right to identify Lamennais as the model for Father Alexis, who is one of *Spiridion*'s main protagonists (letter of 25 November 1838 to Mme Juste Ollivier, in Saint-Beuve, *Correspondance générale*, Paris: Stock, 1936, vol. 2, p. 486). Like the real Lamennais, the fictional Alexis feels the need for the religious system to be completely refounded, but cannot really bring that about. Witness the admission he makes to Brother Angel (*Spiridion*, pp. 117–18), which

It is particularly significant that the story recounted by *Spiridion* ends by turning away from ruminations about the past and ancient traditions – the shift is symbolized by the final destruction of the monastery – and by evoking an intrinsically revolutionary future. This is also why the book ends with a redemptive blasphemy: the soldiers of the French Revolution, those 'terrible avengers of outraged liberty', sack the monastery and destroy, along with all the other religious symbols that bear witness to the survival of a vanished past, a wooden figure of Christ. They trample the gilded image, and hail it as 'Jesus the *sans-culotte*'.[19] Although Sand could obviously not have known it when she wrote these lines, this resurgence of an old millenarian theme also prefigures the revolutionary spirit of 1848, which was to project an identical synthesis of people and true religion.[20] Their synthesis would, it was believed, transcend the

might be a sort of allegorical summary of the 'Lamennais case': 'My reasoning was certainly deplorable, for I was undermining all the authority of the Church without ever thinking of leaving the Church. I was pulling down around me the ruins of a building which can only be attacked from outside. These contradictions are not unusual in minds which are in every other respect sincere and logical. A habitual hostility towards the body of the Protestant Church and a habitual and instinctive loyalty to the Roman Church make them want to preserve the cradle, whilst the irresistible power of the truth and the need for a justifiable independence have completely transformed and enlarged the body such that this narrow bed no longer fits it. In the midst of these contradictions, I could no longer see the main point. I could not see that I was no longer a Catholic.'

19 This is why the fable which, by means of Alexis's narrative, retraces all the episodes in Lamennais's personal history ends, at the point where Spiridion's secret is revealed, with the revelation of a message which is in reality Leroux's message. It is the 'dogma' of the New Trinity, and the prophet of 'socialism' (Leroux was one of the inventors of the term), who sat in the National Assembly in 1848, would later attempt, to the stupefaction of the French clergy, to make it one of the articles of the French Constitution (he himself describes this episode with great verve in his poetic autobiography *La Grève de Samarez*): 'The dogma of the trinity is the eternal religion; true understanding of this doctrine is eternally progressive. Perhaps we eternally go through the three phases of a manifestation – activity, love and science – which is the divine principle that is received by every man when he comes into the world, because he is the son of God. The more we succeed in manifesting simultaneously these three facets of our humanity, the closer we will come to divine perfection. Men of the future, you are destined to fulfil this prophecy, if God dwells within you. That will be the work of a new revelation, a new religion, a new society and a new humanity.'

20 Before he dies, Alexis offers an interpretation of the soldiers' act: '"This is the work of Providence, and the mission of our executioners is a sacred one, even though they do not understand that yet! They said it, and you heard them: it was in the name of Jesus the *sans-culotte* that they profaned the sanctuary of the

worldly institutions that had distorted the true religion. To that extent, fiction anticipated reality, and may even have shaped it.

Corambé, a novel

On the basis of the above commentary, we can conclude that a reading of *Spiridion* cannot be divorced from an interpretation of its speculative content and a reconstruction of the latter's doctrinal sources, as it is the latter that gives it its overall meaning. Our commentary remains, however, inadequate in that it still does not allow us to understand the intrinsic link between the fictional – or, to simplify matters, literary – form, and the religious or philosophical thought that seems to give it a content. At this point we have to go back to the notion of pantheism, to which we have already alluded. This notion helps us to understand that the elementary principles behind a novel like *Spiridion* mean that it is inseparably bound up with speculation, that it is neither a mere commentary nor a more or less arbitrary illustration. It is not speculation dressed up as narrative, but a necessary development of speculative thought. The notion of a 'pantheist' literature now takes on a new meaning. It does not mean that a pantheist 'doctrine', or a doctrine classified as such, is being transposed or translated into a literary exposition which is in itself unrelated to its themes. Pantheism becomes a form of narrative designed to make the real and the fictional communicate. In that sense, George Sand's 'pantheism' is indeed an essentially fictional pantheism: it belongs to the order of a literary philosophy.

At this point, we must turn momentarily away from the text of *Spiridion* in order to look at the personal revelations of Sand's *Histoire de ma vie*: these shed a very definite light on the conditions in which her vocation as a writer developed. We learn, for example, that: 'From my very early childhood, I needed to create for myself an inner world of my own, a fantastic and poetic world; gradually, I also felt the need to create a religious or philosophical world, or in other words a moral or sentimental world.'[21] Brought up in Nohant by her grandmother, who was completely imbued with the ideas of the previous century and was a free-thinker *avant la lettre*, the young Aurore Dupin

Church. This is the beginning of the reign of the eternal Gospel prophesied by our fathers"' (*Spiridion*, p. 270).
21 *Histoire de ma vie* in *Ecrits biographiques*, p. 809.

therefore elaborated, when she was about eleven, a personal religion whose myths were forged out of the books she had read – especially the *Iliad*, which introduced her to the spirit of the pagan world, and *Gerusalemme Liberata*, which was her introduction to Christianity. From the outset, her religion was therefore organized like a fiction: it was constructed like a novel.[22] A close relationship was therefore established between speculation and narration, as the adoption of this system of beliefs meant the simultaneous acquisition of the ability to tell stories, not only by lending them an intellectual content, but also by setting up the framework for their narration.

Sand reconstructs a mythical history and uses her talent as a writer to bring back to life a character called Aurore Dupin. At the same time, she recreates the religion of Corambé:

I said to myself: Given that all religions are fictional, let us create a religion which is a novel or a novel which is a religion. I do not believe in my novels, but they give me as much pleasure as if I did believe in them. Moreover, if I do believe in them from time to time, no one will destroy my illusions by proving to me that I am dreaming. And as I lay dreaming one night, a face and a name came to me. So far as I know, the name meant nothing, and was a random collection of syllables, the sort that takes shape in a dream. My ghost was called Corambé, and the name stayed with him. It became the title of my novel and the god of my religion.[23]

There is some reason to believe that the arrangement of syllables in dreams is not entirely random, and when in the course of one of his successive incarnations Corambé comes to be called Spiridion, the simple change of name is obviously charged with the whole weight of meaning.

What did the cult of Corambé consist of?

Corambé created himself in my brain. He was pure and charitable like Jesus, radiant and handsome like Gabriel; but he lacked something of the grace of the nymphs and the poetry of Orpheus. His form was therefore less austere

---

22 'As I was being taught no religion, I realized that I needed one and created one myself. I did so in great secrecy and in my mind; my religion and my novel developed side by side in my soul' (ibid., p. 810). This personal revelation should not of course be taken literally: autobiography is a literary genre, and it too in its own way contains elements of fiction. A writer who writes his memoirs can be regarded as inventing a childhood for him or herself, in accordance with the specific characteristics of his or her works of fiction. That does not, however, detract from the significance of what Sand writes here: from the point of view of the literary writer, it associates the fact of writing fiction, which will later become real novels, with a religious attitude.   23 Ibid., vol. 1, p. 812.

than that of the God of the Christians, and his feelings more spiritualized than those of Homer's gods. Then I had to complete him by dressing him as a woman on occasion, for the person I had until then loved best, and known best, was a woman: my mother. He therefore often appeared to me in the shape of a woman. Basically, he was sexless and took on all sorts of different shapes.[24]

Sand made this androgynous divinity the emblem of all her novels and of her life, mingling evocations of paganism and Christianity,[25] and creating the object of an essentially syncretic cult. She also called him 'Corambé the designer', as though he were a protean, versatile and palingenetic deity: the God of the thousand and one fictions that haunt the mental universe of a writer.

In another passage in her memoirs, Sand recounts how the figure of

24   Ibid., pp. 812–13. It should be noted that Sand's childhood memories have much in common with a literary reminiscence. The young Aurore Dupin's Corambé recalls too much the 'Sylphide' evoked by Chateaubriand in a famous passage of his *Mémoires d'outre-tombe* (Paris: Bibliothèque de la Pléiade, 1946, vol. 1, p. 93) for the similarity to be the result of coincidence alone: 'I therefore created for myself a woman out of all the women I had ever seen ... This invisible charmer followed me everywhere; I talked to her as though she were a real being; she changed in accordance with my madness: Aphrodite unveiled, Diana dressed in azure and dew, Thalia in her smiling mask, Hebe bearing the cup of youth ... she often became a fairy who helped me master nature. I constantly retouched my canvas; I removed one of my beauty's charms and replaced it with others. I changed her costume, borrowing from every country, every age, every art, every religion. Then, when I had created a masterpiece, I scattered my drawings and my colours; my unique woman was transformed into a multitude of women in whom I worshipped separately the charms I had once adored collectively.' This is no doubt an anonymous myth, unless we regard 'La Sylphide' as a name; what is more, it is innocent of the androgynous ambiguity Sand will give it by inscribing it in a very different erotic schema. But the fact remains, and this is the important point, that it is inspired by the same syncretism which combines figures from paganism and from Christianity: Velleda and Cymodoce. The idea that is being outlined is therefore indeed one that Sand will later make her own: it corresponds to an infinitely malleable composite fantasy and is the product of her poetic fertility. This should come as no surprise: given that autobiographical memory is essentially indirect and that the author is looking at his reflection in the mirror of his works, it is only natural that it should be mediated through literature. Childhood memories start out as memories of the books he has read, and much of their authenticity is borrowed from books. Are not all these 'memories' grafted onto one another in such a way as to make up a timeless portrait of the Writer? Individual writers merely introduce the modifications suggested by their own art.

25   She also associates it with the marvellous world of the rustic tales which play a central role in her literary works.

Corambé appeared to her for the last time in 1832, when 'he' (to follow Sand's habit of always using the masculine pronoun when speaking of herself) had begun to write 'his' first real novel, *Indiana*:

My poor Corambé disappeared forever once I began to feel myself able to persevere with a given subject. He was of too subtle an essence to submit to the demands of form. As soon as I finished my novel, I tried to rediscover the usual abstraction of my daydreams. Impossible! Locked away in a drawer, the characters in my manuscript were quite content to remain there; but I hoped in vain to see Corambé reappear, and with him the thousands of beings who once cradled me every day in their kindly musings, those half-clear, half-distinct figures which would float around me like a *tableau vivant* behind a transparent veil. Those dear visions were no more than the precursors of inspiration. Cruelly, they hid in the depths of the inkwell and would not come out when I dared to seek them there.[26]

Even though the genesis of her activity as a writer is the the object of recurrent descriptions whose value is imaginary or, to be more accurate, fictional rather than historical, Sand does give one important clue when she reveals the link that unites, and at the same time substitutes one for the other, the two forms of 'creation': the literary and the religious. This is why Sand can describe the whole of her *oeuvre* as 'a novel made up of a thousand novels which are linked by one principal, fantastic character called Corambé'. Not only is literature made up of fantasies; it is itself a more or less organized fantasy, or in other words the celebration of a cult.

The relationship between literature and religion is not simply one of equivalence or substitution, for the work of the writer makes them interact still more closely than that. Because of the indefinite and essentially sympathetic – in the strong sense of the term – character of the divinity that inspired it, the cult of Corambé in fact establishes a structure that can both encompass all sorts of heterogeneous representations and actions, and confer upon them a secret unity. Now this essentially literary religion is also the universalist and 'pantheist' religion of *Spiridion*, which has the same power to absorb the most disparate forms of religious belief, to bring out their common features and to make them commune in the framework of an imaginary religion whose outlook is all the more vast and general in that it was originally fictional. Corambé is the 'God' Sand thought she had rediscovered in Lamennais and then in Leroux, and whom she placed at the centre of

26 *Histoire de ma vie*, vol. 2, p. 165.

the world of her novels. It is therefore no accident that Sand should use ideas borrowed from the general tradition of pantheism as raw material for her literary works; she does so because, in order to write, she needs a 'faith' to give unity to all her stories, and because the only system of belief which could support her fantasies as a writer and at the same time allow her to recreate the world in all its diversity is a religion which is no religion because it is not one religion but the very spirit of all religions, brought together in the framework of a never-ending fable of unanimity.

Writing the world means constituting the new reality of a fictional world by describing it. What, from that point of view, was Sand's innovation? Her attempt to reconcile and even fuse very different aspects of life into a universalist vision and to make all beings 'communicate'. By formulating the principles of such an alchemy, in which a pantheist imaginary was at work, Sand was already outlining the poetics of analogical transmutation and depersonalization that would triumph in the second half of the nineteenth century with Flaubert and Mallarmé.

In his work, the author must be like God in his universe: present everywhere and visible nowhere. As Art is a second nature, the creator of that nature must act in analogous ways. One should sense a hidden and infinite impassibility in its every atom, its every aspect. The effect on the spectator must be a sort of humiliation. He must ask: 'How was that done?' And he must feel crushed because he does not know.[27]

These declarations from Flaubert, who was later to cross Sand's path, were inspired by the same syncretism of ideas and forms that gives the literary philosophy of pantheism its very content: from that point of view, *The Temptation of St Antony* can be read as a second *Spiridion*.

Sand therefore turned pantheism into a story-telling machine whose latent manifestations would circulate widely throughout the nineteenth century. That was her way of appropriating the pantheism to which she assimilated her work and even her conscience as a writer. This is why, appearances notwithstanding, *Spiridion* does not belong to the genre of the literature of or about ideas. It is literally not a speculative content that has been given an outward or neutral literary form: the doctrinal elements conveyed by the fiction are worked upon from within by the novel-form, and are therefore completely recreated in such a way that they too are productive of thought.

27 Gustave Flaubert, letter of 9 December 1852 to Louise Colet.

4

The Hegelian musings of
Raymond Queneau

After his early break with surrealism, which he rejected because it had succumbed to the random charms of pure improvisation, Queneau gradually elaborated and theorized a painstaking system of poetics based upon an implicit reference to rules:[1] this was his way of undertaking a return to a sort of classicism. With a sly humour, he therefore took great care to conceal behind apparently insignificant texts mysterious and complex architectures which were constructed with great effort in the course of a deliberately formal research project whose constraints precluded any recourse to artificial automatisms.[2] Although it appears to be whimsical and light-hearted, Queneau's work makes great demands on the reader, and challenges him to 'decipher'[3] the inexhaustible network of allusions on which it is based.[4]

Queneau borrowed the raw materials for this difficult construct, which is by no means the product of sudden flights of inspiration, from

---

1   Notably in the articles published in 1938 and 1939 in the journal *Volontés*, and later reprinted in *Le Voyage en Grèce* (Paris: Gallimard, 1973); the latter title is a direct evocation of the idea of a neo-classicism. Queneau initially claimed that the perfect model was supplied by Joyce.

2   In 'Drôles de goûts', an article published in *Volontés* 11 (November 1938), we read for example: 'Any work has to be broken down if it is to be experienced and understood; any work resists the reader; any work is a difficult thing; not that difficulty is either a sign of superiority or necessity. There must, however, be an attempt to move from less to more', *Le Voyage en Grèce*, p. 140.

3   As is indicated by the title of C. Simonnet's *Queneau déchiffré* (Paris: Julliard, 1962); this was the first study to reveal this hitherto quite unknown aspect of Queneau's writing.

4   Cf. these remarks from 'Drôles de goûts', *Le Voyage en Grèce*, p. 140: 'The work must be amenable to an immediate understanding to ensure that the poet is not divorced from his potential audience (any man who speaks the same language), or cut off from the cultural world in which he lives. And that immediate understanding may later give rise to increasingly deep insights.' This means that reading a literary text is an activity that takes place on several successive levels.

a wide variety of domains: mathematics — and it is this reference that has been most thoroughly explored — but also the rhetorical tradition, the history of cultural forms and, in particular, the history of religions. His literary works are therefore inscribed within an encyclopedic perspective. His field of reference also includes philosophical thought,[5] and especially the elements of Hegelianism bequeathed him by Alexandre Kojève.

In 1947 Gallimard published this latter's *Introduction à la lecture de Hegel*, which brought together the lectures given on *The Phenomenology of Mind* by Kojève at the Ecole des Hautes Etudes between 1933 and 1939. According to the 'publisher's note', they were 'collected and published by Raymond Queneau'. In 1951 Gallimard published Queneau's *Le Dimanche de la vie*, a novel with a Hegelian title, as is obvious from the epigraph taken from the famous passage on Dutch painting in the *Aesthetics*: ' ... it is the Sunday of life which equalizes everything and removes all evil; people who are so whole-heartedly cheerful cannot be altogether evil and base.'[6] In May of the same year, *Critique*, then edited by Georges Bataille, who had assiduously attended Kojève's lectures before the war, published an article by Kojève entitled 'Les Romans de la sagesse'. It proposed a philosophical interpretation of three of Queneau's novels: *Pierrot mon ami* (1942), *Loin de Rueil* (1944) and *Le Dimanche de la vie* (1951). In this review, it was suggested that, although they seemed irreverent and frivolous, these works by Queneau concealed an underlying notion of 'wisdom' modelled on the theoretical concept which Kojève himself had elaborated in his commentary on Hegel.[7]

In the immediate postwar years, to which our investigations will be restricted, there was, then, real exchange between the philosopher and the writer. What was the nature of that exchange? Is it possible to account for it in terms of borrowings? As we shall see from a commentary on three texts by Queneau which revolve around the

5 It should be recalled that Queneau was a philosophy graduate.
6 G. W. F. Hegel, *Aesthetics: Lectures on Fine Art*, tr. T. M. Knox (Oxford: The Clarendon Press, 1975), p. 887.
7 Kojève writes: 'We have to explain why these three seemingly insignificant comic novels demand, or at least agree, to be put on trial before the Hegelian court of universal history. The justification for the trial lies in the fact that the three novels in question deal with Wisdom. Queneau describes three avatars of the Sage, or in other words three of his constituent aspects or moments, and they are both different and complementary.'

problems of the war (*Le Dimanche de la vie*, *Pierrot mon ami* and *Une Histoire modèle*), the answer to these questions is anything but easy and obvious.

With Kojève

We must begin with a brief account of Kojève and of the influence he exerted over his followers in the postwar period. Kojève, a Russian exile in Paris who had studied philosophy in Germany in the 1920s, was given a post at the Ecole des Hautes Etudes, an institution which was both prestigious and marginal, by Alexandre Koyré, a fellow Russian *émigré* who was at this time preoccupied with the religious sciences.[8] In this very curious setting, Kojève, who was never a professional academic, taught a course which, whilst it remained confidential, had a considerable impact in the long term, as we can see from this admission from Bataille: 'From (I think) '33 to '39, I followed the lectures A. Kojève devoted to the exposition of *The Phenomenology of Mind*, a brilliant exposition, quite worthy of the book itself: the number of times Queneau and I came out of that little room dazed, reduced to silence ... Kojève's lectures left me exhausted, crushed, dead to the world.'[9] Queneau and Bataille were joined in the little lecture-room by Lacan, Breton, Merleau-Ponty, Weil, Aron, Klossowski and others. It was more than a casual meeting place; the audience shared in the revelation of a new speculative interest for which Hegel's philosophy was primarily an excuse, even a pretext.[10] Kojève was an irreplaceable intercessor because he introduced his listeners to a language which was largely unknown, at least in France, and whose key words were 'desire for recognition', 'struggle unto

8   His assistant at the time was H. Corbin, who was to become well known in the interwar period for his work on Hamann and his translations of Heidegger, which were the first to appear in France. In order to recapture the very distinctive intellectual climate of the Ecole des Hautes Etudes and the cosmopolitanism that flourished around Kojève, one would have to make an exhaustive study of the review he edited: *Recherches philosophiques*. For a study of all these aspects of Kojève's activities, see Dominique Auffret, *Alexandre Kojève. La philosophie, l'Etat, l'histoire* (Paris: Grasset, 1990).

9   Georges Bataille, *Oeuvres complètes* (Paris: Gallimard, 1973), vol. 6, p. 146.

10 As Vincent Descombes writes in his *Modern French Philosophy*, tr. L. Scott-Fox and J. M. Harding (Cambridge University Press, 1980), p. 11, the dominant reading of Kojève, to whom the first chapter is devoted, 'points to the place where the multiple references of the period converged: it reveals the desire for a *common language*, which it seemed at the time would have to be Hegelian.'

death', 'praxis', 'negativity', 'self-consciousness', 'satisfaction' and 'wisdom' – words which seemed to come from Hegel as read or spoken through Kojève's commentary. At the time, this was the language of modernity, and its reign was to last for several decades.

In order to understand the singular effect produced by Kojève's teaching, it must be recalled that it was based upon Hegel's *Phenomenology of Mind*, a book which had yet to be published in French.[11] In each of his lectures, Kojève would read a few lines from the German text, and then supply a commentary in the shape of a translation, or a translation in the shape of a commentary. He spoke a rather strange language which was neither quite French nor quite German – it was in fact 'Kojèvean' – and adopted a style in which speculation and narration constantly merged. Kojève read the book written by Hegel as though Hegel were telling a story. He told his own version of the story, adding interpretative variations in the shape of an oral commentary.[12] One final lesson emerged from this story, and it was supported by a certain idea of Wisdom, or of the self-consciousness of the man who is fully satisfied because he has succeeded in adopting the point of view of the end of history, or in other words 'the Sunday of life'. Queneau's characters would later adopt the same point of view. Now there was a necessary relationship

11 Jean Hyppolite's full translation of Hegel's text (Paris: Aubier, 1939–41) did not appear until after Kojève had finished giving his lectures. Whilst it was undertaken in a completely different spirit, the completion of his epoch-making translation, whose effects are not confined to the history of Hegelian studies in France, cannot be completely divorced from the intellectual context created by and around Kojève.

12 Here, for example, is an extract from Queneau's version of the 1936–7 Seminar (*Introduction à la lecture de Hegel*, Paris: Gallimard, 1947, p. 140). It deals with Subdivision C of chapter 6 of Hegel's text: '"*Der seiner selbst gewisse Geist*", the Spirit that is certain of itself and self-assured – in the last analysis this is Hegel himself, or his system of philosophy (Phenomenology + Encyclopedia), which is no longer a search for Wisdom, but Wisdom itself (= Absolute Knowledge). Here *Gewissheit* (subjective certainty) coincides with *Warheit* (objective truth = reality revealed by language). Now, a truth is only really true, or in other words *universally* and *necessarily* (= eternally) valid, if the reality it reveals is *fully* accomplished (if *everything* that is *possible* has effectively been *realized*), and therefore perfect, with no possibility of extension or change. This "total" and "definitive" reality is the Napoleonic Empire.' On reading a text like this, one is immediately struck by the strange system of notation – inverted commas, dashes, italics, parentheses and all kinds of abbreviated signs – used to record a spoken commentary. The object is to capture the living concrete reality of what was originally said about another discourse written in another language.

between the final form of this narration – Queneau's transcription of the oral commentary given by Kojève on Hegel's written text – and its content – namely, the idea that certain contemporary events represented the final realization of human destiny in a universal and absolute empire. Kojève's original model was Napoleon. He was later replaced by Stalin.

Kojève's whole interpretation is in fact based upon the following hypothesis: in the history of both the world and thought, Hegel represents the terminal moment in which the circle of human reality closes. Human reality has realized its full potential and has achieved its ideal by giving it a concrete incarnation. This moment coincides with the exemplary actions of history's last hero. After this, nothing can happen that does not already figure in the total system that gives history its rational meaning, and that meaning is reconstructed in its totality in the discourse of the *Phenomenology*.[13] The *Phenomenology* is therefore the 'Book', defined in a sense that reminds one of Mallarmé, who had also read Hegel. Kojève also speaks of the 'Logos' which is the ultimate goal of the whole of human history, the point at which it finds its fulfilment and its completion. At this point, men will begin a new life: life will no longer be dominated by the desire for recognition and the negativity at the heart of desire which forces it to realize itself in struggle and through labour. The new life will be a post-historical existence in which, to adopt Kojève's terminology, the law of *Begierde* ('desire') is replaced by the law of *Befriedigung* ('satisfaction') and in which philosophy, which is literally nothing more than a momentarily unappeased desire to know, becomes wisdom, or in other words the tranquillity of Absolute Knowledge.

These themes no doubt allude to Hegel, and they seem to be stated in Hegel's own words, but, for Kojève, the reference to Hegel functions in the hallucinatory mode of the gloss, whose rightful place is in the margins of the text which he is using primarily as a pretext. His oral commentary on a preexisting written text in fact produces a second text which replicates the first by displacing its characteristics through a transposition which modified both its spirit and its letter. Speaking after and as a follower of Hegel, or after the end of the history which has resulted in the 'Book' that summarizes its whole development, Kojève has apparently only to repeat what is already

---

13 Hegel wrote the final pages of his book to the sound of the cannon of the battle of Jena; Queneau's character Valentin Brû was careful not to forget the fact.

inscribed therein; he has only to read or speak between the lines of a text which is complete in itself and which contains the whole of human destiny within the limits of its text. Quite independently of what it is commenting on, for it has the apparently very Hegelian property of generating its own content as it unfolds, the commentary itself is therefore the preeminent expression of post-historical thought, of the thought of finitude, and it reiterates the end of man in the very terms of its realization.[14] The philosophers of history, from Plato to Hegel, wrote books. Kojève himself claimed to be living in the era of the Sage, to whom nothing new can happen. All that it remains for the Sage to do is to talk about those books, which are now included in the Book which contains them all, and to meditate tirelessly on its message.[15] For wisdom begins where philosophy ends.[16]

14 In an article published in *Critique* nos. 2–3 (1946), Kojève would write: 'It is indeed possible that the future of the world, and therefore the meaning of the present and the significance of the past, depends upon the way in which we interpret Hegel's writings today.' It is as though the world's future lay in the need to understand its past by commenting on it.

15 In the introduction to his article 'Hegel, la mort et le sacrifice', *Deucalion* 5 (1955), Georges Bataille writes: 'It has to be said that the originality and the courage of Alexandre Kojève lay in his having noticed the impossibility of going any further, and therefore the need to abandon the attempt to produce an original philosophy; hence the interminable starting-over that is the admission of the vanity of thought', *Oeuvres complètes* (Paris: Gallimard, 1988), vol. 12, p. 326.

16 What did those who followed, in the strong sense of the term, Kojève's teaching retain of it? They received an indirect philosophical message dealing with a little-known text by Hegel. It spoke of the desire of the Other, of the dialectic of recognition, of struggle, work and death, of the necessary role of violence in history, etc. The message was quite in keeping with the theoretical preoccupations of those who, before the war, took their inspiration from marxism, psychoanalysis, phenomenology, surrealism and existentialism (yet to be born, but already in gestation). All these found a geometrical focus in Kojève's sovereign word. The message, and the echoes it created, was particularly rich: not content with recording it, those who received it appropriated it, consciously or otherwise, and used it in their own work to the extent that they found in it the dynamic element which gave their own investigations a new impetus. One could cite the examples of the implicit reference to Kojève in the theory of the 'mirror phase' elaborated and propagated by Jacques Lacan in the years 1935–40, or of the undeniable relationship between Kojève's 'negative ontology' and *L'Etre et le néant*, which Sartre would begin to write a few years later. The notional and thematic content of Kojève's message was not the only thing to be assimilated: the 'spoken commentary' came to be seen as the modern form of expression *par excellence*. To take only two examples, Lacan's 'seminar', and the return to Freud which defined its programme, and Althusser & Co.'s *Reading 'Capital'*, which proclaims a similar 'return' to Marx, are both the offspring of

Queneau's role in Kojève's very peculiar project may seem subordinate, but it was not unimportant. Kojève spoke as Sages speak,[17] and the preservation and transmission of his discourse required the intervention of a scribe who could preserve its spirit by setting it down in letters that were adequate to it. The scribe was Queneau, who collected the notes and shorthand transcripts he used to produce his exhaustive and disparate anthology. His role is described in the editorial note that prefaces the *Introduction à la lecture de Hegel*: 'The fragments published here are notes on a reading of and a commentary on *The Phenomenology of Mind*. They have been revised by M. Alexandre Kojève, whose present occupations have prevented him from writing the *Introduction to the Reading of Hegel* that we expected of him.' Sages have better things to do, and if they do create an *oeuvre*, it is to be found in the margins of what is written, in an indirect form of expression which requires the intervention of a helping hand, of a complicitous stranger, if it is to be preserved and propagated.

As we shall see, Queneau did not, however, simply record the message of Kojèvean wisdom or become its curator and, in the strong sense, its editor. He appropriated it by transposing it into his own works in forms which remain to be analysed. In order to begin to understand Queneau, I suggest first of all that we reread the last of his works to be marked by Kojève's influence. Here, the influence manifests itself quite explicitly and in a directly visible manner. We will then go back to some earlier texts in which the Kojève-effect comes into play in less obvious ways.

Kojève's teachings. They are more or less legitimate, and there is a family resemblance. It is because of their specific line of descent that they bear the mark of their time.

17 Kojève himself did of course 'write' and publish. He published a number of articles between 1940 and 1950. An *Essai d'histoire raisonnée de la philosophie païenne* and a work devoted to Kant began to appear in 1970, shortly after his death. Other unpublished works have also begun to appear, including the *Esquisse d'une phénoménologie du droit* published by Gallimard in 1982. Kojève's real influence was, however, transmitted through other channels, namely the 'text' of the *Introduction à la lecture de Hegel*, which would not exist without Queneau.

A Kojèvean fiction: *Le Dimanche de la vie*

Valentin Brû, who is the central character in *Le Dimanche de la vie*, is a demobilized soldier. He is married to an over-the-hill and very outspoken haberdasher, and manages a shop selling photograph frames. Harmless and modest almost to the point of self-effacement, he is, however, obsessed by a desire to travel and to visit the battlefield at Jena, where his great-great-grandfather fought and, 'sabre in hand, introduced serious-mindedness into German philosophy'.[18] When he visits the German pavilion at the 1937 World's Fair, Brû picks up a brochure from the tourist branch of the Committee for Franco-German Reconciliation, which is organizing a driving tour of the Napoleonic battlefields, and thus has the opportunity to fulfil his ambition. His memories of his tour are Hegelian: '"At Jena, we were shown the house of a German philosopher who, on the day of the battle, called him the Soul of the World." Called who that?", he is asked. "Napoleon."'[19] Such philosophical allusions are incomprehensible and out of place, coming from a small shopkeeperwho educated himself by reading the *Petit Larousse* dictionary,'which opened the floodgates of knowledge for him',[20]from cover to cover during a period of military service in Madagascar. And they intrigue his neighbours, who begin to look for a hidden meaning in them:

The trip to Germany had caused some disquiet in his neighbourhood. People were lost in conjectures as to the real reasons for such an excursion and the word 'spy' had actually been mentioned. The mystery seemed all the greater in that Valentin's answers to the various questions left his questioners even more perplexed than before. Eventually, and even though Valentin had learned the value of prudence, it was no secret that he thought war inevitable.[21]

Brû is gradually revealed to have a prophetic gift which will finally lead him to take up the profession of clairvoyancy, dressed as a woman and using the name 'Mme Saphir'.

With the help of these details and a few others which the attentive reader can readily identify in Queneau's text, we can recognize Valentin Brû as an incarnation of Kojève's Sage who, because he regards everything from the viewpoint of the end of history – the

18 Raymond Queneau, *Le Dimanche de la vie* (Paris: Gallimard, 1951), p. 151.
19 Ibid., p. 233.   20 Ibid., p. 75.   21 Ibid., pp. 240–1.

empirical moment of which supposedly coincides with the battle of Jena and therefore with the moment when Hegel wrote his *Phenomenology* — understands them in terms of their profound necessity, or in other words in terms of their immanent rational meaning. He 'sees' reality in the systematically accomplished order of its overall development and accepts its inevitable unfolding dispassionately, even indifferently. Brû is a prophet because he knows that everything was finally settled at Jena in 1807, and that, henceforth, the future can be no more than a meditation on the past: that was the lesson he learned during his stay in Jena.[22] Valentin Brû can foresee and predict a new war in 1937 — it will be recalled that Queneau wrote his novel fifteen years later — because he thinks that its necessity is inscribed in the course of a history that has already taken place and will simply repeat itself indefinitely in a time which has become undifferentiated. The coming world war is also a repetition of the end of history, which has already taken place and after which nothing really new can happen.[23] It is the same method that allows Brû to exercise, not without some mystification but to general satisfaction, his profession as a clairvoyant: what he reveals to his clients is their past, which contains all their possible hopes and fears, and about which he has taken the trouble to learn in advance.

It must also be recalled that, for Kojève, the Sage is the individual who, having reached the end of history, attains self-consciousness or Absolute Knowledge. In Brû's case, self-consciousness takes the apparently surprising form of instincts and feelings which do not even have to be expressed to produce their effects.[24] When he reaches the

22 Cf. ibid., p. 236: '"So why did you go on your journey?" said Chantal. "Am I pissing you off by talking about it?" said Valentin. "You told us more about it than about Madagascar" said Chantal. "In Madagascar", said Valentin suddenly, "they rebury the dead." "What?" said the others. "They bury them", said Valentin, "and then, after a while, they dig them up and go and bury them somewhere else." "What savages", said Julia. "It's like in history", said Valentin. "Victories and defeats never end where they took place. You dig them up after a while so that they can go away and rot somewhere else."' The lesson learned in Madagascar is the same as the lesson of Jena: when history is finished, all that remains to be done is to 'dig up' the past and 'rebury' it elsewhere.

23 'According to him, there will be no postwar. Or, rather, there will be nothing afterwards. Or it will be unthinkable. After such a war, there will be no after' (ibid., p. 289).

24 This is why Brû shares his prophetic gift with the tramp Jean sans tête, whose innocence, which is apparently the very antithesis of wisdom, predisposes him to

limits of language and reason, he discovers infallible knowledge. But what then remains of self-consciousness? An analogous difficulty arises in Kojève's own discourse: in his view, complete wisdom finally reverts to the almost animal existence of post-historical man, who has nothing left to know because nothing more can happen to him.[25] Once it becomes real, Absolute Knowledge ceases to be knowledge in any real sense, or at least is no longer the knowledge that is reflected in the consciousness of an individual. After the advent of the perfect man, realized according to Kojève in the Hegel/Napoleon dyad, and in the period that follows the end of history, there will only be non-conscious Sages for whom time no longer exists, or at least not in the form of a possible future, since time is no more than the dismal repetition of a past that is over.

Such is the secret privilege enjoyed by Valentin Brû and which, despite his personal mediocrity and the banality of his way of life, differentiates him from those around him. He is a man apart because he enjoys a specific relationship with time: that of the man of the end of history, who has recognized and accepted himself for what he is.[26] The Sage's asceticism empties his existence of all preoccupations and all empirical desire; literally transcending the images of day-to-day life, he is concerned only with an undifferentiated and monotonous time which passes without anything coming to pass in it, and which, whilst it is Time itself when grasped in its integrality, is not quite

sense what is going to happen.'"Happy New Year", he said. "Happy New Year. Happy New Year. Happy New Year. Pra pra pra pra pra pra pra pa pra. Happy New Year." Valentin said the same, and slapped his thigh in mirth. "Happy New Year", went on Jean sans tête. Crooking his index finger, he went on: "Tac, tac, tac, tac, tac, tac, tac, tac, tac." "Boom, boom", he shouted so loudly that he gave himself a fright and went to hide behind a chair' (ibid., p. 242). The premonition of the coming cataclysm drives those who sense it mad.

25 'The end of history is the death of man as such. After that death, there remain: 1. living bodies with a human form but no Spirit, or no Time or creative power; 2. a Spirit which exists empirically, but in the form of an inorganic reality that is not alive; in the form of a Book which, not even having animal life, has nothing to do with Time' (*Introduction*, p. 388 n.). Similarly, at the end of *Pierrot mon ami*, when the Luna Park of human history is completely ravaged and destroyed by a fire, a menagerie is built on its old site. Now that the 'philosophers' have gone, it becomes a home for wise animals. At this point, Queneau's 'Book' ends.

26 'All that was left to him was the vacuity of time. And so he tried to see how time passes' (*Le Dimanche de la vie*, p. 199). Passing the time, making time pass, watching time pass: these formulas signify an attempt to transcend time, or to understand it and put an end to it.

time.[27] On the indistinct frontier which scarcely divides wakefulness from sleep, absolute consciousness coincides with absolute unconsciousness.[28]

To the extent that *Le Dimanche de la vie* looks like an enigma that has to be deciphered — as did Queneau's first novel *Le Chiendent* which appeared twenty years earlier in 1933 — Kojève's thought is of course one of the keys to the enigma. Yet is there not a deeper and more complex relationship between the novelist, who rather than 'doing' philosophy, 'plays' at it in his own fashion, or in other words very freely, and the philosopher-story-teller who rearranged the text he was expounding in a very non-academic way? We cannot read or understand Queneau without referring to Kojève. But does not Queneau for his part urge us to reread Kojève, whose project now appears in a rather new light? It is clear from even a summary account of it that the doctrine of the end of history professed by Kojève is terrifying, assuming that it is meant to be taken seriously and that we do take it seriously. Kojève was, of course, an intellectual terrorist and provocateur. It is, however, difficult to believe that this conception and the terms of its formulation could have been taken literally: did

27 Cf. ibid. p. 222: 'The time that passes is neither beautiful nor ugly; it is always the same. Perhaps it sometimes rains for a few seconds, perhaps at four the sun holds back a few minutes as though they were rearing horses. The past may not always be as well-ordered as the present because there are no clocks there, and the future might arrive in chaos, with each moment pushing and shoving to be the first to be cut into slices. And perhaps there is some charm or horror, some grace or abjection, in the convulsive movements of what is going to be or what has been. But Valentin had never taken any pleasure in these suppositions. He still didn't know enough about them. He wanted to content himself with an identity that was neatly cut into pieces, of different lengths but all of the same kind, without being tinted with the colours of autumn, washed in the April showers or mottled like the changing clouds.' This dissociation of lived time and clock time could perhaps be read as a memory of Heidegger, again transmitted through the intermediary of Kojève, but exploited *a contrario*.

28 This is why Valentin Brû feels particularly close to Jean sans tête, whose immediate individuality evokes both an absolute indeterminacy and a sort of universality. 'Thanks to your broom, I have been able to follow time, nothing but time, for more than seven minutes. But now I understand that I should kill it, not follow it. Having escaped from myself after paying so much attention, I found myself in the place I started out from. I hadn't moved. Is that like sleeping without dreaming?' (ibid., p. 244). For the post-historical man who knows that there is no future, but only a past, the present itself dissolves into an undifferentiated contemporaneity, in which there is nothing more to hope for or desire. 'There really was nothing left for him to do but kill time and sweep into time images of a world that history was about to absorb' (ibid., p. 293).

pre- and postwar French intellectuals really believe that they were living 'after' history, and that that situation determined their practical and intellectual activities? When he summarized Kojève's thought in his article 'Hegel, la mort et le sacrifice', Bataille lucidly recognized: 'This vision of things can justifiably be regarded as comic.'[29] Queneau's disenchanted humour and the casually sardonic grace of his story which, without seeming to touch upon them, deals with the basic problems of human existence, the sympathetic and pathetic nature of his characters, who are above all anti-heroes, reduce the vision expounded by Kojève to its true dimensions. It is this that gives us its authentically provocative value. It refers to a very specific and topical issue, namely the threat of a new world war. By transposing that issue into the fictional realm of the end of history, and perhaps the end of the world, conjured up by Kojève's thesis, Queneau forges a paradoxical representation that is at once familiar and unfamiliar. Its meaning, however, is essentially an interrogative meaning. Queneau, who is in every sense of the word Kojève's reader and scribe, reveals the hypothetical, and ultimately allegorical, character of a philosophy of history which remains credible only because of this ironic transposition. It is the transposition that gives it its authentic spirit at a sub-literal level, and it is to be taken *cum grano salis*, or read as a discourse that echoes its own disavowal.

Pierrot mon ami: the history of the end of history

Pierrot mon ami, another 'novel of wisdom', was written ten years before *Le Dimanche de la vie*. Its plot describes, in making it the motif of a fable, a universal conflagration long before the second novel retrospectively announces the signs that foretell it. In terms of the issue that concerns us here, namely that of the relationship between a literary discourse and a philosophical discourse, the two books are quite similar, but they differ in one important respect. In *Pierrot mon ami*, the allusions to a philosophical content, which can actually be expounded in an abstract way, go completely unnoticed on a first reading, whereas our attention is expressly drawn to them in *Le Dimanche de la vie*. It is as though, as in the earlier *Le Chiendent*, Queneau had erased every trace of the theoretical scaffolding that invisibly supports his text.

29   Georges Bataille, *Oeuvres complètes*, vol. 12, p. 329.

In *Pierrot mon ami*, the only explicit allusion to philosophy is the grotesque presence of the 'philosophers' who haunt the noisy spaces of a 'Uni Park' (a fairground), where they persistently try to find the right sight lines that will allow them to look into the depths and see the underwear of the girls as it is fleetingly revealed by a blast of air in the Palace of Fun. These unattractive and completely idle characters adopt the purely theoretical pose of the voyeur; they passively enjoy a spectacle which is theirs for the price of an admission fee without ever really becoming involved in it. Queneau later describes them in similar terms when he speaks of them as 'philosophical cows'.[30] These philosophers are not Sages, nor are they wise. 'Convulsed with expectancy, the philosophers spotted choice morsels and leered at them with staring eyes and dilated pupils.'[31] They embody a representation of an inactive knowledge which is totally out of step with reality. It brushes past reality without ever becoming committed to it, simply following its meanderings and contradictions without succeeding in mastering them, or even in understanding them.[32] The philosophers' behaviour is ambiguous because their lack of involvement is artificial; when their curiosity is frustrated by the prudishness of the moralistic pimps who want to protect the modesty of their girls from indiscreet eyes, the philosophers start a memorable fight which will lead to the temporary closure of the Palace of Fun on grounds of immorality. They are later found 'standing in front of a roundabout where the girls, skirts hitched up high, are perched on pigs'.[33] After the fire which completely destroys the Uni Park, the philosophers are the first to be suspected, wrongly, of starting it; it transpires after the event that the fire was in fact started by an Idea.

Are we to see a philosophical meaning in these figures, which seem to be eminently caricatural? Yes, if we recall that Kojève's concept of 'wisdom' is based on the distinction between wisdom and philosophy proper. The latter is no more than the temptation of and the desire for an absent wisdom, which is why its expectations are usually frustrated and disappointed. As Kojève was later to point out in his article on Queneau, true wisdom is a combination of satisfaction and self-

---

30 Raymond Queneau, *Pierrot mon ami* (Paris: Gallimard, 1942), p. 160.
31 Ibid., p. 13.
32 'There's a lot of satyrs – that's the only word for them – who come to get an eyeful. We call them the philosophers. They're lechers. You have to be sick or a bit touched to spend your time like that' (ibid., p. 105).
33 Ibid., p. 117.

consciousness, and it therefore precludes the incomplete forms of both instinctual and irrational unconscious satisfaction,[34] and the unhappy consciousness, of which the Sartre of *La Nausée* is, according to Kojève, the prime representative. Within the trajectory of consciousness, the schema for which Kojève claims to have copied from Hegel, philosophy therefore corresponds to a wisdom which is incomplete because it is unfulfilled and unappeased. Conversely, the ideal of wisdom is inseparable from the possibility of its realization, not in the sense of an individual or particular realization, but in the sense of an objective and collective incarnation whose one real locus is universal history. Wisdom therefore exists only when all the contradictions of history have unfolded and been transcended, or when the end of history has come about.[35]

The lunar Pierrot dreamed up by Queneau is of course detached from the conflicts of history but, unlike the 'philosophers', he does not succumb to the illusion that it is possible to adopt a passively contemplative attitude towards them. His possession of this type of post-historic wisdom relates him to Valentin Brû: his myopia, his constant bad luck, his 'inner twilight, shot through from time to time by flashes of philosophical lightning',[36] mean that he is indeed a speculative animal who has renounced all activity because he has pursued all activities to the very end, and has learned that they were meaningful only in terms of the overall perspective that abolishes them by unifying them. In the article he devotes to Queneau's novels, Kojève describes Pierrot more fully as being 'the disinterested Proletarian with an aristocratic bearing and tastes', or in other words as the slave who has freed himself from his master's desire because he

---

34   In *Le Dimanche de la vie*, Queneau was to adopt a rather different position in this respect. Ten years earlier, he had not yet finished settling accounts with the surrealist cult of spontaneity and chance, and the way in which it privileged the unconscious from a viewpoint quite different from that of his own aesthetic.

35   This idea is made explicit in a footnote to the first appendix to the *Introduction à la lecture de Hegel* (p. 506): 'Truth to tell, the Sage is no longer an individual in the sense that he is essentially different from everyone else. If Wisdom consists in the possession of the truth, there is no difference between one Sage and another. In other words, he is not human in the sense that Historical man was human (and nor is he free in the same sense, since he no longer negates anything through action); he is, rather, "divine" (but mortal). The Sage is, however, an Individual in the sense that it is in his existential particularity that he possesses universal Science. In that sense, he is still human (and therefore mortal).'

36   *Pierrot mon ami*, p. 165.

has been able to control his own desire and has thus put an end to the conflicts of reality, at least insofar as they are reflected in his consciousness.

Queneau's novel, which from this point of view is not reducible to a verbal game or a formal construct, does have something to do with a philosophy of history. It consists of a description of the contrasting destinies of the Uni Park and the Poldève Chapel, which gives the whole narrative its theme. The narrative is essentially about an encounter between two worlds. On the one hand, there is the artificial world of the Uni Park and its din.[37] In the story told by Queneau, its unstable, changeable and conflict-ridden reality represents the realm of both pleasure and labour. In terms of the Kojèvean system it corresponds to the profane world of *Diesseitigkeit*, which is torn apart by the conflicts of economics and politics. On the other hand, there is the Poldève Chapel: it is always in silence and darkness, because it is dedicated to the celebration of a heroic cult observed only by a small elite of initiates.[38] Peaceful, religious and cultural, this world exists with constant reference to an ideal beyond (the *Jenseitigkeit*, as opposed to the *Diesseitigkeit*): in total contrast with the variations and opposition of the real world, it preserves a space for memory and legend.[39]

---

37 'The sprawling Uni Park was ablaze with light, swarming with people and noisy. Music, noises and screams mingled together; they assaulted the ears like a single noise. Above the many lights, some of them motionless, others swaying, the aeroplanes attached to a tall pylon circled silently in a zone that was already dark and therefore poetic. But below it looked very much like a cheese crawling with black larvae and lit by glow-worms' (ibid., p. 47). With slight modifications, this passage could be transformed into a description of an air raid. Because of its aggressivity, an image of a fairground serves as an image of war.

38 When Pierrot asks the labourers who work just beside it to explain its purpose, they are incapable of doing so; Posidon, who for twenty years has kept a café on the corner of the street where it stands, admits to having never noticed its existence (ibid., pp. 59, 168).

39 This is how Kojève summarizes this episode in the novel in his article on Queneau: 'Does he not venerate, like a true Hegelian Sage, a Grave containing the remains of a haughty but absurd aristocratic past which is never to return, and which remains present in memory alone; not that that prevents him from calling conservative and mechanized firemen when the cataclysmic fire destroying the eminently bourgeois Luna Park that surrounded it and would sooner or later absorb the last resting place of the vaguely Slav martyr-prince, threatened (without actually succeeding in doing so) to sweep this vestige of the heroic past into the void?' This sounds curiously like the historical culture of the Crusades, and their tireless quest for an empty Grave symbolizing an ideal beyond, as

How does the encounter between these two worlds come about, and what meaning emerges from it? Queneau's novel offers two successive interpretations. The first is the lengthy story told by Mounnezergues in chapter 3. It describes the concurrent creation of two worlds that resulted from the splitting of a sort of primal chaos; what he is in fact describing is the genesis of myth, in the form of what might be termed a 'small, portable mythology' containing, encyclo-pedically, a small-scale model of all religious speculation. But the Epilogue also contains Voussois's fragmentary revelations, which strip the myth of its sacred content and attest that, to use the formula with which Hegel sums up the spirit of Christianity, 'the grave is empty'. Voussois, a character who undergoes many transformations, and who is successively called Mouilleminche, Chaliaqueue and Torricelli, would thus appear to symbolize the cunning of history, which plays on the internal contradictions of both worlds, and eventually resolves them by revealing the real principles on which they were built. It then transpires that the cult centred on the Poldève Chapel revolved around an absent object: Prince Luigi never existed, or rather Voudzoï was merely Voussois, and it was Voussois who, in order to halt the uncontrolled spread of the Uni Park and to keep it within the limits of its 'system', used an imaginary corpse to organize a hoax.

It is primarily the clash between myth and corresponding reality that provides *Pierrot mon ami* with its subject matter. Two essential lessons emerge from it. The first is that the sacred and profane worlds are in fact a single world which split as it came into conflict with itself; it therefore exists in the form of two complementary and exclusive aspects which are meaningful and purposeful only when they are related to one another.[40] A single reality can, that is, be seen in the alternating forms of an externalized and a completely internalized world: there can be no Palace of Fun without a rue des Larmes (Street of Tears), because economic growth and the cult of the Gods express the conflict-ridden development of the same overall content, and because the whole of human history has unfolded in the space that opens up between these two poles. The second lesson to emerge from

described by Hegel in the section of chapter 4 of the *Phenomenology* devoted to the 'unhappy consciousness' (this passage was discussed by Kojève in 1934–5; see Introduction, pp. 69–70).

40 Queneau attaches great importance to the fact that the Uni Park and the Poldève Chapel share a single territory whose contours form a perfect parallelepiped: their layout means that the two fit together perfectly.

Queneau's story is that both worlds and the contrast between them must vanish together; the Poldève Chapel does of course survive the fire in the Uni Park, 'basking in the same oblivion',[41] but it is clear that its survival is temporary and that the cult will fall into oblivion. Now that it no longer stands alongside the Uni Park, it has no *raison d'être*. That is in fact how the novel ends: with a great clear-up operation that liquidates the entire cycle of all previous history.

The final conflagration in the Uni Park, which begins when the aeroplanes catch fire and is followed by 'the most terrible fire of modern times',[42] leads to the complete destruction of the building, whose fragility is now revealed – it will be recalled that Queneau's novel appeared in the middle of the war. This represents the final moment of human history: the moment of its self-suppression. After the disappearance of the 'historical' world of the Uni Park – and its destruction must also obliterate every trace of its past struggles with the sacred world that is its pathetic reflection – history itself comes to an end at the moment when opposites disappear because they are dialectically absorbed into one another. Significantly, Queneau indicates, in a sort of return to a reunified and pacified nature, that the setting for the main events is taken over by a zoo.[43] This too can be seen as a discreet and ironic allusion to one of Kojève's themes: once history is over, historical man disappears to make way for wise animals.[44]

It is clear from the way the story ends that the subject of *Pierrot mon ami* is the end of history. Does this mean that we must try to extract from the novel a 'philosophy' which is being indirectly expressed through stylistic and narrative devices? Certainly not: *Pierrot mon ami*

---

41 *Pierrot mon ami*, p. 216.   42 Ibid., p. 137.

43 On this theme, which is of particular importance in Queneau's work, see also the poem 'Génèse d'un zoo', in *Battre la campagne* (Paris: Gallimard, 1968).

44 This is illustrated by a note in the *Introduction à la lecture de Hegel*: 'Man's disappearance at the end of history is not a cosmic catastrophe: the natural world remains what it has been throughout all eternity. Nor is it a biological necessity: Man lives on as an animal in harmony with Nature or being-as-given. What does disappear is man in the true sense, or in other words the Action that negates the given and Error, or, in general, Subject as opposed to Object. The end of human Time or of History, or the final annihilation of Man in the true sense or of the free, historical individual simply means that Action, in the strong sense of the term, ceases' (p. 434; cf. the passage cited in note 2 above). The theme of 'the death of man', which created a scandal when it was taken up by Foucault, was, then, not really new.

is as much, or as little, a philosophical novel as it is a detective story. Queneau did not simply take an abstract idea from the philosophical tradition and dress it up in the seductive colours of fable. He did, however, use the idea of the end of history as raw material to be so worked as to become one element in a narrative. The philosophical references we have identified, and which an inattentive or uninformed reader would simply fail to notice, do not provide the key to its whole meaning: they weave, beneath the linear narrative, a network of allusions and meanings in which they intervene as potentialities indicating the form of one possible reading within an apparently inexhaustible combinatory that is not reducible to an exclusive and fixed structure.

What defines a literary text in its relationship with philosophy is the opening up of a variable space within which any one term echoes the others, splits and is absorbed into the movement of its own transformations.[45]

Towards the absolute science of history

To conclude, let us read one last text, which was written at practically the same time as *Pierrot mon ami*. It will allow us to specify the speculative implications of philosophical fiction, as practised by Queneau.

In 1966, Queneau published *Une Histoire modèle*, which is one of his most enigmatic texts, not least because it is unfinished. This little book takes the form of a sequence of ninety-six 'chapters', emphatically numbered in Roman numerals. Some are only a few lines long, and the most fully developed barely fill a short printed page. In them, Queneau succinctly deals with topics such as: 'Is History a Science?' (I and II), 'Origin of Religion' (x, six lines), 'Basic Elements of History' (XLIII), 'The Exploitation of Man' (LXI). Their seriousness is counterbalanced by the presence of other considerations, which seem more incongruous: 'The Comic Novel' (xv), 'On Childhood' (xxxII), 'Love and History' (LVII), 'Monsters' (LXXVI) and 'Stocking Old Men' (LXXXIV). The disproportion between form and content is so blatant that it would appear difficult to take its author's intentions seriously.

When *Une Histoire modèle* was published, Queneau prefaced it with an introduction which briefly sketched its genealogy and explained

45 Queneau gives a dazzling demonstration of this in his *Exercices de style* (Paris: Gallimard, 1947).

why he had exhumed a text written in 1942 but abandoned before the project had been completed: 'I am publishing this text now, even though it is incomplete (I have changed only the title), because, on the one hand, it seems to me that it provides more information for those who were kind enough to take an interest in my *Les Fleurs bleues* and because, on the other, it can at least be regarded as a diary, even if one takes the view that it makes no contribution to quantitative history.' The interval of almost twenty-five years separating the writing of the text from its revelation to the public had, that is, introduced a split between distinct, or even divergent, levels of meaning. It is as though this little book contained several different books, despite (or because of) its laconic manifest content, as though its superimposed strata echoed and challenged one another in accordance with the strategy of a complex and very deliberate game which was very typical of Queneau.

Let us begin with the text that was published in 1966. In his essay on Queneau, Jean Queval recalls that the book appeared in a wrapper announcing: 'This book is not a novel.'[46] This formula, which seemed to come from an instruction manual, was also intended as an ironic warning: although it was 'model' in the sense of being a fine history, this 'history' was not a history, or at least was not the history of a new Zazie or a new Sally.[47] Queneau was also making the point that this is not a novel, but something else. It is an abstract theory of universal history, presented in a formally deductive manner, inscribed within a scientific and philosophical context, and unrelated to fiction. But is this an indication that it is to be taken seriously? Nothing could be less certain. The formula 'This is not a novel' sounds very much like a denegation, and it recalls the title of the most famous of Magritte's paintings: *This is not a Pipe*. The latter formula also refers to a double ambiguity and turns the canvas, which Magritte glosses by naming it, into a sort of 'model painting'. This is not a pipe; this is not a novel ... And yet it looks very much like one, the only difference being that this is not a real pipe or a real novel ... But what is a 'real' pipe or a 'real' novel? And what is a painting which depicts a fake pipe, a pipe which is not a pipe? What is a model history which displays certain characteristics of the novel, let us say the novelistic element within the

---

46 Jean Queval, *Essai sur Raymond Queneau* (Paris: Seghers, 1971 (third edn)), p. 23.
47 See Raymond Queneau, *Zazie dans le métro* (Paris: Gallimard, 1959) and *Les Oeuvres complètes de Sally Mara* (Paris: Gallimard, 1962).

novel, without being what we call a 'novel'? That it is possible to raise these questions reveals that, when he published it in 1966, Queneau no longer took seriously the theory of history which is evoked rather than elaborated in his book. He did not believe in it, or no longer believed in it.

Hence the indirect warning, which only the naive could fail to notice: careful, all this is no more than literature! Queneau thus hints at the possibility of applying two lines of interpretation to his text. On the one hand, it is the source for later novels such as *Les Fleurs bleues*, which also deals with history in what might be described as a 'model' way. On the other hand, it takes the form of an autobiographical document, of a 'diary' which preserves the memory of an earlier stage in Queneau's intellectual and literary itinerary. In that sense, *Une Histoire modèle* provides an account of Queneau's theoretical pre-occupations in 1942, when he was writing *Pierrot mon ami*. We therefore cannot avoid the following question: did Queneau's project have the same meaning when he began it in 1942 as it did in 1966 when, despite the apparent failure indicated by the fact that he had left it unfinished, he decided to publish his findings and at the same time suggested a new interpretation, which was now literary rather than scientific and which might change its meaning? Was it, or was it not, more serious in 1966 than it had been in 1942? And what relationship can we establish between what is serious and what is not? And, for Queneau, is not the 'serious' something that is, like Magritte's pipe, at once serious and not serious?

Queneau published the text he wrote in 1942 unchanged, but he did alter the title: when the book appeared, its title underwent an inversion which indicated the author's change of attitude towards his earlier investigations. What had initially been presented as a theoretical model for history, in the sense of a rational exploration of its mechanisms, now became a 'model history' which had more in common with a story: it was now no more than a 'history'.

In the preface to his book, written in 1966, Queneau reveals that he originally gave his work the following title: *Brouillon projet d'une atteinte à une science absolue de l'histoire* ('Unsystematic Outline for an Attempted Absolute Science of History'). This was a tribute to the *Brouillon projet d'une atteinte aux événements des rencontres du cône avec un plan* ('Unsystematic Outline for an Attempted Meeting between a Cone and a Plane') published by Girard Desargues in 1639. Desargues was a whimsical geometrician and a near-contemporary of Descartes, but was attracted to different subjects and dealt with them in different ways. In the first half of the seventeenth century, he was famous for the acuity of his insights, and for his confused expositions.[48] He certainly has his place in an encyclopedia of the exact sciences, but it is in that grey area where the exact sciences merge with the 'curious sciences' (which are now well known, thanks to the work of Baltrusaitis). It is thanks to the mediation of the curious sciences that the exact sciences also seem to come into contact with what Queneau calls the 'inexact sciences'.

In the original version of his text, Queneau borrows from Desargues the marvellous expression, *Brouillon projet d'une atteinte*, and then reworks it for his own purposes. The borrowing is significant, for it shows from the outset that the unfinished nature of the text that was later to be entitled 'Une Histoire modèle' was inscribed in its original title. It was never an attempt to elaborate a definitive or a closed system, with all the serious-mindedness involved in such an undertaking. Queneau freely entered into an open-ended research project whose muddled or confused lucidity constantly colluded with a spirit of playfulness.[49] The playfulness became obvious when, on his own authority, Queneau modified Desargues's original title by using it to form the apparently incongruous collocation: *Brouillon projet d'une atteinte à une science absolue de l'histoire*. The formula seems to fall apart as soon as it is stated, since it reduces the obviously radical project of an 'absolute science' to an unsystematic project which is by definition incomplete and lacunary.

What might this 'absolute science' be? It is allusively evoked in paradoxical, even contradictory terms which undermine the serious-nesss of the expression. Another reference given by Queneau in his prefatory note provides the explanation: it is to Vito Volterra's *Leçons*

48 He was the first to think of applying projective methods to the problems of pure geometry: this is in fact the subject of the *Brouillon projet*. The title itself may have been a pun on 'projection', and Queneau certainly read it as such. Another of Desargues's mathematical treatises, now lost, had the rather provocative title of *Leçons de ténèbres* ('Lectures on shadows'). An adolescent with a particularly astute mind whose family background made him receptive to new ideas was to demonstrate his precocious genius by clarifying in a few pages the ideas that Desargues had discussed in an impenetrable and interminable treatise. The text in question was the *Essai sur les coniques* written by Blaise Pascal in 1640.

49 When, in the texts collected in *Bords* (Paris: Hermann, 1963), Queneau discusses mathematicians in theoretical terms, he explains that the important thing about them is that they never stop 'playing'.

sur la théorie mathématique de la lutte pour la vie ('Lectures on the Mathematical Theory of the Struggle for Life'). This too is an incongruous title, notable mainly for the contradictory effect it produces: what do abstract 'lectures on mathematical theory' have to do with the concrete problems of the 'struggle for life'? Judging by the title alone, one might be tempted to believe that this is a further reference to the domain of an encyclopedia of inexact sciences. The Italian mathematician Vito Volterra was born in 1860 and died in 1940. For a long time, he taught at the University of Rome. He was the inventor of functional analysis, which led him to concern himself with the problems of the mechanics of heredity. His name, no less than that of Descartes, belongs to the authentic tradition of the history of the sciences. The books by Volterra that caught Queneau's attention were written in the latter part of his career. From 1925 onwards, by which time he was collaborating with the biologist Umberto d'Ancona, Volterra's initial interest in pure mathematics developed into an interest in questions of biometry, more specifically in the analysis of variations in animal populations considered in their mutual relations.[50]

Volterra's research was therefore inscribed in what was already an old scientific tradition which attempted to apply mathematical methods to the study of animal and human phenomena. Earlier representatives of this tradition include Condorcet, Malthus, Quételet, Galton and Pearson; later examples postdating both Volterra's studies

50 The starting point for this research was provided by the study made by Ancona in Genoa of the effects of the 1914–18 war on fishing and on the development of certain marine species. In 1928–9, Volterra, who had been forced by Mussolini's regime to leave Italy and settle in France, was invited to lecture on the mathematical theory of the struggle for life at the Institut Henri-Poincaré. His lectures were written up and published in 1931 in the *Cahiers scientifiques* published by Gauthier-Villars. These are the works cited by Queneau. A number of other complementary and contemporary publications on the same topics could also be cited: Volterra and Ancona, *Les Associations biologiques au point de vue mathématique* (*Actualités scientifiques et industrielles*, no. 243, Paris: Hermann, 1935, series edited by G. Tessier) — this work was written with biologists in mind, and for their benefit the mathematical part of Volterra's theory was trimmed and simplified; Volterra, *Fluctuations dans la lutte pour la vie, leurs lois fondamentales et leur réciprocité*, a lecture read to the Société mathématique de France, and published by Gauthier-Villars in 1938. Mention should also be made of the Russian mathematician Kostitzin's little book on *Biologie mathématique* in the Armand Colin collection (no. 200, 1937). It was prefaced by Volterra and was an introduction to these questions for the general reader.

and Queneau's reading of them include the development of scientific ecology and, the new fields opened up by cybernetics, the general study of regulation and systems theory. Within this tradition, and his position in it is far from being marginal, Volterra's problematic was eccentric and it is by taking stock of its eccentricity that we can understand why it was of particular interest to Queneau.

In his 1944 article on 'Mathematics in the Classification of the Sciences', Queneau again alludes to Volterra's work in his description of mathematical attempts to appropriate the totality of the world, including biological and sociological phenomena, and to elaborate an exhaustive knowledge or 'absolute science' of the concrete.[51] Now the distinguishing feature of Volterra's approach is the attempt to extend mathematical research, not by 'applying' its findings outside its own field of investigation, but, according to Queneau, by 'logically' formulating problems in transcendent analysis.[52] The goal is to formulate and solve the integral-differential equations known as 'Volterra equations', which are, in their own terms, capable of explaining phenomena that seem, *a priori*, to be beyond the competence of mathematicians. One such phenomenon is the competitive development of species (or 'the struggle for life'). It is in that sense that Queneau announces at the end of his article 'the formation of a completely new logical mathematics capable of absorbing sociobiology (the phenomena of so-called consciousness and life)'.[53] It is therefore no coincidence that Queneau should choose to base his own investigations on Volterra's work, and to transpose it to the consideration of human history, with all the problems that entails, and not least the drift to what would come to be called sociobiology. When, in 1966, he published the text that was now called *Une Histoire modèle* twenty-five years after it was written and despite the fact that it was unfinished, Queneau was no doubt more aware of the risks inherent in 'extending' Volterra than he had been in 1942, when he had been forced to abandon his work. In his view, the project now had no more than a metaphorical or purely 'literary' value. This was a further reason for concealing anything that might

---

51 The article first appeared in 1948 in the issue of *Cahiers du sud* (ed. F. Le Lionnais) devoted to 'Les Grands Courants de la pensée mathématique'. It was subsequently reprinted in the first edition of *Bâtons, chiffres et lettres* (Paris: Gallimard, 1950) and then in *Bords* (Paris: Hermann, 1963).
52 The term 'logical', used in precisely this sense, appears several times in the text of *Une Histoire modèle* (pp. 88, 96, 108).   53 *Bords*, p. 129.

suggest a direct link between his text and some theoretical and scientific ambition, and for describing it as quite the opposite, or in other words as a 'novel-essay'.

Let us now try to understand the difference between the method used by Volterra and earlier work in the domain of biometry. His originality lay in the way he stated the problems. Volterra had already made a completely theoretical and abstract study of the question of the balance between species, rather than the more usual descriptive analysis. Rather than starting out from an empirical census of variations in animal populations and then using probability calculus to present his findings in statistical form, he worked with 'models' or ideal types which were simplified images of reality. In order to do that, he had to imagine, *a priori*, fictional situations,[54] initially simple and gradually more complicated, so as to come closer and closer to a concrete reality. The statistical interpretation was made later, when the time came to verify the findings.[55] A deductive approach thus appeared to use abstract general hypotheses to generate the most concrete forms of existence, the medium for their genesis being a mathematical analysis.[56] In this way, Volterra succeeded in mathematically demonstrating general tendential laws which could later be subjected to experimental verification.[57] This, then, is the meaning of the

54 It is clear that at this point the work of the mathematician converges with that of the novelist, whom he provides with 'models'.
55 In order to obtain a better idea of how Volterra's demonstrative argument works, one has only to look at the table of contents of his '*Leçons*':
   Chapter 1. Coexistence of two species:
   1. Two species fighting for the same food.
   2. Two species, one of which eats the other.
   3. Two species; various instances of mutual action.
   Chapter 2. First study of coexistence between a random number of species:
   1. Species fighting for the same food.
   2. Species that eat one another.
   3. An equal number of species that eat one another.
   Chapter 3. Study of the coexistence of *n* species, with wider hypotheses. Systems of dispersal and conservation.
   Chapter 4. On comparative hereditary actions in biology and mechanics.
56 Queneau alludes to this method in chapter xxv of *Une Histoire modèle*, p. 34.
57 This, for example, is how Volterra explains the 'law of the disturbance of asymptotic averages' in the second chapter of his *Leçons sur la théorie mathématique de la lutte pour la vie* (Paris: Gauthier-Villars, 1931), p. 52: 'If species that devour and species that are devoured exist in equal numbers, if a certain state of immobility can be reached, and if the destruction of each species is both constant and proportional to the number of individuals (but small enough to

expression 'absolute science', which was used by Queneau in the original title of his project: it refers to a completely deductive theory which claimed to come into contact with the real concrete world as though it were the result of its own internal development.

Insofar as it is an 'absolute science *of history*', Queneau's essay is, however, also based on another system of reference, namely Kojève's description of human history as a rational process which produces the real forms of its manifestation as it progresses. Queneau's wartime project can therefore be interpreted as an attempt to combine the implications of Volterra's mathematical theory and those of Kojève's lectures on the philosophy of history. This explains why the writing of the *Brouillon projet d'une atteinte d'une science absolue de l'histoire* coincides with that of *Pierrot mon ami*, which deals with the same problems in different terms.

Volterra's theory had one more unusual feature, this time at the level of the solutions to the problems raised by the abstract deductive method outlined above. Volterra used the so-called functional method. The fourth chapter of his *Leçons* is devoted to an exposition of the method; there, Volterra stresses that the construction of his earlier 'models' had led him to study 'hereditary' phenomena, and that this involved the application of appropriate forms of mathematical analysis.[58] In very general terms, his notion of 'hereditary phenomena' concerned the evolution of systems whose future transformations were determined not only by their present state, as classical mechanics would have it, but also by the sequence of their earlier states. The persistent and cumulative effects of those states would influence their later modifications. In other words, the processes in question were determined by memory or history, and their study would naturally

allow a state of immobility and, therefore, non-reversible fluctuations), the asymptotic average will increase for some devouring species, and will decrease for some of the species that are devoured.' One can just imagine the jubilation Queneau must have felt on reading such a pronouncement, and on seeing the incongruous effects that derive from its literary 'style'.

58 The notion of 'hereditary phenomena' relates, not to the traditional acceptation of the term 'heredity' in the specific domain of biology, but to the elaboration of a new scientific concept, which was originally developed in the context of the study of the phenomena of hysteresis in mechanics. When the concept is applied to questions pertaining to the biological realm, care must be taken not to use it in its original (and current) sense; in other words, it has nothing to do with the general problems of descendance and lines of descent. For a definition of hereditary phenomena, see *Leçons*, chapter 4.

result in the formulation of tendential laws of transformation. According to Volterra's mathematical interpretation of these phenomena, their evolution was not reducible to the repetition of periodic cycles, but tended towards limit-states beyond which any further modification was unthinkable.

From Queneau's point of view, this theory was of considerable interest. The hereditary mechanics whose principles Volterra had extended to the consideration of the general problems of life had simultaneously produced a general theory of evolution which would, ultimately, include every aspect of human history, and that was *Une Histoire modèle*'s programme.[59] What was more, the laws that gave this history its overall direction, and which could be understood in strictly theoretical and deductive terms, made it possible to identify, at least hypothetically, its necessary direction. The latter took the form, not of a regular process modelled on a fully objectified cosmic evolution, but of an irreversible evolution leading in a single direction. It then became possible to discuss the question of the meaning of history in purely logical terms, as though it were a problem in pure mathematics. Now we know that Queneau was literally obsessed with this question during the period of the Second World War. His search for an absolute science of history led him to the notion of the end of history, and it was now possible to discuss it without lapsing into inaccurate speculations or vague and arbitrary philosophical interpretations. The notion of the end of history would also be central to his 'novels of wisdom'.

The history that interested Queneau at this time was both history as it is lived, history as it is understood and history as it is recounted: the history of men, the history of scientists and philosophers, but also the history of writers, or in other words fiction. Queneau began to weave the tissue of this polysemy in *Une Histoire modèle*. Let me cite some passages that establish the connection between reality, knowledge and fiction: 'If there were no wars and revolutions, there would be no history, no subject-matter for history ... History is the science of human unhappiness.'[60] 'If there were no unhappiness, there would be nothing to recount.'[61] 'Imaginary stories are always about human

59 *Une Histoire modèle* touches, either directly or indirectly, on the theme of the end of history in chapters VIII (p. 16), IX (p. 17), XVII (p. 25), LXXXVI (p. 103), LXXXVIII (p. 105), LXXXIX (p. 106) and XCI (p. 108).   60 Ibid., p. 9.
61 Ibid., p. 15.

unhappiness; there is nothing else for them to recount.'[62] 'Literature is the projection onto the imaginary plane of man's real activity; labour is the projection onto the real plane of man's imaginary activity. The two are born together. One refers metaphorically to Paradise lost and takes stock of man's unhappiness. The other progresses towards Paradise regained and tries to make men happy.'[63] Insofar as it attempts, in its own way, to resolve the conflict between the real and the imaginary, is not literature too a form of struggle and labour? Can we not say that, in its attempt to take stock of human unhappiness, it also helps to make men happy?

62 Ibid., p. 21.   63 Ibid., p. 103.

❖❖

PART II

Into the depths

❖❖

5

❖❖

On Victor Hugo: figures of the man from below

❖❖

The proletariat, the lowest stratum of our present society, cannot stir, cannot raise itself up, without the whole superincumbent strata of official society being sprung into the air.

Marx and Engels, *Manifesto of the Communist Party*[1]

Elements announcing the birth of a literature of the depths can be found at the end of the eighteenth century in the Gothic novel and in Sade. Its actual birth was an event that can be situated and dated, and its significance is at once aesthetic and political. It implied a new relationship with the world, a new way of seeing things and saying things. 'He resembled the creatures of the night, groping his way in an invisible element, lost underground in seams of darkness.'[2] Even independently of the fact that it has come down to us under the signature of Victor Hugo, such a sentence could not have been written in any other period but his. A sentence like this is also inspired and supported by ideas which, even before they became part of the conscious speculations of their author or scribe, were the ideas of his era. How did literature become the site where thought of this kind could be elaborated and communicated? If we can answer that question, we may perhaps know a little more about the preconditions for the formation of a literary philosophy.

A new literary form: the serial

In 1836, a considerable mutation occurred in the domain of the press in France and it coincided with the emergence of new means of expression. They were formally adapted to messages whose very

1 Karl Marx, *The Revolutions of 1848. Political Writings Volume 1* (Harmondsworth: Penguin Books in association with *New Left Review*, 1973), p. 78.
2 Victor Hugo, *Les Misérables, Oeuvres complètes* (Paris: Club français du livre, 1969), vol. 11, p. 886.

content was new, and corresponded to the birth of a new public.[3] The development of mass journalism went hand in hand with both technical innovations and a real ideological transformation, which was well described by one of its initiators. In the editorial he wrote for the first number of *La Presse*, which appeared in July 1836, Emile de Girardin commented:

We have created this newspaper because we think that differences of opinion have to do with a diversity of concerns, with different points of view, but that this divergence is more apparent than real. At a superficial level, this diversity can be found everywhere; at a deeper level it is almost non-existent. A careful examination and then a serious reading of their works soon showed us that the most eminent minds build on a substratum of almost identical ideas. As we dug deeper, we found the same strata beneath the edifice of all their discourses and writings.

De Girardin's goal was, in other words, both to homogenize public discourse and to move its point of application by displacing it downwards to the level where forms of opinion which, when grasped at the level of their effects, seemed disparate, in fact converged. At this point, the new figure of subterranean man emerged.

In writing of the need to 'dig deep' in order to see what was happening in the depths of public opinion, Emile de Girardin signalled the need to look beyond, or rather beneath, particular differences and contrasts in order to find the 'substratum of identical ideas' that supplied the object of collective exchanges. Being subjected by the need for universality to generalized norms, public opinion could be defined as an average. It coincided in an almost statistical manner with the common residue that existed in or between individual opinions once their differences had been removed or erased. In the depths that gave it its cohesion, public opinion was a mass phenomenon.[4] The

3 The introduction of advertising allowed the cost of subscriptions, which had previously been very high, to be reduced. Periodical publications therefore ceased to be the preserve of strictly categorized groups of readers, and began to be addressed to a wider public.

4 A few years later, Sainte-Beuve responded to Girardin's initiative by publishing an article on 'industrial literature' in the *Revue des Deux Mondes* (1 September 1839). In it, he denounces the levelling down of literary discourse that had resulted from the new practices of the popular press: the attempt to transmit that discourse to the greatest possible number of readers has robbed it of its original characteristics, and simultaneously denied it the means of achieving distinction.

movement that drew thought downwards also drew the eye of the reader to the lower part of the pages of the newspaper, to the basement of writing where a prime form of the literature of the depths was being elaborated and put on display: the serialized novel, an authentically popular mode of expression which, together with the irruption of subterranean man, completely transformed conditions of public communication by promoting collective forms of reading and writing.

In the mid-nineteenth century, Eugène Sue was the classic example of the 'people's writer', and the trajectory he followed to achieve that status is a revealing one. He originally specialized in sea stories, and then moved on to writing social novels. French society had been periodically shaken by the groundswells of 1789 and 1830, and a new storm would come in 1848. For those who had witnessed these storms, French society was made in the image of the sea and its ceaseless movement.[5] Michelet and Hugo make constant use of this image, as though the power of the crowd emerged from the depths of the sea. The metaphor gave rise to a style: the sea was a form, or rather – and Hugo was to exploit this idea to the full – the sea was that

Sainte-Beuve therefore makes a stand against the transformation of the writer's function, which he interprets as its degradation, and explains it in terms of a combination of two phenomena: the debasement of literary writing brought about by the development of new means of mass communication and the simultaneous professionalization of the writer. Sainte-Beuve's text coincided with the foundation of the Société des gens de lettres, which was set up to defend the rights of the writers who had become the salaried employees of the new distribution system. Sainte-Beuve's text ends thus: 'For all those with a profound love of letters, this is a time for vigilance. The lower depths are now constantly rising, and are rapidly becoming the common level as everything else collapses or is debased ... Above all, we must summon up our intellectual courage and dare to resist. Let industrial literature exist, but let it flow in its own bed, and let it gouge it out slowly. For it has an all too natural tendency to spread. To conclude: two literatures coexist in very unequal proportions, and will increasingly coexist, mingling as good and evil will mingle in this world until judgement day: let us attempt to anticipate and nurture that judgement by identifying the good and firmly restricting the rest.' Sainte-Beuve therefore recognized that great changes were taking place in the depths of society; but for him, the depths meant the 'lower depths', or in other words the rabble and its scandalous mysteries.

5 One of Sue's early works begins thus: 'Listen to the dull, melancholic murmur of the Ocean; it sounds like the hubbub of a great city waking up; see how the waves rise up at long intervals and calmly unfurl their immense curls; sometimes, white, tremulous spray is dashed from the diaphanous crest of two waves as they meet, crash into one another, rise up together and fall back into dust after a slight impact', *Atar Gull* (1831), vol. 1, chapter 1.

which gave form to the formless. This form developed out of the appearance and unexpected disappearance of isolated sequences dealing with individual events or situations which were fleetingly glimpsed and then immediately plunged back into, and literally drowned in, the immensity from whence they had emerged and into which they now merged once more. A new form of novel was being woven, and it was no longer organized around a central subject defined by essentially psychological characteristics. It was fragmented and dispersed into a multiplicity of actions whose singularity was swallowed up by a never-ending collective movement. Collective movement was no longer the result of initiatives on the part of individuals, but of the unpredictable and fatal logic of events of which individuals were mere playthings.[6] Novels about the people thus came to consist of separate and unconnected episodes. Their anarchic proliferation is still impressive because it hints enigmatically at hidden connections that exist, not at the superficial level of conscious actions and motivations, but in the muddy depths of a hidden and widely shared life.

Les Misérables: a novel of the depths

Hugo raised the techniques of the mass-consumption novel to the heights of great art; indeed, in his view, did not the sublime come from below? *Les Misérables* was not originally published in serial form, but

6 In the letter to Fenimore Cooper that was published as the preface to *Atar Gull*, Sue describes the narrative technique, specifically adapted to sea stories, which he used again in the popular novels he wrote some ten years later: 'Do you not feel some vague sympathy for that singular being who, when he appears alone in the midst of this noisy, tumultuous world, seems almost fantastic, because there is something so unexpected, so charmingly mysterious about the encounter?... Now, I have always wondered, Sir, why we should not attempt to include this unexpected element, these sudden apparitions which gleam for a moment, fade and then disappear forever, into sea stories, which encompass so much, whose scenes are often separated by thousands of leagues. Why not, rather than obeying the strict rule that gives equal importance to a given number of characters who are there at the beginning of the book and who must, willy nilly, get to the end of it so that each can make his contribution to the denouement? If we accept that a philosophical idea or a historical fact can run through the whole book, why not use it to group characters who, rather than following in the wake of the moral abstraction around which the book revolves, can be abandoned by the wayside when the opportunity arises or as the logic of events demands.'

it was written using the techniques specific to the genre, which thus
acceded to literary dignity. It was in every sense the book of the
people: written for, and perhaps by the people, and not on it or about
it. In it we find, transposed and transfigured in the sublime space of
myth, the jerky reality of the world of the serial novel, with its tonal
clashes, its tangled plots and its unresolved destinies. Hugo amplifies
figures from a 'minor' literature in such a way as to elaborate a new
form of fiction which, being no longer based upon the psychological
analysis of individual passions, depicts the complexity and, so to
speak, the density of a social structure.

Throughout this immense book, which from beginning to end is an
ode to the man from below, the image of the sea, which Hugo had so
often exploited in his poetry to evoke crowds, is associated with
another metaphor: that of night. Night is another figure of the dark
abyss from which there emerge the ill-defined silhouettes of characters
who are uncertain as to their own identity and destiny. They emerge
only to disappear back into the depths of a society as though they had
been drawn into a chasm.[7] In order to give a name to these limitless,
countless masses, to this sundered and fragmented mass of disjointed

---

7   See, for example, *Les Misérables*, p. 814: 'Having said that, Gavroche went off or,
to be more accurate, flew back like an escaped bird to whence he had come. He
plunged back into the darkness as though he were making a hole in it, with the
rigid rapidity of a projectile: the ruelle de l'Homme armé was once more silent
and deserted; in the twinkling of an eye, this strange child, who had something
shadowy and dreamlike about him, had plunged into the mists amongst the rows
of black houses, and was lost there like smoke in the darkness. One might have
thought he had melted away or vanished, had it not been for the sound of glass
shattering a moment later, as the splendid crash of a streetlight smashing onto
the cobbles suddenly awakened the outraged bourgeois once again. Gavroche
was on his way.' The Parisian street urchin, who is the city's critical consciousness,
is absorbed into it so as to be reborn of it, as in the 'elephant at the Bastille'
episode. The unpredictable trajectory he traces across Paris as he disappears or
vanishes provides a map of the complex network of the city.
    Hugo uses similar devices to sketch the silhouettes, which are no less heroic
in their own way, of the marginal wretches he describes in the 'Patron-Minette'
episode: 'They seemed to have vanished completely ... Thénadier and his
daughter Azelma, the only two of the wretched group to have remained, had
plunged back into the darkness. The gulf of the social unknown had silently
closed over these creatures. On the surface, not even faint ripples were to be
seen, not even the mysterious concentric circles which announce that something
has fallen in and that a line could be thrown there' (ibid., p. 935). The people
suffer because they are fragmented, crushed, literally forced into the abyss,
permanently in search of their incomplete unity.

members, Hugo is forced to use the language of darkness, to employ
words dredged from the very sewers of the city. He haunted the gates
to the city, witnessed these births and separations, and became their
poet: 'Anyone who has wandered as I have in the lonely spots near
our suburbs, and which we might call the limbo of Paris, will have
glimpsed here and there ...'[8] In this darkness, one glimpses no more
than tattered images of a people who will appear in the solidity of their
collective reality only in the harsh glare of a riot.

The ends of writing are therefore inverted situations, things and
people have to be 'deindividualized' by becoming dissolved in the
masses. They then reemerge as fleeting apparitions whose ghostly and
ephemeral appearance testifies to the permanent existence of a literally
unfathomable mystery.[9] Here, Hugo is following Sue, the inventor of
these new forms, which were specifically adapted to the social novel.[10]
In the labyrinth of the great city, people lost their individual existence,
which was absorbed into a shapeless mass. Sue invented the poetic
technique of the social supernatural, and it was far removed from
realism. Marx failed to understand it, and his mockery of Sue is facile
indeed: the unlikely Rodolphe, prince and worker, was anything but
the embodiment of a real person. His anonymity allowed him to break
the strictest taboos, to establish links between the extremities of social
space, and therefore to reveal its opacity and density.[11]

Hugo both borrows and transcends Sue's discovery. His Jean

8 Ibid., p. 435.
9 Louis Chevalier, *Classes laborieuses et classes dangereuses* (Paris: Livre de
   poche/Pluriel, 1978), p. 201, demonstrates how the socialization of its content
   modified the function of literature: 'The description of criminal groups offers a
   semblance of truth, or at least provokes horror, only when it depicts gatherings,
   masses or crowds, when, that is, it merges men and things. The slow and
   monstrous progress of the chain gang as it grows out of the shadows and, so to
   speak, rises out of Paris, inspires a horror that convicts do not evoke when they
   are described individually. Once the description attempts to individualize one or
   another character, it loses both its efficacy and its verisimilitude.'
10 Cf. J.-L. Bory, *Eugène Sue* (Paris: Hachette, 1962), p. 264: '*Les Mystères de Paris*
   marks the transition from Balzac's individual criminals, who are described
   meticulously, to Hugo's criminals, who are shadowy fragments of a shadowy
   crowd.' Here, Bory is following the thesis advanced by Chevalier.
11 Cf. R. Bozzetto, 'Eugène Sue et le fantastique', *Europe*, November–December
   1982, p. 108 (special issue on Sue): 'His social transgressions seem to allow him
   to take a unified view of society as a whole. But because he is so unstable and so
   difficult to situate, the viewpoint he constructs is strictly imaginary and illusory,
   since only he can adopt it.'

Valjean bears witness for the whole of humanity: being no one in particular, he is the whole world, and a world in himself.[12] This is also the secret of his saintliness, for he must consequently atone for others. 'Man has even greater depths than the people.'[13] This statement must not, above all, be seen as an index of a return to a traditional psychological perspective which reduces the individual to the illusory subjectivity of consciousness, for the same depths can be found in man and crowd alike. The individual reflects the crowd that exists within him. Jean Valjean is both man and crowd. Thanks to a sequence of rebirths and reincarnations, his palingenetic nature is transformed into a multitude of individual existences which are in secret – and subterranean – communication with one another. In this multiple life, the contrasting elements of the diurnal and the nocturnal change places, just as they do in the sublime and vulgar existence of the people. The destiny of the people is symbolically summed up by the destiny of a man who is no longer 'an individual'. Plunging into the depths of darkness and then soaring into the heights of luminosity, this transient figure represents, thanks to his metamorphoses, the permanent transformation of darkness into light, and the alchemy of that transformation is a perfect illustration of both the history of humanity and the contemporary structure of a society.

It thus transpires that the mass cannot survive outside the individual, just as a machine cannot move without dragging its component parts with it. The mass inhabits the individual, haunts him and at the same time creates within him a world of troubles. That is the subject of the 'storm inside a head' episode. Inside a man's head, there is a sea, and in that sea there lives a hydra. Gilliath's struggle against the octopus is a continuation of Jean Valjean's struggles in a different sea.[14] Thanks to the evocative power of his words, the poet conveys

12 'To write the poem of human consciousness, if only that of one man, if only that of the least of men, would be to merge all epics into one higher and definitive epic', *Les Misérables*, p. 201.   13 Ibid., p. 807.

14 'Many men have a secret monster of this kind, an evil that feeds on them, a dragon which gnaws at them, a despair that haunts their nights. Such a man looks like other men, and comes and goes. No one knows that inside him there is a terrible parasitic pain with thousands of teeth, which lives inside the wretch who is dying of it. No one knows that this man is an abyss. He is stagnant but deep. From time to time, a disturbance of which we understand nothing can be seen on the surface. A mysterious ripple spreads, disappears and then reappears; a bubble of air comes up and bursts. It is nothing, but it is also terrible. That is the unknown beast breathing' (ibid., p. 972).

the fathomless depths of the social abyss in which men drown, as in Hugo's metaphor of a man drowning in the sea.[15]

The ambiguous semantics that give this epic of the masses its title indicates in its own way the feeling of vertigo that is produced by looking into the abyss: 'There is a point where the unfortunate and the infamous mingle and merge in a single word, a fatal word: *les misérables*.'[16] Working people, dangerous people: *misérable* is the switch-word, the password that brings about the transsubstantiation.[17] When we see into its depths, society becomes 'the lower depths'. And it was this mutation which Hugo wanted to transcribe in a transitional form of literature that dealt with boundaries and marginality. It could be created only by someone who haunted the city gates. It is because it allows us to grasp the process of becoming and the metamorphosis that the novel is elevated to the status of myth. The *misérables* also have to pay a price and to bear the weight of sins they did not commit.

The figure of Jean Valjean is in that respect exemplary. As we have already seen, he is a drowning man, but he is also a survivor, and a man who literally supports society's misery by taking its full weight on his shoulders.[18] In one of the most striking passages in his book, Hugo

15 'He slipped, he fell, it was over. He is in the monstrous water. Beneath his feet, everything flows and runs away. Torn and shredded by the wind, the waves surround him hideously. The rolling abyss is carrying him away. Tatters of water swirl around his head. A rabble of waves spits on him, shapeless openings half devour him. Every time he goes under, he sees precipices of darkness; terrible unknown plants seize him, wrap themselves around his feet, draw him to them. He feels that he is becoming an abyss ... The implacable advance of human societies! The men and the souls that are lost on the way! The Ocean into which there falls all that the law allows to fall! The sinister disappearance of help! Moral death! The sea is the immense abyss into which the law casts those it has damned. The sea is an immense expanse of poverty. When it drifts with the current in this abyss, the soul can become a corpse. Who will bring it back to life?' (ibid. pp. 116–17).   16 Ibid., p. 547.
17 Cf Chevalier, *Classes laborieuses*, p. 221: 'There is a certain indeterminacy [about this word] ... an ambiguity of usage which arises because it is applied to changes that are difficult to grasp ... it designates a situation midway between an unhappy condition and the criminal condition, or rather the transition from one to the other ... it depicts a situation which might be said to be, as Hugo said of poverty, "a nameless thing"'.
18 'Whenever he twisted his neck to look up from the darkness in which he lay, he saw, with mingled terror and rage, a sort of terrifying accumulation of things, laws, prejudices, men and deeds whose outlines he could not make out, level after level, rising as far as the eye could see. Its bulk terrified him, and it was none other than the amazing pyramid we call society. All that — laws, prejudices, deeds, men and things — came and went above him, obeying the mysterious motion God

depicts in visual terms a man being crushed. In this passage, Jean Valjean, who has become Monsieur Madeleine, lifts the cart that has fallen onto old Fauchelevent by taking it on his back. The act which consecrates him as a hero in the eyes of the crowd also unmasks him to the law; it prompts Javert, who has urged him on, to say: 'I've met only one man capable of doing that. He was a convict.'[19] Nicknamed 'Jean-le cric' ('John the Jack') in prison because of his extraordinary strength, Valjean begins to resemble a caryatid. When he takes on his shoulders the whole mass of a 'cart' symbolizing a wretchedly poor society, he 'supports' it — in every sense of the word — through his suffering. And he can support it and atone for it only because of the position with which he identifies himself completely: below, beneath, at the bottom. He is subterranean man.[20]

Hugo was the visionary writer of the depths; he made the descent that took him down to the point where things seemed to vanish into infinity. 'When it is a matter of sounding a wound, a gulf or a society, since when has it been wrong to descend too far, to get to the bottom?'[21] At this point — the lowest point — the novel becomes History: to write a novel about society is to 'know' it, and therefore to expose its full reality.[22] Literature is now Philosophy too:

imprints on society, trampling him and crushing him. There was something tranquil about its cruelty, something inexorable about its indifference. Those condemned by the law are souls who have fallen to the lowest possible depths of misfortune, wretches lost in the nethermost limbo into which no one looks; they feel the whole weight of human society pressing on their heads, the weight of a society that is so terrible for those who are outside it, so fearful for those who are beneath it. In this situation, Jean Valjean dreamed, and what could be the nature of his dreams? If a grain of millet in the mill could think, it would probably think what Jean Valjean was thinking' (ibid., p. 114).   19 Ibid., p. 171.

20 Unlike Valjean, Javert — is the assonance a coincidence? — is the man of law and right, of rectitude and the surface. When, at the end of his interminable quest for the 'wretch', he finally finds him, he also destroys himself or, as Hugo puts it (p. 91) with extraordinary inventiveness, 'goes off the rails'. All that remains for him to do is to plunge into the abyss into which Valjean has led him: he throws himself into the Seine. 'It seemed to open onto infinity. It was not water beneath him; it was the void ... And darkness alone knew the secrets of the convulsions of that vague shape as it disappeared beneath the water' (ibid., p. 917). When Javert disappears, so too does the rigid structure of society, which is swallowed up by the milling, tormented masses, whose murky depths are periodically stirred up.   21 Ibid., p. 697.

22 'Studying social deformities and infirmities and describing them in order to cure them, is a task which leaves no room for choice. The mission of the historian of morals and ideas is no less austere than that of the historian of events. The latter

The social observer must enter that darkness; it is a part of his laboratory. Philosophy is thought's microscope. Everything tries to flee it, but nothing escapes it. To compromise is useless: what side of oneself does one show by compromise? The shameful side. Philosophy pursues evil with its unflinching gaze and does not allow it to escape into nothingness. Amid the vanishing and the shrinking, it detects all things.[23]

This admirable final sentence is emblematic of the whole of Hugo's poetic and political thought; it sums up all his attempts to see things as they emerge from the nothingness of the darkness like indeterminate figures of the infinite.

The man of the crowd

In about 1848, there developed a form of literature that was popular in terms of the content of its message, the forms of its style, the mode of its exposition and the interplay of its imagery, and it echoed the social upheavals that marked the entire period. This literature had to adapt to the rules of a particularly sophisticated rhetoric capable of restoring a presence to indistinct things that came from the depths of night and the abyss of the sea. Both *Les Mystères de Paris* and *Les Misérables* attempt to capture the general wretchedness [*misère*] of the city by depicting a boundless space that stretches, or plunges, as far as

deals with the surface of civilization, struggles between crowned heads, the birth of princes, the marriages of kings, battles, assemblies, great public figures, revolutions ... Everything takes place outside, in the light of day. The other historian deals with the inside, with the depths, with the people – working, suffering and waiting. He deals with overburdened women, with the people in its agony, with the silent, secret wars that set man against man, the mysterious ferocities, prejudices, and confessed iniquities, the mysterious side-effects of the law, the hidden evolution of souls, the slight tremors of the multitude, the starvelings, the bare-foot, the half-naked, the disinherited, the orphans, the unfortunate and the infamous. All these larvae crawl in the darkness. The historian must go down, down into the impenetrable casemates that swarm with those who bleed and those who strike blows, those who endure evil and those who do evil. Are the duties of the historian of hearts and souls any less onerous than those of the historian of external facts? Do you think that Alighieri has less to say than Machiavelli? Is the underside of society less important than its surface, because it is deeper and darker? How can we understand mountains if we do not understand caves?' (ibid., pp. 699–700). This passage seems to anticipate those Queneau devotes to the general problems of history in his discussion of Volterra's analyses of the clash between species that devour and species that are devoured. 23 Ibid., p. 877.

the eye can see. Walter Benjamin dates the birth of an aesthetic of the crowd, seen as a direct expression of the establishment of a modern capitalist society, to the 1850s, and finds the most perfect form of its expression in Baudelaire, the inventor of the theme of 'modern life'. According to this view, Baudelaire is the poet of the new social relations.[24] Like the arcades which so fascinated Benjamin, these relations run through a society symbolized by the space of its city: they cut through it, make holes in it and reproduce it in such a way as to reveal a hidden texture whose logic is that of dispersal. Poe's story of the 'man of the crowd', which Baudelaire translated, is the story of a man lost in this secret organization, whose structure — by definition always hidden and elusive — consists of the vistas opened up by a perspective that stretches to infinity.[25]

Benjamin contrasts this 'modern' representation, which is appropriate to the new forms of a capitalist society, with Hugo's epic style which, rather than dispersing the crowd, makes it denser and concentrates it in order to make it a 'subject' with which the poet can identify in order to describe it, rather than abandoning it to its shapeless objectivity. Baudelaire's wanderer remains on the surface, walks aimlessly and appears to get nowhere; the people and the myths of its depths are tendentially forgotten and effaced. In that sense, the *flâneur* who wanders through the modern crowd is essentially different from Hugo's passer-by who, without taking a leading role in revolutions, does accept responsibility for the revolutionary process so as to reveal its latent finality. 'To Baudelaire the crowd never was a

---

24 Cf. Baudelaire's letter to A. Houssaye, reprinted as the preface to *Le Spleen de Paris*, and first published in *La Presse* in 1862: 'Which of us has not dreamed, on his ambitious days, of the miracle of a poetic, musical prose without rhythm and without rhyme, supple enough and jerky enough to adapt to the hybrid movements of the soul, the swaying of daydreams, and the jolts of conscience? It is above all familiarity with enormous cities, and the encounter with the countless relations that exist in them, that gives birth to this obsessive ideal.' There is something of Hugo in this quest for a new form of expression, midway between prose and poetry, and designed to occupy the unexplored space that lies between light and shadow.

25 It seems that Balzac was one of the first to evoke such a perspective and to make a literary theme of it: 'You cannot imagine how many adventures are lost, how many dramas are forgotten, in this city of pain. So many horrible and beautiful things! The imagination will never really grasp the truth that lies hidden there, and that no one can discover. One would have to go too far down to find those admirably comic or tragic scenes, those masterpieces born of chance' (*Facino Cane*, 1836, *Préambule*).

stimulus to cast the plummet of his thought down into the depths of the world.'[26] To put it rather differently: Baudelaire's Paris no longer had any depth because it was the post-1848 city, and because he was writing after the failure of the democratic revolution. His city is therefore the shapeless, almost absurd, setting for a directionless and desperate quest that takes him through a world which is itself in crisis, so much so that it has lost all substance, has no meaning in itself and consists in a network of mere appearances. The Paris described by Hugo, in contrast, evokes the pre-1848 period,[27] the rise of the revolution and not its decline; here, the masses are in unanimous communion with their destiny. For Hugo, history certainly has a meaning insofar as it unfolds, from beginning to end, within a space polarised into 'above' and 'below', whereas for Baudelaire, who, even before Schopenhauer began to be known in France, inaugurated the aesthetic tradition of pessimism, history no longer has any meaning.

Benjamin is therefore no doubt right to make a distinction between the poetics of Hugo and Baudelaire by showing that they derive from systems of representation, or world-views, that are historically and socially irreducible. One wonders, however, whether he is justified in contrasting them so starkly in his attempt to clarify the implications of his own argument. After all, neither Hugo's nor Sue's vision of the masses is as simplistic or devoid of complexity as Benjamin claims it to be. In neither *Les Mystères de Paris* nor *Les Misérables* do the people have the obvious presence that would allow them to perceive — immediately, directly and completely — their reality as having already been constituted in itself. The representations of subterranean man which we have been analysing have certainly not abandoned the attempt to give a dynamized image of their subject-object, which they identify through its incessant metamorphoses. The exfoliated, fragmented and, one might almost say, liquid reality of the popular novel is glimpsed in the shape of mythical figures which reveal an absence

---

26 Walter Benjamin, 'The Paris of the Second Empire in Baudelaire', in *Charles Baudelaire: A Lyric Poet in the Era of High Capitalism*, tr. Harry Zohn (London: Verso, 1976), p. 61.

27 *Les Misérables* was written under the Second Empire, but Hugo had gone into exile because of his hostile reaction to the reversion to Caesarism that had been generated by the perversion of universal suffrage: the combination of the celebration of a future and the commemoration of a past had led to a withdrawal from all that the present represents. The context reflected by the novel does not correspond mechanically to the moment of its composition.

rather than an opaque reality.[28] Non-representable in itself, the figure of the people makes its presence felt in the gaps in the narrative. It is the gaps that give it its evocative meaning. Hence the need to resort to poetic fiction to show, or rather to suggest, something which, by its very nature, belongs to the shadows: the dark mass of the man from below.

'Well grubbed, old mole!'

To what extent does this mythology of darkness and the depths allow us to understand the transformations in French society that coincided with its establishment as a system of representation? Contemporary analyses of this mutation were developed on very different grounds and were in principle intended to provide a rigorous and objective explanation for it, but they were based upon precisely the same schemas of thought, since they presuppose, in analogous fashion, a downwards displacement of theoretical interest, and an inversion of the relations that effectively determine social reality.

In his study of 'The Class Struggles in France', written in 1849 and published in 1850, Marx, for instance, attempts to find behind the sequence of political events that makes up the 'surface' of history the latent principle which gives the impetus to this development. He thus succeeds in demonstrating that the indisputable failure of the revolutionary movement of 1848 was merely the visible and superficial aspect of an overall process, the truth of which in fact lay at a different level, namely in the depths of the social body and its historical movement. This meant that, whilst the recent history of French society did have a meaning, that meaning remained occult, or even occulted; in order to grasp its meaning, things had, so to speak, to be approached from below through a constant process of excavation. The precondition for its revelation was a constant and expanding interplay between what had been uncovered and what

---

28 'The central aim of *Les Mystères de Paris* is, like that of any fantastic text, to capture the advent of the unnamed. Its advent takes two forms: the destabilization of a familiar viewpoint (in this case by Rodolphe), and the emergence of disparate fragments in the margins of this destabilized vision. Evil and violence are evoked in the distortions and ruptures that the text produces as it advances. At the same time, it uses scenes to punctuate the difficulties it experiences in arriving at a self-representation' (Bozzetto, 'Eugène Sue et le fantastique', pp. 109–10).

remained hidden. Having attacked the superstructure of the building, the erosion would eventually attack its base: here, Marx is picking up and interpreting in his own way the Hegelian concept of a 'civil society' that exists apart from the political state. Civil society exists beneath and prior to the state; it is the real locus where all social conflicts are rooted, and where their outcome is decided.

At precisely the same moment, Tocqueville gave his explanation for the revolution of 1848. In political terms, his explanation is diametrically opposed to Marx's, and yet it too refers to the same dissociation between higher and lower phenomena, and it too could be interpreted in terms of base and superstructure, even though Tocqueville interprets both notions in different terms. In the *Souvenirs* Tocqueville wrote in 1850–51, which are devoted in their entirety to the events that followed February 1848, we find an astonishing passage in which analysis and evocation mingle in a mode of recollection inherited from Chateaubriand. It is based upon images which also act as concepts:

The country was at this time divided into two parts, or rather two unequal zones. The upper part, which alone contained the whole political life of the nation, was the realm of pure languor, impotence, immobility and boredom; in the lower part, in contrast, political life began to manifest itself through feverish and irregular symptoms which the attentive observer could easily feel. I was one of those observers and although I certainly did not imagine that the catastrophe was so close at hand or that it would be so terrible, I had doubts in my mind which gradually increased, and the increasingly deep-rooted conviction that we were heading towards a new revolution. That marked a great change in my thinking, for the universal calm and the respite that had followed the July revolution had led me to believe for a long time that I was destined to spend my life in an enervated and peaceful society. And indeed, anyone who had looked only at the inner fabric of the government would have been convinced of it. Everything seemed to combine with the mechanisms of freedom to produce a royal power that was so oppressive as to be almost despotic; and in reality that result was effortlessly produced by the regular and peaceful movement of the machine. King Louis-Philippe was convinced that, if he himself did not touch that fine instrument and left it to operate in accordance with its own rules, he was safe from all danger. His sole concern was to keep it in order and to make it work as he saw fit, forgetting the society on which the ingenious mechanism rested; he was like the man who refused to believe his house had been set on fire because he still had the key to it in his pocket. I could not have the same interests and preoccupations, and that allowed me to see through the mechanism of institutions and the fog of petty day to day events and to consider the state of the country's morals and opinions. At that level, I could clearly see the appearance of several signs which habitually announce the approach of revolutions, and I began to think that in 1830, I had mistaken the end of an act for the end of the play.[29]

The text is based on a symbolism of signal (premonitory indices), of machinery (the mechanism of the State, which seems to work automatically) and of obscure impulses (which work mysteriously on society, as though something from the depths had come to the surface). One could even say that this symbolism is auditory rather than visual; Tocqueville describes himself as the man who 'heard' the revolution coming because he had noticed, beneath the usual noise of what was going on above (the workings of government and its wheels), the muted grumblings of imperceptible mutations occurring in the secret history of everyday life. In his view, the irresistible movement leading to the democratization of society could therefore be explained in terms of an inversion of relations between society and state. That inversion both revealed the social question by bringing it into the light of day, whereas it had long been buried in the silence of the great abyss where it had been slowly elaborated, and displaced the centre of gravity of political action downwards by rooting it in the mass existence of the people, the *demos*, who were the object of democracy rather than its subject.

The similarity between the analyses made by Tocqueville and Marx is striking. We find in both the same fascination with 'lower' phenomena, interpreted as elements and symptoms of a necessary historical evolution whose meaning is perceptible only if one abandons the limited and superficial viewpoint of 'politics', in the everyday sense of the term, and looks behind and beneath politics for the great silent movement that supports and explains it. In the series of articles written in 1852 which he later devoted to 'The Eighteenth Brumaire of Louis Bonaparte', Marx would succumb to the same tendency to interpret, as we can see from a passage that has become famous:

But the revolution is thoroughgoing. It is still journeying through purgatory. It does its work methodically. By December 2, 1851, it had completed one half of its preparatory work; it is now completing the other half. First it perfected the parliamentary power in order to be able to overthrow it. Now that it has attained this, it perfects the *executive power*, reduces it to its purest expression, isolates it, sets it up against itself as the sole target, in order to

---

29 Alexis de Tocqueville, *Souvenirs* (Paris: Gallimard, 1942), part 1, pp. 30–1.

concentrate all its forces of destruction against it. And when it has done this second half of its preliminary work, Europe will leap from its seat and exultantly exclaim: Well grubbed, old mole.[30]

This text leaves the careful reader perplexed: the revolution is personified and described as the intentional and inventive subject of its own history. It plays tricks with events to make them produce, in the long term and without their knowing it, a meaning which is diametrically opposed to the meaning they seem to have in the immediate present. It manipulates men and institutions to its own ends. The personification of the revolution irresistibly reminds one of Hegel's teleology as it draws the whole of history towards the goal it has assigned it and acts as its rational principle. In adopting these Hegelian themes, Marx may have been trying to produce – and to dramatize for highly polemical ends – an inverted, grating and caricatural picture of a process which had, for anyone who could get to the bottom of it, a very different nature.

From this point of view, the expression 'Well grubbed, old mole' is of particular interest. It was originally a quotation from Shakespeare: it is Hamlet's reply to his father's ghost, whose revelations from beyond the grave have shaken his confidence in the social and familial order.[31] Now this quotation had already been used by Hegel in the conclusion to his *Lectures on the Philosophy of History*. Hegel uses it to express the fact that the new spirit will not emerge, by erupting from beneath the earth, until its gestation has been fully accomplished.[32] The image of a mole grubbing through the earth is superimposed on

30 'The Eighteenth Brumaire of Louis Bonaparte', in Karl Marx and Frederick Engels, *Selected Works* (New York: International Publishers, 1968), p. 170.

31 The (adapted) quotation is from Act I, scene v. It echoes the worries and suspicions that have already developed in Hamlet's mind: 'Foul deeds will rise, though all the earth o'erwhelm them, to men's eyes' (Act I, scene ii).

32 Cf. Hegel, *Lectures on the Philosophy of History*, tr. E. S. Haldane (London: Kegan Paul, 1896), vol. 3, pp. 546–7: 'For in this lengthened period, the Notion of Spirit, invested with its entire concrete development, its external subsistence, its wealth, is striving to bring spirit to perfection, to make progress itself and to develop from spirit. It goes ever on and on, because spirit is progress alone. Spirit often seems to have forgotten and lost itself, but inwardly opposed to itself, it is inwardly working ever forward (as when Hamlet says of the ghost of his father, "Well said, old mole! canst work i' the ground so fast?") until grown strong in itself it bursts asunder the crust of earth which divided it from the sun, its Notion, so that the earth crumbles away. At such a time, when the encircling crust, like a soulless decaying tenement, crumbles away, and spirit finds itself arrayed in new youth, the seven league boots are at length adopted.'

that of a child emerging from its mother's womb and literally coming into the world. It is as though both mole and child had dug forward and upward to appear, propelled by their impetus, in the light of the sun.[33]

Marx borrows the Shakespeare quotation from Hegel, and uses it as a model for an overall representation of history, but he does so in ironic terms. For Marx — and this naturally reminds one of the materialist 'inversion' of idealist philosophy — the mole of history constantly grubs deeper and deeper so as to lay bare the hidden mechanisms of the revolution; the revolution will take place not in spirit's sunshine, but in the dark subterranean passages through which the proletariat is trying to make its way in the dark. In contrast with Hegel's providentialism and progressive optimism, we can therefore give Marx credit for attempting to take stock of the dark reality of the struggles of the workers, from whose point of view history and the revolution can only advance by their bad side, making no promises and giving no guarantees.

These divergences can, however, appear only because they have a common basis: no matter whether history is moving upwards or downwards, the fact remains that its movement can only be perceived thanks to the mediation of an imaginary schema relating to a sort of eschatology. When he describes the revolution going deeper and

33 The latter comparison is made explicit in another text. 'The spirit of man has broken with the old order of things hitherto prevailing, and with the old ways of thinking, and is in the mind to let them all sink into the depths of the past and to set about its own transformation. It is indeed never at rest, but carried along the stream of progress ever onward. But it is here as in the case of the birth of a child; after a long period of nutrition in silence, the continuity of the gradual growth in size, of quantitative change, is suddenly cut short by the first breath drawn — there is a break in the process, a qualitative change — and the child is born. In like manner the spirit of the time, growing slowly and quietly ripe for the new form it is to assume, disintegrates one fragment after another of the structure of its previous world. That it is tottering to its fall is indicated only by symptoms here and there. Frivolity and again ennui, which are spreading in the established order of things, the undefined foreboding of something unknown — all these betoken that there is something else approaching. This gradual crumbling to pieces, which did not alter the general look and aspect of the whole, is interrupted by the sunrise, which, in a flash and at a single stroke, brings to view the form and structure of the new world' (G. W. F. Hegel, 'Preface' to *The Phenomenology of Mind*, tr. J. B. Baillie, New York and Evanston: Harper Torchbooks, 1967, p. 75). It will be recalled that, at the end of his *Lectures on the Philosophy of History*, Hegel uses the metaphor of sunrise to interpret the French Revolution.

deeper to get to the bottom of things and shake their foundations, Marx himself surrenders to the tendency to daydream that had inspired Hugo's vision of 'people without number',[34] communicating in its lower regions with the cosmic immensity.[35] When he flees into the sewers of Paris and is regenerated there, Jean Valjean takes the same path. A secret correspondence seems to have been established between theoretical analysis and poetic vision: it is as though, even before any premeditated reflection had taken place, a logic of images – images of verticality and darkness – had imposed its stereotypes on discourses about the masses.[36]

Subterranean histories

Three examples will serve to show how this imaginary of the depths took shape, and to illustrate the role it played in the development of visionary theories about the man from below.

The first is borrowed from Heine, whose work stands at the very point where speculation and fiction meet; its influence on Marx is well known. In the dedicatory letter prefacing the articles he published between 1840 and 1845 in the *Allgemeine Augsburger Zeitung*, and then republished in French under the title *Lutèce*, and in which he included his observations on recent changes in French society, Heine writes, in a text dated 1854:

I did not describe the storm, but the heavy, fearfully dark clouds that carried it in their bowels as they rolled towards us. I wrote frequent and accurate reports on the sinister regions, on the troglodytic titans who were lying in wait in the bottommost strata of society, and I hinted that they would rise up

34 Victor Hugo, 'La Pente de la rêverie', *Les Feuilles d'automne*, no. 29 (dated 28 May 1830), line 47. *Oeuvres complètes* (Paris: Club français du livre, 1967), vol. 4.

35 'A gentle slope/Leads from the real world to the invisible sphere/The spiral is deep, and as one descends it,/Moves constantly downwards and widens/And because you have touched upon some fatal enigma/You are often pale on returning from this dark voyage/ ... And so my spirit dived beneath this unknown wave/In the depths of the abyss it swam, naked and alone/Always moving from the ineffable to the invisible' (ibid., lines 5–10, 139–41).

36 It comes as no surprise to learn that Hugo also heard the noise the mole made as it grubbed along: 'Everywhere else, even in the most peaceful states, something wormeaten is falling to pieces, and attentive ears can hear the dull noise of revolutions, still tunnelling away, digging their subterranean tunnels, spreading the ramifications of the great central revolution whose crater is in Paris, beneath all the kingdoms of Europe' (Preface to *Les Feuilles d'automne*, dated 24 November 1831, ibid., p. 367).

from their darkness when the moment was right. At the time, those shadowy beings, those nameless monsters to whom the future belonged, were usually examined through the wrong end of the telescope and, seen in that way, they really did look like demented aphids. But I showed them life size, in their true light, and seen in that way, they looked more like the most fearful crocodiles, the most gigantic dragons ever to have emerged from the slime of the abyss.[37]

Wagner may not have read these lines, but he must have been drawing on the same sources when, still reeling from the events of 1848, he later developed his own vision of a dwarf people shut up in the deep caves where they worked gold for their exploiters. In the same series of articles, Heine predicts the development of social struggles in the apparently peaceful France of the July Monarchy. He describes 'Occult powers hiding in the shadows ... in the basements of official society, in the catacombs where, in the midst of death and decomposition, a new life is germinating and coming into bud.'[38] Two ideas and two images are being superimposed here. One is that of the advance of the people; it is analogous to being born into the bright light of day, and is preceded by a gestation in the dark. The other is that of a struggle taking place beneath society (in the basements), and involving not only individuals but social classes. Heine's vision is midway between Hegel's analyses and those of Marx.

The second example is the description of Coeur-Saignant's hovel in *Les Mystères de Paris*, which was published in 1842:

The wan, trembling candle shed a feeble light on the shabby corridor, throwing the black shadow of the hideous child onto the greenish walls, which were cracked and dripping with moisture. At the end of the corridor, through the half-darkness, one could see the low arch of the entrance to the cellar and the thick door, reinforced with iron bands. Chouette's red and white tartan bonnet stood out against the darkness. When he pushed at it with the help of Tortillard, the door opened, groaning on its rusted hinges. A breath of damp vapour escaped from the lair, which was as dark as night. The lantern on the floor shed a gleam of light on the bottom of the stone stairway, whose upper treads were completely invisible in the shadows. A cry, or rather a savage roar, came from the depths of the cellar.[39]

In the dim light of this melodramatic scene, there lurk the shadowy monsters evoked by Heine. Their very real existence had recently

---

37 Heinrich Heine, *Lutèce* (Geneva: Slatkine, 1979), p. 9 (facsimile reprint of the 1855 edition).   38 Letter 44 of 20 June 1842, ibid., p. 248.
39 Eugène Sue, *Les Mystères de Paris*, vol. 7, chapter 7, 'Le Caveau' (1842–3).

been revealed by Villermé's investigations. They were the people of the abyss, sapped by the darkness of poverty, the prisoners of a society which wove, in its mysterious depths, the sinister network of its necessities.

Finally, in *Spiridion*, the novel George Sand wrote between 1838 and 1842 and which first appeared as a serial in the *Revue de Paris*, the paradigm of the descent into hell fulfils a similarly revelatory function, but in this case it reveals the secret of the whole of human history:

I reached the *Hic est* stone, raised it without any great difficulty and began to descend the stairway. I was gripped by a feverish chill and my teeth were chattering with fear; I dropped my lamp; I felt my legs give way beneath me ... I went on down into the darkness; but my mind was slipping and falling prey to illusions and ghosts. It seemed to me that I was going deeper and deeper and that I was plunging into the depths of Erebus. Finally, I came slowly to a level spot and heard a lugubrious voice pronouncing these words, which it seemed to be confiding to the bowels of the earth: 'He will not climb the stairway again.' All at once, I heard around me the sound of thousands of terrible voices chanting to a strange rhythm: 'Let us destroy him! Let him be destroyed! What does he want here amongst the dead? Let him be restored to suffering! Let him be restored to life!' Then a feeble light pierced the shadows, and I saw that I was on the last step of a stairway as dark as the foot of a mountain. Behind me there were thousands of red-hot iron steps; before me, nothing but the void, the abyss of the ether, the deep blue of night beneath my feet and above my head. I was seized with vertigo and, leaving the stairway and abandoning the idea of reclimbing it, I threw myself into the void, screaming blasphemies. Scarcely had I pronounced the blasphemous formula than the void was filled with jumbled colours and forms, and eventually I found myself on a level with an immense tunnel, into which I advanced trembling ... [40]

There are considerable differences between this frenetic, Dantesque text, with its literary pretensions, and the prosaic excesses of Sue's text, and yet both are working raw materials born of the same historical imaginary. In both Sand and Sue we find subterranean visions of a world of the depths, and it is as though the same stairway plunged into both the cloaca of the lower depths of Paris and the vertiginous abyss where humanity fulfils its common destiny. And when the descent is complete, we find the same swarming crowd in both texts.

40 Sand, *Spiridion* (Paris: Editions d'Aujourd'hui, Collection 'Les Introuvables', 1976), pp. 161–3.

Whilst he did amplify its effects, Hugo therefore did not invent the typical literary thematic of the literature of the man from below which, unbeknownst to those who transcribed it, had been the object of a collective elaboration in the period 1840–50. This thematic expressed a concern to recognize and to understand the emergence of a new reality: the masses.

A historical mythology

As we have seen, the discovery of new forms of sociality went hand in hand with the specific development of symbolic schemata. They were an inverted expression of a world plunged into the intense and terrifying intimacy of its subterranean existence. When we catalogue these images of the man from below, are we in fact doing anything more than exploring an archetypal imaginary whose thematic recalls that recorded by Bachelard in his *La Terre et les rêveries de la volonté*? If that is the case, these elementary figures are a projection of timeless ideas which emerge from an idle and archaic dream only to be plunged back into it as they surrender to unconscious models of representation. It might even be thought that these models have always had the ability to function automatically, without having to be produced, without, that is, being historically determined. That description, and the immobility-effect it induces, is unsatisfactory for two reasons. On the one hand, whilst it claims to reveal the mechanism behind a fantasy or illusion, it in fact reproduces it by deferring the possibility of actual knowledge of its objective content, which it dissolves into the movement of its images. On the other hand, by reproducing a fantasy, it perpetuates indefinitely and eternalizes a mechanism by divorcing it from the social determination on which it depends. That is why it is not enough to identify images: we also have to understand how and why, and therefore within what limitations, those images can actually intervene in such a way as to act not only upon the thoughts and discourses, but also the actual lives of men. The notion of a historical mythology should allow us to resolve these interrogations.

In a widely discussed passage written in 1857, Marx describes industrial capitalist society as having reached a stage of 'social development which precludes a mythological attitude towards nature, i.e., any attitude to nature which might give rise to myth; a society therefore demanding from the artist an imagination independent of

mythology'.[41] Its relationship with dreams relating to a lost childhood
is therefore a purely nostalgic one, as is the relationship between
Greek art and its sources of inspiration. This analysis takes on its full
meaning only if we relate it to the assumptions that implicitly support
and justify it, namely a progressive theory of stages of social
development, which either erases or absorbs traces of earlier stages as
it advances, and the idea that a supposedly 'advanced' society is one
that has completely distanced itself from intellectual models which,
like mythology, are considered archaic. We see here the return, in an
over-simplified form, of a number of theses put forward by Hegel: that
of the death of art, interpreted as a privileged expression of symbolic
thought; that of a rational teleology which determines historical
development and constantly leads it in the same direction, rather in the
manner of a 'providence'. It is on the basis of such speculations that
Marx succeeds in identifying a new form of imagination 'independent
of mythology'.

So-called 'developed' societies do, however, have their primitive
systems of symbolization, and they are essential if those societies are
to establish their characteristic relationship with the real. Frankenstein,
Captain Nemo and Tarzan are to the modern world what the fairies
and monsters of the Odyssey were to Homeric culture. They are
heroic figures that breathe life into collective representations, into
fictional incarnations of the imaginary relations men have with their
real conditions of existence. It is not because they are rooted in some
primal civilization, from which they borrow their primal naivety, that
these representations usually seem archaic; it is because they project
into a mythical realm of origins relations of which they are a
circumstantial expression.

Every mythology is historical in both its form and its meaning, and
every great period in history elaborates the mythology that suits its
material and cultural needs. That mythology allows it to propagate,
through a system of images, an interpretation of its conditions of
collective existence that is acceptable to all, together with the hopes
and fears that characterize those conditions. This is why the figures of
the man from below that move through the narrative and theoretical
texts we have been analysing are not the timeless archetypes of a
universal imaginary that exists independently of the historical and

41 Karl Marx, *A Contribution to the Critique of Political Economy* (Moscow: Progress
    Publishers, 1970), p. 216.

social reality it expresses through them; they are part of that reality, and they contribute to its constitution. Our understanding of nineteenth-century French history would remain incomplete if we did not take the trouble to include in it this mythical production, whose fantastic system developed out of the transformation of relations between State and society, and the related emergence of what was at the time coming to be called the social question.

The suggestions made by Marx notwithstanding − in, it is true, a draft which he left incomplete and which he himself did not publish − taking stock of a collective mythology does not lead to the misrecognition of the social reality it supposedly reflects. On the contrary, it is essential to take it into account if we are to understand the workings of social reality. It is an essential element in its workings. When we describe the imaginary figures of the man from below painted by the major and minor writers of this period, we are not moving away from an objective analysis of the effective forms of sociality it established; we are restoring to them an essential dimension by reconstructing, not something that might be described in pedestrian terms as a 'mentality', but a veritable structure of thought, a form of knowledge immanent in that society and specifically adapted to its historical conditions. By comparing texts borrowed from Marx or Tocqueville with texts written by Sue or Hugo, and by demonstrating that comparable schemas of representation are at work in them, we are not attempting to deny the originality of their content by arguing that, ultimately, everything is mere literature; the point is to call attention to that content by showing how fictional texts can, in their own way, not only convey but produce forms of speculation which are directly expressive of a determinate historical reality. They allow us both to understand it and to imagine it.

In arguing this thesis, we are not too far removed from the concept of '*episteme*', as introduced and theorized by Foucault in *The Order of Things*. That concept designates the historical form of knowledge [*savoir*] that exists prior to the acquisition of particular knowledges [*connaissances*]. It organizes in advance the space they will occupy, and which will supply their meanings and objects. It is as though that *savoir* preceded itself and supplied the conditions for its own concrete manifestations. According to Foucault, the nineteenth century saw the emergence of a new order of knowledge which was, no doubt, related to the establishment of new and 'democratic' forms of society. It broke completely with the forms that preceded it. The break was one between a type of knowledge deployed within the flat surface of an infinite repesentative space with no depth, and a type of knowledge which moves inwards along a vertical and not a horizontal axis.[42] The three basic activities that define human reality – life, speech and labour – began to be understood in terms of the rootedness that both situated their elements and allowed them to communicate through the intermediary of the new in-depth perspective that also gave them their consistency.

In terms of this *episteme*, the configuration revealed by the existence of the man from below became the essential truth about Man, a truth enigmatically turned in upon itself by a process of internalization which gave its subject-object an ideal autonomy. The images used to suggest this new truth were therefore inseparable from the metaphysics of finitude, which was unknown to the classical or metaphysical representative order. According to classical metaphysics, human reality was comparable only to itself and to its world, and could therefore be explained in terms of the development of its essence, which was also the product of its activity. What was at stake in the adventures of Rodolphe and Fleur-de-Marie, and in those of Jean Valjean, was the birth of both this truly – or supposedly – human world and the anthropological speculation which would, it was assumed, allow it to be correctly interpreted.

What stance does Foucault adopt in order to dismantle these mechanisms of knowledge and identify their mutations? He answers that question by describing his project as an 'archaeology of knowledge'. His conception of the *episteme* cannot mean a neutralized

---

42 'The space of Western knowledge is now about to topple: the *taxonomia*, whose great, universal expanse extended in correlation with the possibility of a matheis, and which constituted the down-beat of knowledge ... is now about to order itself in accordance with an obscure verticality ... Thus, European culture is inventing for itself a depth in which what matters is no longer identities, distinctive characters, permanent tables with all their possible paths and routes, but great hidden forces developed on the basis of their primitive and inaccessible nucleus, origin, causality and history. From now on things will be represented only from the depths of this density withdrawn into itself, perhaps blurred and darkened by its obscurity, but bound tightly to themselves, assembled or divided, inescapably grouped by the vigour that is hidden down below, in those depths. Visible forms, their connection, the blank spaces that isolate them and surround their outlines – all these will now be presented to our gaze only in an already composed state, already articulated in that nether darkness that is fomenting them with time' (Michel Foucault, *The Order of Things*, London: Tavistock, 1974, pp. 251–2).

theory capable of remaining outside the field of its object; it implies research into those mysterious and hidden events that exist beneath systems of knowledge and weave the tissue of their conditions of possibility. It belongs, of necessity, to the order of the *episteme* of depth that appeared at the beginning of the nineteenth century and which still dominates our thinking. Anyone who doubts that this is the case should read the note on the back cover of *The Order of Things*: 'This book is not a "history" of the human sciences, but an analysis of their foundations, a reflection on what makes them possible now, an archaeology of contemporary modes of thought.' A knowledge which plunges its object into the depths of history and life is recognizable as such only when it is related to its 'basement' in terms of its essential verticality.

Knowledge of this kind looks obsessionally downwards towards the prime locus where its truth is produced. It therefore does not have the value of a primitive paradigm, even if it is refracted through a rhetoric of origins. It is bound up with the existence of a certain type of society: one in which the man from below is assigned a place. The symbolic figures that allow the society to which he belonged to identify him as belonging to that place are no more than the expression of its 'knowledge', of the self-knowledge that this society elaborates as it establishes its functional organs. For as it constructs the more or less stable structures that guarantee its order by allowing it to shape the power relations on which it is built, any society calls upon all the shared notions it uses to reflect that order and all its effects. For the democratic society whose model was gradually organized after the end of the eighteenth century, the idea that 'the truth lies below' was the shared notion that acted as a regulating principle and assigned all its discourses their object.

Writers played a major role in the constitution of this figure of thought: it was they who invented its concrete forms of exposition by giving them the appearance of their fictions. But 'behind' and 'beneath' these fictions, we must recognize the knowledge that originally shaped them and was embodied in them: the literary philosophy of an era, as incarnated in the historical mythology of the man from below.

6

Georges Bataille: materialism inverted

No insurmountable problems arise when we attempt to reconstruct the thought of 1848 by situating it historically on the basis of the testimony of writers who both learned its lessons directly and helped to produce it. This is because that thought, which it is tempting to describe as a form of mysticism, seems to be so closely bound up with an era that is quite different from our own. Thanks to the distance that separates it from us, it seems easy to discern its features to the extent that they stand out against a background that is now a thing of the past. Are we therefore to conclude that, when replaced in the symbolic network within which they acquired their full meaning, the thematics of darkness and depth, as identified from our reading of texts by Hugo in particular, are now outdated and that the literatures of the twentieth century have lost their fondness for them, have been won over to a new modernity, and generate or exploit new cultural schemata based upon other references? The passages from Foucault evoked at the end of the last chapter demonstrate that this is far from being the case, and further confirmation will come from a reading of texts by Bataille and then Céline. These texts demonstrate the reappearance of comparable obsessions. They too are bound up with representations of verticality and of inversion which were of particular significance at a moment – the 1930s – when the works of the young Marx were being rediscovered. This might be an indication that, when they are characterized in terms of the speculative and fictional modes that make up what we have called their historical mythology, the 'thought' of the nineteenth century and that of the twentieth exist within a mutual relationship of continuity that makes them contemporaries, rather as though their discourses were deployed within a single system.

The texts by Bataille that we will be studying do not belong to the realm of narrative fiction, but to the genre of the essay. They have much in common with philosophical speculation, but at the same time they still have a poetic dimension. Although they deal directly with a basic theoretical question, namely that of materialism, they eschew abstraction and generality and are therefore still bound up with specifically literary issues, even if the latter are to some extent divorced from a narrative context. More than any other, Bataille's writing is marked by this oscillation, this exchange between fiction and speculation. When he 'inverts' materialism, Bataille also attempts to make a poetic critique of materialism by using notions that function simultaneously as images and as concepts. We have already seen notions of this type at work in apparently very different contexts.

Bataille obviously adds nothing, or very little, to the doctrinal history of materialism; he cannot even be considered *a* materialist in that he does not elaborate a 'materialist' theory of materialism, and never claims to be doing so. Although he does, in a bid for recognition, take materialism as a reference in certain of his earliest works, he does so in the sense that he makes demands of it from the position of someone who is interrogating materialism and calling it into question. Bataille's stance can be characterized as materialist to the extent that it helps to reveal what is problematic about the materialist attitude. The theoretical interventions that will be discussed here were made in the years 1929–30, when Bataille was editing the journal *Documents*;[1] by privileging this specific moment, which coincides with the publication of Bataille's first works, it may be possible to grasp this materialist attitude in its nascent state, at a point when its features were sharply, even excessively, outlined and when they therefore revealed the antagonistic aspects of its intellectual and cultural conjuncture. Those aspects are particularly well illustrated by the debate that arose between Bataille and Breton.

The young Bataille

In 1929, Bataille was thirty-two. In 1922, he had been awarded the Ecole des Chartes's diploma for his edition of *L'Ordre de la chevalerie*, a twelfth-century tale in verse. He then started work in the Bibliothèque Nationale, working first in the Department of Numismatics before moving to the Printed Books Department. He had published little. After spending almost a year in a seminary, he had

---

1 See Michel Leiris, 'De Bataille l'impossible à l'impossible *Documents*', *Critique* 195–6 (August–September 1963), pp. 685–93.

published a short text inspired by neo-Catholicism on 'Notre-Dame de Reims'.[2] The selection of nonsense [*fatrasies*] published anonymously in *La Révolution surréaliste* had been his sole contribution to the surrealist movement.[3] A few articles on antique oriental coins had appeared in the journal *Aréthuse* in 1928, whilst a major review of an exhibition of Mexican art, published under the title 'L'Amérique perdue' in *Cahiers de la République des lettres, des sciences et des arts*, had begun to outline the themes of expenditure and sacrifice. Finally and most importantly, *L'Histoire de l'oeil* appeared in 1928 under the pseudonym 'Lord Auch'; this was the first scandalous text to be published by Bataille, who was to return constantly to the general problems of eroticism.[4]

Let me give a few details about his philosophical formation. Bataille studied for his *baccalauréat* in isolation, and sat it as an independent candidate during the First World War, at a time when he had taken refuge in the Auvergne with some of his family. In 1920, he was working at the British Museum in London to further his studies at the Ecole des Chartes, and probably attended a lecture by Bergson, the revised text of which was later published in *La Pensée et le mouvant*.[5] We know the titles of the books he read in the Bibliothèque Nationale, and they indicate the range of his interests; the authors include Nietzsche, whom Bataille first read in 1922,[6] Hegel, studied in 1925 in Vera's old translations, which Breton was also reading at the same time, and Freud, read in about 1926 at the time when Bataille was in analysis with Dr Adrien Borel, who also analysed Leiris and

2 This text, which was exhumed after Bataille's death, marks a sort of point of repulsion for all his later work, the stages of which seem to have been undertaken in order to negate it. On this point, see Denis Hollier's reflections in his major study of Bataille, *La Prise de la Concorde* (Paris: Gallimard, 1974).

3 *La Révolution surréaliste, seconde année*, no. 6, pp. 2–3.

4 For Bataille, erotic writing no doubt represents a privileged method for the artificial establishment of the preconditions for a clandestine, parallel or marginal literature. It conforms to the aims illustrated by one of his most famous formulae: 'I write in order to efface my name.'

5 The lecture was an exposition of the principal themes of Bergson's philosophy, and it ended by inverting the conventional image of relations between the possible and the real: 'It is the real that becomes possible and not the possible that becomes real' (*La Pensée et le mouvant*, 3rd edn, Paris: PUF, 1955, p. 115). The dynamic and expansive tendency within Bergson's thought may have struck, and to a certain extent inspired, Bataille.

6 He seems to have been particularly impressed by his reading of *Beyond Good and Evil*.

Queneau.[7] By 1925, Bataille was in close contact with the Russian philosopher Léon Chestov, who had emigrated to France;[8] it was presumably Chestov who awakened his interest in the 'tragic' thought of Pascal, Kierkegaard and Dostoievsky. It should also be mentioned, finally, that, thanks to Alfred Métraux, who had been his fellow student at the Ecole des Chartes, Bataille had been introduced to the work of Mauss, whose *Essai sur le don*, published in *L'Année sociologique* in 1924, ends with a discussion of the possibility that sociology and psychoanalysis might collaborate on a study of the social and affective phenomena of ambivalence. We know from Métraux's account that Bataille was particularly impressed by a formula used by Mauss in one of his lectures: 'Taboos are meant to be broken.'[9] All these intellectual experiences shed light upon the texts written and published by Bataille in 1929–30; it must not be forgotten that these texts predate both his collaboration on Souvarine's *Critique sociale*, which would allow him to meet Simone Weil, and the later encounter with two other Russian philosophers who had emigrated to France, namely Koyré and Kojève, who would give a new dimension to Bataille's philosophical culture.

Nothing in the references we have listed evokes materialism, nor even appears to come close to it. And yet, the series of articles Bataille published in *Documents* – and certain of them have the characteristics of genuine philosophical texts – constantly deal with materialism, and do so in such a way as to give a dynamic impetus to all his speculations. Why materialism? And what materialism?

Bataille contributed to every issue of *Documents*, which was originally a kind of art journal. He wrote on apparently disparate and incongruous subjects, the only thread that connected them being his attempt to sketch a mythology of everyday life.[10] One might be tempted to compare this project with the quest for the marvellous and

7 See Elisabeth Roudinesco, *La Bataille de cent ans. Histoire de la psychanalyse en France* (Paris: Ramsay, 1982), vol. 1, pp. 358–9.
8 Bataille collaborated on the French translation of Chestov's *L'Idée du bien chez Tolstoï et Nietzsche. Philosophie et prédication* (Paris: Editions du Siècle, 1925, reprinted, Paris: Vrin, 1949).
9 Alfred Métraux, 'Rencontre avec les éthnologues', *Critique* 195–6 (August–September 1963), p. 683.
10 The same aim was spelled out in the general text, probably written by Bataille, that introduced the journal: 'We will, in general, be looking here at the most disquieting facts, facts our knowledge of which have yet to be defined. In these investigations, the sometimes absurd character of the findings or methods will, far from being concealed as happens when one obeys the rules of propriety, be

the strange that was being systematically undertaken by the surrealists at the same time, and Bataille's path may seem to have crossed theirs as they attempted to bring about a poetic transformation of reality. It was, however, over precisely this point that Bataille disagreed with Breton from the outset; Bataille's deliberately rambling and ever-ambivalent quest – and it was quite crucial to his position – was intended, not to reassure or to seduce, but to disconcert and disturb. His favourite weapon was a form of derision that could not have been further removed from the serious-minded solemnity professed by Breton. The texts published in the seven issues of the first series of *Documents* are a perfect illustration of Bataille's attitude and of the desire for scandal that inspired it.

The first series of *Documents*: the use of ignominy

In the first issue of *Documents*, dated April 1928, Bataille published a study of 'Le Cheval académique'. It begins with a series of remarks on the depiction of animals on Gaulish coins and ends with general comments on the domains of the philosophy of nature and the philosophy of history. The central idea behind the text is that both natural evolution and human civilization develop between two extreme systems of reference: on the one hand, a classical order based upon discipline and a sense of proportion, and on the other, a barbarian violence characterized by its excess. From the outset, Bataille describes as 'idealist' the mind's spontaneous tendency to characterize this excess negatively, or in terms of an absence or lack.[11] He contrasts this with the need to regard the powers of formlessness as a 'positive extravagance',[12] and to consider them, therefore, in terms that preclude any reference to negativity. Bataille is beginning to outline the twin schemata that will reappear in all his subsequent speculations. On the one hand, we find the idea that a polarity governs the alternating phases of a dual and divided movement. In this connection Bataille speaks, presumably in order to rule out any preoccupation with their resolution, of oppositions and not contradictions. Bataille's

deliberately underlined, both out of hatred of fullness and for humorous reasons.' (Cf. Bernard Noël's introduction to his edition, *Documents*, Paris: Mercure de France, 1968, p. 12.)

11 One might find here an echo of the arguments put forward by Bergson in his 'Le Possible et le réel' about the interpretation of disorder as an absence of order.

12 D, p. 160. All references to the texts published by Bataille in *Documents* (D) are to Georges Bataille, *Oeuvres complètes* (Paris: Gallimard, vol. 1, 1970).

oppositions are repetitive and not developmental, and they eternally rend reality apart. The reference is therefore to a Nietzschean rather than a Hegelian concept, and Bataille's general argument is essentially anti-dialectical. On the other hand, we have the schema of reversal, which is to be taken literally. Authentic thought turns upside down or inverts the visible appearance of things; this inevitably reminds one of the obstinate presence of the same themes in the work of the young Marx.[13]

The second issue of the first series of *Documents*, which appeared in May 1928, included two contributions from Bataille. His study of 'L'Apocalypse de Saint-Sever' is devoted to an eighth-century Spanish illuminated manuscript, in which Bataille finds a naive and wild apology for the powers of horror: 'the immediate expression of the unintelligible – and therefore all the more significant – metamorphoses that result from certain fatal inclinations'.[14] The same issue saw the inauguration of a new column which would feature regularly in later issues of the journal, namely the *Dictionnaire critique*, represented on this occasion by Bataille's note on architecture, which is described as a manifestation of 'the ideal being of society, as the being that orders and prohibits authoritatively'.[15] This 'architecture' symbolizes the incarnation of a form in an idea which it uses to establish a relationship of domination so as to repress the formless. The 'materialist' inversion will of course attack this representation by revealing its essentially negative and reactive character.

The following issue (June 1929) again included two texts by Bataille. They were perhaps the most important to appear in the first series of *Documents*: an article on 'Le Langage des fleurs' and a new entry in the *Dictionnaire critique* on 'Le matérialisme'.

The text on the language of flowers is a commentary on enlargements of photographs showing the sexual organs of plants.

---

13 A sort of wild Heracliteanism seems to provide the means to synthesize the thought of the young Marx and that of Nietzsche: 'All these inversions, which seem to be specific to the human night, may be no more than one aspect of that alternating revolt, of that rigorous oscillation that swells in moments of anger and which, if we look at arbitrarily brief segments of endless revolutions, crests and foams like waves on a stormy day' (*D*, p. 163). To cite another passage: 'The ignoble apes and horse-like gorillas of the Gauls are supremely ugly animals with unspeakable mores, but they are also grandiose apparitions and prodigious inversions, and they therefore represent the definitive answer that the burlesque and fearful human night gives to the platitudes and arrogance of idealists' (*D*, p. 162).   14 *D*, p. 169.   15 *D*, p. 171.

Bataille uses them as a starting point for his reflections on the natural logic of existence, which he terms 'the obscure intelligence of things'.[16] The principle behind this logic is a fundamental clash of values governed by a polarity of above and below which testifies to 'an obscure decision on the part of the plant world'.[17] The decision is expressed in a sort of pre-linguistic language: the language of 'aspect', which exists prior to the language of words, introduces 'values that decide things'.[18] These evaluations are not reducible to judgements that assess reality in accordance with the external criteria of affinity and utility; they are, rather, the judgements of reality itself as it asserts, primitively and immediately, its basic tendencies. According to Bataille, this direct expression, which exists prior to any symbolization, means that the truth of things, illustrated here by the vegetable kingdom, does not lie in the idealizing tendency that seems to raise them, in a progressive or progressivist way, from 'below' to 'above', but, on the contrary, in the tendency that degrades them by constantly dragging them from 'above' to 'below' or, to borrow an expression used by Marx at the beginning of *The German Ideology*, bringing them down from heaven to earth.[19] Thanks to the same cyclical dynamic of the inversion of values and of their apparent relations that will, following Feuerbach, support the speculations of the young Marx and then those of Nietzsche, the attempted sublimation that aspires to elevating nature above and beyond is inverted into its opposite, and nature is dragged down into its bottommost depths. Once again, the themes of polarity and inversion overlap.

L'Anus solaire, a text by Bataille written slightly earlier in 1927 but not published until 1931, gives, in a frenetic form, a political translation of this inversion of values:

Those in whom the eruptive force accumulates are necessarily below. To the bourgeois, communist workers look as ugly and dirty as the sexual and hairy

16 *D*, p. 174.   17 *D*, p. 173.   18 *D*, p. 174.
19 'The roots in fact represent the perfect counterpart of the visible parts of the plant. Whereas the latter rise up nobly, the ignoble and sticky roots wallow in the soil; they are in love with rot, just as the leaves are in love with light. It is also to be noted that the indisputable moral value of the term 'base' is bound up with this systematic interpretation of the meaning of roots: in terms of movement, that which is evil is necessarily represented by a movement from above to below. That is a fact which it is impossible to explain unless we do not attribute a moral meaning to the natural phenomena from which that value is borrowed precisely because of the striking character of this aspect, this sign of the decisive movement of nature' (*D*, p. 177).

parts, or the lower parts; sooner or later, the result will be a scandalous eruption in the course of which the asexual and noble heads of the bourgeois will be cut off.[20]

In outlining the cyclical complementarity of love and death, which is the principle behind the whole of his erotic philosophy, Bataille likens the revolution to a natural fire, to an explosive device concealed in the darkest and innermost reaches of things which will bring things lower still, in accordance with their deepest impulses.

The conception of materialism formulated in the same issue's 'Dictionnaire critique' now takes on its full meaning. Rejecting attempts at idealist recuperation, Bataille argues the need to rematerialize materialism by linking it to the assertion of its authentic values, those of 'below', and thus outlines the notion of a base materialism.[21] The particular significance of this claim is that it reveals the paradoxical aspects of the inversion thesis by simultaneously establishing its limits. Bataille means precisely this: once we posit a relationship between an 'above' incarnated in the mind or an idea, and a 'below' rooted in a material nature, it is not enough to modify the poles that determine it by inverting the order of their values. To give matter a new position within that relationship, or to give it a foundational or causal role by making spirit dependent upon it, would leave intact the hierarchical structure that subordinates one value to the other. Ultimately, such a reversal would merely produce a new and disguised idealism by assigning to matter the position once occupied by mind. Both the idealization of matter and the materialization of ideas mean inscribing the reversal in a hierarchy of domination and privileging a high value over a low value by making implicit reference to a negativity.[22] A true materialism, in contrast, would be one which is

---

20 *Oeuvres complètes* (Paris: Gallimard, 1970), vol. 1, pp. 85–6. This text echoes the passages from Hugo cited in the previous chapter.

21 Let me cite, for purposes of comparison, the first and last sentences of this short text on materialism: 'Although they want to eliminate all spiritual entities, most materialists have succeeded in describing an order of things which, being hierarchical, has specifically idealist characteristics … It is time, when the word materialist is used, for it to designate the direct interpretation, which precludes idealism, of raw phenomena and not a system based upon fragmentary elements of an ideological analysis elaborated under the aegis of religious relations' (*D*, pp. 178–9).

22 'They [materialists] have placed dead matter at the top of a conventional hierarchy of facts from various orders, without noticing that they have therefore

capable of escaping this architectonically or juridically inspired attempt at legitimation, and of restricting itself to 'the direct interpretation of raw phenomena'.[23]

How can 'below' be revalorized without it being idealized? How can its specific determinations be asserted without being elevated and therefore distorted? In order to bring out the difficulties inherent in such a project, Foucault speaks in the text he devotes to Bataille of a 'non-positive assertion'.[24] The assertion opens up the space for the deployment of an authentically critical thought that no longer identifies assertion with legitimation. On the contrary, it contrasts the two. In order to restore their effective power to lower things, Bataille establishes in the 'Matérialisme' entry in his *Dictionnaire critique* a dichotomy between an abstract materialism based upon 'dead matter', and a concrete materialism 'based immediately upon psychological or social facts, and not upon abstractions such as artificially isolated physical phenomena'.[25] This major idea was taken up again and developed a few years later in an article on 'La Critique des fondements de la dialectique hégélienne' written in collaboration with Raymond Queneau for *Critique sociale*.[26] In this text, the model for a materialist process incarnated in a 'dialectic of the real' is represented by the phenomena of the instinctual opposition studied by psychoanalysis, whose polar 'logic', which is based on a principle of ambivalence, is extended to the consideration of nature and history. At the same time, it is argued in terms that could also be found in Politzer's writings of the period, that the idea of the concrete must be divorced from the subjective-objective opposition, which is now described as being artificial. The attempt to reduce the objective to the subjective, or the subjective to the objective, is thus invalidated.

surrendered to the obsession with an ideal form of matter, with a form that comes closer than any other to what matter should be' (*D*, p. 178).

23 *D*, p. 179. A handwritten note dating from the same period makes a similar point: 'Materialism certainly does not mean that matter is the essence. That view is simply one of the forms of the idealist philosophy that identifies matter with the idea. Nor does it mean that man submits only to something more base than himself, to something more base than his reason – matter is his reason's *base*. But it betrays it by its very nature, which becomes irreducible to reason once it no longer finds any higher authority to confirm it as God or idea' (*Oeuvres complètes*, vol. 1, p. 650).

24 Michel Foucault, 'Préface à la transgression', *Critique* 195–6 (August–September 1963), p. 756.   25 *D*, p. 179.

26 Bataille, *Oeuvres complètes*, vol. 1, pp. 288–9.

To end this introduction, we will simply list the titles of the articles published by Bataille in subsequent issues of the first series of *Documents*: 'The Human Face' (on late-nineteenth-century family and group photographs); 'Around the World in Eighty Days' (on a play at the Châtelet); 'The Big Toe' (on an enlarged photograph of this 'low' organ); 'The Lugubrious Game' (on a painting by Salvador Dali). The following entries also appeared in the *Dictionnaire critique*: 'Black Birds'; 'Eye'; 'Camel'; 'Misfortune'; 'Dust'; 'Hollywood'; 'Abattoir'; 'Factory Chimney'; 'Metamorphosis'; 'Formless'. All these texts, which are significant primarily because of the apparent thematic disparity, illustrate 'the present need to resort to ignominy'.[27]

Polemic with Breton

In late 1929, by which time all the texts by Bataille that we have been discussing had been published, André Breton published his second Surrealist Manifesto in the twelfth issue of *La Révolution surréaliste*. It appeared at a crucial moment in the evolution of the movement, which was attempting to purge itself and get its second breath so as to place itself in the service of the revolution, to use the new title under which the journal continued to appear (*Le Surréalisme au service de la Révolution*). This second manifesto, which is exactly contemporary with the texts by Bataille that we have been discussing, is a fundamental text expounding the preconditions for a reconciliation between the poetic imagination and political action. It centres upon a dialectically inspired thesis to which Breton and his disciples would frequently refer in subsequent years:

Everything leads one to believe that there exists in the mind a certain point from which life and death, real and imaginary, past and future, the communicable and the non-communicable cease to be perceived as contradictory ... The point in question is *a fortiori* the point where it becomes

27 *D*, p. 212. The formula appears in a note to 'The Lugubrious Game', which also includes the following: 'The only weapon against the half-measures, evasions and delusions that betray complete impotence is a black rage and even an indisputable bestiality; it is impossible not to behave like a pig guzzling in the dung and mud grubbing everything up with his snout. Nothing can put a halt to its repugnantly unstoppable greed' (ibid.). How can one fail to hear in these disgusting grunts, the 'voice' of St Antony's pig, as described by Flaubert? That pig too wallows in mud which reminds one of the dung heap of 'The language of flowers' in the first version of the *Temptation of St Antony*.

impossible for construction and destruction to be used as weapons against one another.[28]

In this passage, which deals, among other things, with communication between above and below, Breton would seem to intersect the path taken by Bataille when, the previous year, he wrote in *Histoire de l'oeil*: 'This appears to me to be the culmination of my sexual excesses: a geometrical and perfectly blazing incandescence (among other things, the point where life and death, being and nothingness, coincide).'[29] The same blaze does indeed seem to shine through Breton's text and Bataille's, but the sublime point between life and death, which both are trying to locate, is also the point over which they were to disagree fundamentally, all the more so because they had been so close. The result was a bitter debate in which the main point at issue was the question of the dialectic.

The final pages of Breton's manifesto are devoted to a long diatribe against 'M. Bataille'. Breton does at least recognize that Bataille's position was indisputably rigorous; hence the privileged role he gives him in this generalized settling of scores. Above all, he denounces Bataille's 'phobia about ideas', which, in his view, lies at the origin of his attempt to redefine materialism.[30] At the beginning of this diatribe, Breton, no doubt carried away by his irritation, makes an extraordinary slip by misquoting a passage from the entry on materialism in the *Dictionnaire critique*. He writes:

With M. Bataille, nothing that is not already well known; we find an offensive return of the old antidialectical materialism, which is now gratuitously attempting to work its way through Freud. 'Materialism', he says, 'direct interpretation of raw phenomena, *precluding all idealism* [Breton's emphasis], materialism which, if it is not to be regarded as a senile idealism, must be immediately based upon economic and social phenomena.' As there is no specific mention of 'historical materialism' (and indeed how could there be?), we are indeed obliged to observe that, from the philosophical point of view, the expression is vague and that, from the poetic point of view of novelty, it is meaningless.[31]

28 *La Révolution surréaliste* 12 (December 1929), p. 1.
29 Bataille, *Oeuvres complètes*, vol.1, pp. 288–9.
30 *La Révolution surréaliste* 12 (December 1929), p. 16. In his memoirs, Luis Buñuel records that Breton found Bataille 'too crude, too material', *Mon Dernier Soupir* (Paris: Ramsay, 1986), p. 148.
31 Breton, *La Révolution surréaliste*, 12, p. 16.

Now, as we have already had occasion to note, Bataille wrote: 'Materialism will be regarded as a senile idealism to the extent that it is not based immediately upon *psychological* [my emphasis] or social facts, rather than upon abstractions such as artificially isolated physical phenomena.'[32] By replacing the term 'psychological' with the term 'economic', Breton, either because of a lapse in concentration or for polemical purposes, erases the innovatory effect of Bataille's text, and brings it back to the well-trodden paths of economic and social determinism, which is identified once and for all with an anti-idealist materialism.

Breton therefore attacks Bataille for his materialism, and he does so in the name of what appears to be an idealism:

M. Bataille is of interest to me only insofar as he flatters himself that he can oppose the harsh discipline of spirit, to which we have every intention of submitting everything – and I see no disadvantage in giving Hegel prime responsibility for this – with a discipline which does not even succeed in appearing more cowardly, as it tends to be the discipline of non-spirit (and that is where Hegel lies in wait for him).[33]

Reading these lines, one could almost think that Breton had some foreknowledge of the theses Bataille would put forward some ten years later in *L'Expérience intérieure,* and of the ascetic practice of non-thought advocated in that book. Even though that practice would, like a spiritual exercise, take the form of an extremely harsh and radical discipline, in Breton's view, the struggle against spirit, even and especially when waged by spirit, inevitably meant degradation, and precluded the poetic transmutation and idealization of the real advocated by surrealism.

The debate centres on the interpretation of Hegelian philosophy. At this time Breton is seeking in the dialectic a means to reconcile opposites (above and below, real and imaginary, revolution and poetry): he devotes an entire work to this question. *Les Vases communicants* (1932), which was written before Kojève began his lectures, is a far from negligible moment in the history of Hegelianism in France. As we have seen, Bataille, in contrast, is concerned with an undialecticized materialism, so to speak, and is prophesying a return to the raw and immediate forms of natural reality in the name of a

32 D, pp. 178–9.   33 Breton, *La Révolution surréaliste,* p. 15.

Nietzschean inversion of values. That automatically rules out any possibility of the oppositions of the real reaching the moment of their final resolution, which would imply the reduction or recuperation of below by above in the name of a 'senile idealism'. And Bataille uses precisely that expression to describe surrealism.

Bataille's initial response to Breton's attack was a very short but particularly virulent contribution to 'Un Cadavre', the collective pamphlet published by the victims of the 'Second Manifesto'. The text he wrote for the pamphlet is entitled 'Le Lion châtré'.[34] Here, surrealism is described as a 'new religion', as a resurgence of idealism taking the form of a flight from reality and its most sordid aspects, which surrealism replaces with a completely poetic, imaginary and marvellous world. Bataille's answer to this ideology of liberation, whose conventional character he denounces, is this: 'With the exception of some rather unsavoury aesthetes, no one wants to lose himself in blind and idiotic contemplation. No one wants to have anything more to do with mythical freedom.' Elsewhere, and on a very different level, Bataille was to give a more theoretical and less polemical answer to Breton's arguments. This was the article entitled 'Le Bas Matérialisme et la gnose' which opened the second series of *Documents* at the beginning of 1930.

Base materialism: a new anthropology

In his 'Le Bas Matérialisme et la gnose', Bataille develops, in the margin of reproductions of some gnostic intaglios held in the collections of the Cabinet des Médailles, a certain number of philosophical considerations which are of particular interest, if only because they elucidate in advance all the later evolution of his thought.[35]

As in the earlier article on 'Materialism' in the *Dictionnaire critique*, Bataille begins by challenging what he sees as the artificial way in which the materialism-idealism opposition has traditionally been presented. Because both tendencies have been described as coming into conflict within the framework of a hierarchical relation of authority, in which both struggle to gain and maintain a dominant

34 Bataille, *Oeuvres complètes*, vol. 1, p. 218.
35 See Denis Hollier, 'Le Matérialisme dualiste de Bataille', *Tel Quel* 25 (1966). The same ideas are developed in Hollier's *La Prise de la Concorde*.

position, a 'metaphysical scaffolding' has been erected, and their real polarity has been obscured because it has been reduced to univocal criteria ensuring the hegemony of one or the other tendency. In such a context, it is ultimately irrelevant whether it is materialism or idealism that emerges victorious, the main point being that, whatever happens, one preeminent term survives.[36] In demonstrating that, over and beyond the apparently speculative issues that are at stake, the conventional debate about matter and form is in fact still a debate about power – and he stresses in his analysis that the primacy accorded to one tendency or the other is meaningful only within a 'social order', metaphysics being a translation or transposition of the political – Bataille therefore has to deal with the philosophical problem of monism. He demonstrates that the real dichotomy is not one between materialism and idealism: it exists within 'materialism' itself. Bataille suggests two possible interpretations of materialism. The real opposition is therefore one between a monist or metaphysical materialism, which reduces the whole of reality to a single principle ('abstract matter') and asserts its authority, and a dualist materialism which asserts the basic division of all that exists, and refuses to reconcile its immanent oppositions.

To support his conception of a dualist materialism, Bataille introduces a largely mythical reference to gnosticism in the context of a reevaluation of the Hegelian dialectic. His interpretation of the dialectic is somewhat unexpected, as he relates it to its distant gnostic origins: 'Hegelianism, no less than the classical philosophy of Hegel's era, seems to derive from very ancient conceptions developed by, amongst others, the gnostics at a time when metaphysics could be associated with the most monstrous dualist cosmologies and could

---

36 Cf. *D*, p. 178: 'If we consider a single object, it is easy to distinguish between matter and form, and an analogous distinction can be made concerning organic beings; form now takes on the value of the unity of the being and its individual existence. But if we consider things as a whole, and transpose distinctions of this kind, they become arbitrary and even unintelligible. We thus have two verbal entities which can be explained solely in terms of their constructive value in the social order: abstract God (or simply the idea) and abstract matter, the head warder and the walls of the prison. Variants on this metaphysical scaffolding are no more interesting than different styles of architecture. A lot of effort has gone into finding out whether the prison or the prison warder came first; although those efforts were, historically, of primordial importance, today they would probably provoke a belated astonishment, if only because of the disproportion between the implications of the debate and its radical insignificance' (*D*, p. 220).

therefore be strangely debased.'[37] The historical reality of this line of descent is of little importance for our purposes; the main point of interest is the comparison Bataille makes between the dualist perspective and the way in which forces from below are given a new value in the context of a 'debased metaphysics', to use his own terminology. This clearly means that the authentic spirit of materialism cannot be divorced from a dualist doctrine of separation and division, regardless of whether or not we call it 'gnostic'. It follows that only the doctrine of division is capable of giving a real and effective content to a dialectic.[38] In short, Bataille could have used the famous formula 'One divides into two'. In his view, the raw experience of sexuality is the exemplary instance or primal figure of that formula. In their article on 'Les Fondements de la dialectique hégélienne', published two years later in *La Critique sociale*, Bataille and Queneau would of course explain, in the framework of what was later known as 'Freudo-Marxism', that, by theorizing that primal experience and by revealing the phenomena of affective ambivalence to be found within it, psychoanalysis had opened the way for a redefinition of materialism and of the dialectic. Arguing on those grounds, Bataille could recuperate and interpret in his own way, which went against all 'rationalism', the thesis that the dialectic has a 'rational kernel'. He shows that, by reestablishing a teleology in the contradictory processes of the real, or by turning 'one splits into two' into 'two are reconciled in one', Hegel shaped a primitive dualism into a new monism, and therefore described the dialectic in 'a reduced and emasculated state'. Yet despite that repression, there remained a trace

37 *D*, p. 221.
38 This is the note added by Bataille to the text cited: 'Since Hegel's doctrine is above all an extraordinary and quite perfectly reductive system, it is obvious that the base elements that are so important in gnosticism are found only in a reduced and emasculated state. For Hegel, the intellectual role of those elements is still a destructive role, even though destruction is seen as a necessary element in the constitution of thought. This is why, when Hegelian idealism was replaced with dialectical materialism (through a complete inversion of values that gave matter the role that thought once had), matter was no longer an abstraction, but a source of contradictions. And there was no longer any question of contradiction being providential; contradiction simply became one of the properties of the development of material facts' (*D*, p. 221). As we can see, in 1930 Bataille, no less than André Breton, claimed to be a dialectical materialist, but his conception of the dialectic, which he reduced or 'debased' to its gnostic origins, was quite different from that adopted by Breton who, in keeping with the basic programme for a sur-realism, constantly looked upwards.

of the primal movement of the scission that separates and divides all reality. His 'idealism' was, of course, a disavowal of that very scission.

Bataille came back to these same problems much later when he reviewed S. Pétrement's book *Le Dualisme dans l'histoire de la philosophie et des religions* for *Critique* in 1947.[39] What particularly caught Bataille's attention in Pétrement's work was the idea that dualism took historical and theoretical primacy over monism, for this meant that the monist thought characteristic of traditional metaphysics was a reductive reinterpretation of a primal dualism. Pétrement speaks in this connection of a 'transcendental dualism', and finds its exemplary figure in the Platonic philosophy from which, in her view, Aristotle later derived a system of monist thought. This analysis confirmed Bataille's initial interpretation of the gnostic spirit, which asserted the irreducibly primal character of the scission and denied any possibility of recuperation or reconciliation. Everything was therefore from the outset divided and dual; reality itself, considered in all its aspects, must stem from that basic division prior to which no other, and no unity, could be thought.

Why is the recognition of this primal scission ascribed to gnosticism? No doubt because gnosticism is for Bataille a model for a clandestine culture which drowns its own principles in ignominious derision. But, having said that, according to this interpretation, gnosticism is no more than a secondary elaboration that conceals a much deeper process behind a mythological facade. The dualism of which Bataille is thinking is not in fact an ontological dualism that merely contrasts 'things' or regions of reality; and it is at precisely this point that the thesis put forward by Pétrement, mainly on the basis of her reference to Platonism, reveals its limitations. It is, rather, an axiological dualism whose privileged manifestation is provided by the divorce between the sacred and the profane. Here, we find the heaven-earth opposition, as formulated in Feuerbach's *Essence of Christianity*, and as then transmitted to the writings of the young Marx, which were, of course, rediscovered in the 1920s. Bataille is therefore proposing both to reread Plato by comparing his work with the mysteries of gnosticism, and to decipher the meaning of intellectual

39 Paris: Gallimard, 1946. Bataille's article was entitled 'Du Rapport entre le divin et le mal', *Oeuvres complètes*, vol. 11 (Paris: Gallimard, 1988), p. 198. Pétrement was Simone Weil's biographer and the author of *Essai sur le dualisme chez Platon, les gnostiques et les manichéens* (Paris: PUF, 1947); this was her doctoral thesis.

developments whose implications were at once closer to home and more remote.

According to Pétrement, the 'religious' conflict between the divine and the worldly, as thematized by Christianity, is a transposed echo of a basic philosophical debate between Plato and Aristotle over a fundamental issue in metaphysics that took place in the context of pagan Greece; the gnostic theses were no more than a later expression of that debate. Bataille himself thought it necessary to go beyond that specifically philosophical discussion, and to take up still more primal questions which had been asked in a very different context.

In 'Préface à la transgression', the text he devoted to Bataille in 1963, Foucault offers his own interpretation of the position Bataille defended. This interpretation, which is heavily influenced by Heidegger, tries to establish that the primal experience of division, which gave rise to the splitting of openness, is to be found in the very first manifestation of thought in Greece, which preceded metaphysics and its history of being. It is, therefore, in the pre-Socratics, and in Heraclitus in particular, that we will find the primal, almost naive, form of the dualist dialectic of 'one divides into two'.

If, however, we go back to the texts written by Bataille, we find that he is attempting to privilege a still more radical origin, which exists prior not only to metaphysics (Pétrement's thesis), but also to Western thought as such (Heidegger's thesis, as restated by Foucault). He traces it back to the very beginnings of human evolution.[40] Indeed, what Bataille is trying to get at with his aesthetic and poetic reference to gnostic dualism is the ante-historical experience of the division of values that must have come about as a result of the nature-culture articulation. The division arose when culture became divorced from nature. Although the allegorical explanations authorized by the mysteries of gnosticism should not, in historical terms, be taken too seriously, Bataille's base materialism therefore finds its real meaning in a theoretical vision whose categories are essentially those of an anthropology. At this level, he also exploits the teachings of Mauss, as refracted through the speculative models he simultaneously borrows from Marx and Hegel. Bataille borrows from Mauss the principle of a dual and divided structure of human behaviour and of correlative forms of consciousness. Once it has been established that

---

40 *Lascaux et la naissance de l'art* (Skira, 1955), which is one of Bataille's last works, is a good illustration of this conception.

this behaviour and those forms of consciousness cannot be reduced, except in an imaginary mode, to the homogeneous unity of a subject or an ego, it follows that they arise from the immediate and conflictual relationship that binds them not only to others, but to the Other as such. It is the figure of the Other that introduces an internal symbolic division.

This explains why the human act *par excellence* is that which contrasts the profane and the sacred; it constitutes the human essence by marking it at birth with an insurmountable division. It is therefore religion, and not technology, that defines the human as such, constituted in its relation to a limit that traverses it internally, and which prevents it from identifying itself with or contenting itself with the abstract fullness of a being that is simply given. We can now understand how the theory of desire [*Begierde*] expounded by Kojève would in later years give a new impetus to these speculations, even though Kojève himself relates it to the promise of satisfaction [*Befriedigung*] that coincides with the moment of the end of history. Some unpublished notes drafted by Bataille in 1930, or in other words in the same year that he wrote his article 'Le Bas Matérialisme et la gnose', contain the astonishing formula: 'Man is what is lacking in man'[41] which, to remain within the same theoretical horizon, might be seen as the initial germ of Lacan's theory of the *Spaltung*. The same formula also contains *in nuce* all the themes of the 'sociology of the sacred' which Bataille was to develop in the context of the Collège de sociologie after 1936. To a certain extent, these ideas derive from Mauss and, through his intermediary, Durkheim's *Elementary Forms of Religious Life*,[42] which has proved to be an important source for the entire history of modern thought.

Man is what is lacking in man. Man is therefore not a being of need but, as Mauss discovered by combining in his own way the teachings of Durkheim and those of Freud, a symbolic animal. Unlike a thing, a symbolic animal is not constituted through the economic accumulation of property or commodities; it is a divided 'subject', and is traversed, thanks to flows of gifts and sacrifices, by the collective relations that allow it to communicate with other men and, through them, with the whole of nature. In *La Part maudite*, which was published after the Second World War, Bataille would combine these flows and cycles of exchange into a 'general economy' working on the basis of

---

41 Bataille, *Oeuvres complètes*, vol. 2, p. 419 n.   42 First published in 1917.

expenditure, as opposed to the 'restricted economy' that functions on the basis of appropriation. All this was the logical outcome of his defence and illustration of 'base materialism'.

On the basis of the points made above, it is now possible to reread the conclusion of 'Le Bas Matérialisme et la gnose',[43] and to comment on it as we read: '*It seems that, ultimately, gnosticism, in its psychological process* [this confirms that Bataille was not interested in gnosticism as a hypothetical historical doctrine, but as a symptom of a mental structure establishing a divide between the human and the non-human] *is not very different from a modern materialism, by which I mean a materialism implying no ontology, a materialism that does not imply that matter is the thing in itself* [we can now understand what Bataille means when he speaks elsewhere of a 'materialism of psychological or social facts']. *The most important thing of all is not to surrender oneself and one's reason to anything higher* [here, Bataille is outlining the theory of sovereignty, which coincides with the rejection of a principle of authority exercised for the exclusive benefit of 'above', and therefore with the recognition of the values specific to 'below'] *to anything that can give a borrowed authority to the being that I am, to the reason which arms that being. That being and its reason cannot in fact surrender to anything lower, to anything that can be used to ape any authority.* [Communication can thus be established between the divine and evil; effecting an inversion of values does not mean putting what was below in place of what was above by cleansing it of its heterodox dimension; on the contrary, it meant asserting, and in a sense rooting, the baseness of the base by sanctifying it, and by relegating upwards – and therefore into the profane – anything that claims to have the authority of a higher principle.] *I therefore surrender completely to what has to be called matter, as it exists outside me and outside the idea, and in that sense I do not accept that my reason becomes the limit of what I have said, for if I did so, matter, being limited by my reason, would immediately take on the value of a higher principle ... Base matter is external and alien to ideal human aspirations and refuses to be reduced to the great ontological machines that result from those aspirations.*' Authentic materialism is a materialism which surrenders to matter insofar as, unlike a thing, matter is not subject to external or rational limitations and insofar as it is a product of its own immanent dynamic. Matter is, in other words unlimited and self-determined by its own expansive power. It has no goal, and

43   *D*, pp. 224–5.

cannot possibly be recuperated or used. There is no possibility of salvation, either economic or theological.[44]

It has become conventional to regard Bataille's thought as a sort of meteor which is unrelated to anything else. Even a casual study of his early texts shows the inadequacy of that view. On the other hand, the opposite approach, which would absorb his thought into a tradition and see it as an illustrative extension of a tradition to which it adds nothing, is equally inadequate. We have to reconstruct its historical inscription, which locates it at the moment of transition between the great intellectual tendencies of the nineteenth century and those of the twentieth century. In Sartre's very polemical review of *L'Expérience intérieure*, we read:

With the words 'nothing', 'night' and 'the not-knowing that lays bare', M. Bataille has quite simply prepared for us a nice little pantheistic ecstasy ... Replace M. Bataille's absolute nothing with the absolute being of substance, and you have Spinoza's pantheism ... Spinoza's pantheism is a white pantheism; M. Bataille's is a black pantheism.[45]

Sartre intended the comparison to be derogatory. One could, however, borrow the principle behind it and interpret it differently: Bataille's project, midway between philosophy and poetry, could then be seen as a resurgence – an occult resurgence – of the great pantheist tradition which has been a heterodox parallel to the classical forms of materialism since the end of the eighteenth century.

The most interesting feature of its resurgence is that it brings in its wake an obscure fascination with 'lower things'. In giving them an irreplaceable value in his attempt to refound materialism in both literary and theoretical terms, Bataille, perhaps without knowing it, was perpetuating an intellectual trend which had begun a century earlier and which determines his position in the realm of literary philosophy.

---

44 *La Part maudite* will return to this theme of how matter expands within a world that is infinitely open to the cycles of the general economy. This theme will allow Bataille to find a meaning in human sacrifice. In this connection, mention should be made of a very interesting text which marks the transition between the writings of 1930 and the post-war texts: 'Le Labyrinthe', which was published in 1934 in *La Critique philosophique*, the journal edited by Koyré at the Ecole des Hautes Etudes (*Oeuvres complètes*, vol. 1, pp. 433f).

45 Jean-Paul Sartre, 'Un Nouveau Mystique', *Situations I* (Paris: Gallimard, 1947), pp. 184–5.

7

A rhetoric of abysses: Céline's magic metro

It is possible to tell stories about the depths. Hugo and the popular novelists did so, but so too did certain nineteenth-century theorists. It is also possible to undertake a philosophical and poetic exploration of the preconditions for a new evaluation of base forms of existence. Bataille did so at the beginning of his career when he outlined a materialist anthropology centred on the theme of ignominy, which he would later develop throughout the whole of his literary *oeuvre*. One might, however, wonder if these stories and these speculations are talking about the same thing. And what do they have to say about it at the point where their discourses appear to intersect? If they did speak the truth about a depth that existed almost in itself and opened onto reality itself so as to reveal its mysteries and vertiginous perspectives, literature could indeed be regarded as a prime way of taking cognizance of objective reality's being, as defined in the ontological sense. And yet is not the basic knowledge that is communicated in fiction simply one more illusion? And is not the playfully deceptive character of that illusion the very thing that has to be taken seriously? Rather than attempting to take off the mask behind which it conceals its so-called revelations, as we would do if we surrendered to the temptations of hermeneutics, we must preserve the illusory element and thus maintain the autonomy of its exposition. We must abandon the attempt to look behind literature's statements for the other discourse of which it is the distorted and deformed expression, and which constitutes its authentic meaning. For if literature does deal with truth, the truth in question has no value other than that conferred upon it by literature. It is the truth of its style. Literature establishes a real stylistics of depth rather than a metaphysics, and stylistics is in itself a partial substitute for philosophy.

Céline's rhetorical position, which he describes in a carnivalesque mode in his *Entretiens avec le professeur Y*, helps to illustrate this general thesis. The *Entretiens* uses the seemingly incongruous metaphor of the metro to develop it in literary terms. Céline spins the metaphor out to the very end – to the end of night, one might say – and in the dark extremities into which it leads him, the shade of literature emerges. This is literature's last word on literature, and it talks about nothing.

A celebration of movement

The natural place for a metro is below ground: the communication it establishes is essentially subterranean, or *underground* [English in the original], as we would now say. The initial referential schema Céline uses to develop his image of the metro is a surface/depth opposition. 'In my emotive metro, I leave nothing on the Surface.'[1] He leaves nothing on the surface, or in other words he takes everything away. He takes away all reality, in order to drag it into the depths. Like a metro, Céline's style carries off everything that exists on the surface in a reassuring and immediately consumable form, carts it off and sweeps it away so as to denounce its apparent attractions. 'The surface is much more pleasant to visit.'[2] The surface freezes what it displays, limes it, and falsifies it by making it conform to the stereotyped norms of reception and reproduction which transform it into a cliché. On the surface, everything is superficial. It is a 'cinematic' world of chromo, like the American cinemas described in *Voyage au bout de la nuit*, where 'You plunge right into a lukewarm forgiveness.'[3] Céline prefers the raw emotion that 'comes from the core of being'[4] to this facile contentment – and consent – and the compromises it involves. This presupposes that raw emotion can be rendered and captured by a ruptured style that prevents it from becoming banal and maintains it in its essential verticality. In that respect, Céline's model for the subterranean writer is Pascal. Like Pascal, Céline tries to destabilize usage and rejects the world and its superficialities.[5]

1 Louis-Ferdinand Céline, *Entretiens avec le professeur Y* (Paris: Gallimard, 1955), p. 104. 2 Ibid., p. 102.
3 Louis-Ferdinand Céline, *Voyage au bout de la nuit*, in *Romans I* (Paris: Gallimard/Bibliothèque de la Pléiade, 1981), p. 201. 4 *Entretiens*, p. 36.
5 Cf. *Entretiens*, pp. 97–9. 'I'm a chap who takes after Pascal ...' (p. 98), 'the same fear as Pascal! ... The feeling of the abyss! ... but in my case it's not the bridge at Neuilly ... No!!! It happened to me in the metro ... in front of the stairs in the metro ... the North-South line! ... I owe the revelation of my genius to the Pigalle metro station' (p. 99) 'The depths or the surface? What a choice of infinities!' (p. 101).

Such a stance presupposes, not secrecy and dissimulation – Céline launched and published his 'metro' quite openly – but at least a certain obscurity which ultimately takes the form of confinement: from the very outset, Céline is a potential prisoner or exile. For discourses from the depths are, of necessity, denied the modes of apprehension and acceptance appropriate to a literature designed for immediate consumption. That is why this discourse should provoke, if not a lack of success, at least incomprehension and refutations, and may even be banned. It is the very opposite of a seductive and saving mode of speech looking for acquiescence and identification: it is intended to be repulsive. It calls for defiance and opens up an internal abyss of uncertainty and incompleteness. 'Night' is its natural habitat: insofar as it is the bearer of an assignable meaning, receiving the message it conceals – or conveys, given that it is a metro – means following it into the lower depths, into remote and secret depths that conceal a dark and difficult revelation.[6] No positive certainty lies at the bottom of this abyss, merely an unending fall that takes us deeper and deeper, towards absolute ignominy and horror.[7] We flee into ludicrous, grotesque precipices where human pretensions are lost and swallowed up, where they collapse and literally vanish into the abyss.[8]

There is, however, a form of transport in these depths. Céline runs a metro. 'Everything into my magic transport.'[9] Céline's entire *oeuvre* is carried along by a celebration of movement, which is the subterranean and therefore sovereign principle behind real emotions. 'Nothing but emotion ... breathless emotion.'[10] This breakneck discourse is never stable and is constantly displaced, for the man who

6 'There is a moment when you are quite alone, when you have come to the end of all that can happen to you. It's the end of the world' (*Voyage*, p. 348).
7 An episode from the Great War in *Voyage au bout de la nuit* (pp. 82–3) describes people going down into the shelters: 'Those minor panics in which a whole neighbourhood in pyjamas, following the candle, would disappear clucking into the depths to escape an almost imaginary peril, give you an idea of the harrowing futility of these beings, who are sometimes like frightened chickens, and sometimes like smug, consenting sheep. Similarly monstrous inconsistencies are enough to disgust forever the most patient and stubborn of sociophiles. As soon as the siren sounded, Musyne forgot that she had just seen what heroism really was in the *Théâtre des armées*. She insisted that I had to rush with her to the deepest tunnels, into the metro, into the sewers, anywhere, provided it was a shelter in the bottommost depths, and, most important of all, we had to do it now ...'
8 'Scandale aux abysses' was the title of the script for an animated film published by Céline in 1950.   9 *Entretiens*, p. 104.   10 Ibid., p. 105.

voices it sweeps it away in the incessant flight that allows him to escape from himself. 'Never the slightest halt anywhere.'[11] From the *Voyage* to the hellish journeys of the war and the post-war years, Céline's own books depict him as a man in perpetual motion who can never stay in one place because he has no place, who is constantly caught up in an endless quest that prevents him from settling down or standing still. The emotional transports that keep dragging him deeper into the depths are the inevitable effect, or symptom, of this uncertainty, in the face of which no illusion can be sustained because all illusions are dispelled by the unknown and the night.

This exasperated speech rejects the appeasement of silence, and it makes a noise. It rumbles, thunders and gets louder, like the elevated railway that Bardamu can hear in his hotel room in New York. It stops him from sleeping, or in other words from dreaming.[12] Céline's sentences, with their jerky lines, their unexpected digressions and their sumptuous rises, but also their platitudes and their falls, accelerate and decelerate, swell and collapse as they move to an alternating, irregular and broken rhythm, like that of a metro. His noisy transports cut through the normal softness of ways of speaking and writing. His discourse derives immense power from this internal rupture, which constantly dashes it against silence in an attempt 'to get to the bottom of life',[13] where it pursues its violent trajectory and interrupts it only to plunge once more into the insidious fissure of a suggestion, an appeal, or an insatiable unsatisfaction. 'Into the abyss, I told myself!'[14] That is Bardamu's exhortation to himself as he wanders through the streets of New York, and it will lead him to a hallucinatory vision, at once repellent and magical, of collective defecation that sums up the whole nauseous reality of the city. The city's reality comes directly from its belly, from its guts. The truth lies at the bottom of the hole.

This impassioned speech constantly finds new internal stimuli, and they make it set off again in pursuit of its own end. If, and only if, the

11 Ibid., p. 102.
12 'In my room, the same rolls of thunder would shatter the echo again and again. First, the thunder of the subway, which seemed to rush towards us from far away, carrying away all the aqueducts as it crossed them and breaking the town with them, and then, in between, the incoherent cries of the machines that came up from the street far below, and then the muted noise of the shifting crowd, hesistant, always boring, always on the point of going and then hesitating again, and coming back. The great stew of men in the city ... Men, pushing before them life, day and night' (*Voyage*, pp. 208–9).   13 Ibid., p. 240.
14 Ibid., p. 195.

secret behind the tumult it bears within it could finally be revealed, it could return to the void from whence it came. But it must always remain separated from the silence that could appease it by its destiny, which is to go to the limit of what it can say, of what can be said.[15] It must keep rushing onwards in the hope of reaching that limit. It is this perpetual headlong flight that gives Céline's sentences their very characteristic rhythm. They are decentred and off centre. Every sentence flings itself into the next in a vain attempt to find the equilibrium that eludes it. This is a rhetoric of wanderings and collisions.

Only the *Voyage*, Céline's first great work, still borrows the traditional form of narrative fiction and exhibits the deceptively ideal closure of a complete text. Its final lines read: 'It [the tugboat] called to its side all the barges on the river, all of them, and the city itself, and the sky and the countryside, and us, and carried it all away, the Seine too, everything, so that we don't have to talk about it any more.'[16] Céline's later works will twist this speech that sweeps the whole world along with it, dismember it and tear it into smaller and smaller pieces, so as to keep it in the gaping openness of a painful disquiet that can be neither exhausted, expiated nor satisfied. His books do not end in a silence that finally brings everything together. The silence is dispersed throughout them in the gaps signalled by the famous three suspension points. It is impossible to fill or conceal the void by which discourse seems to be decomposed just as it is being composed. The exorcism of silence: this broken voice is damned, inexorably out of step with everything it tries to say, and void of meaning. It can never be 'satisfied'.

The little trick

This impossible trajectory can be pursued only if it is kept on the rails which set it, not a definite goal or course, but the minimal element of invariance essential to its perpetuation and communication. This construction, which is anything but spontaneous, means that a style has to get under way on 'quite special rails',[17] on trickily bevelled and streamlined rails. It is the rails that allow emotion to be recaptured in

15 'We will not rest until everything has been said once and for all, and then we will be quiet, and unafraid of being quiet. We'll get there' (ibid., p. 327).
16 Ibid., p. 505.   17 *Entretiens*, p. 110.

an accurate rendering. They produce the effect of a break, of an open wound from which emotion pours and pours. This is the 'trick', the little invention of the 'emotive style' that allows Céline, somewhat surprisingly, to describe himself as a successor to the impressionist painters: 'Not so much *plein air* as *plein air* rendered'.[18] In order to render this emotion in its raw crudity and cruelty, it is not enough to 'reproduce' it by photographing it or by taking a sort of snapshot which claims to freeze it, and which thus distorts its essentially mobile qualities.[19] This is what Colonel Réséda, who is both Céline's interlocutor in the *Entretiens* and professeur Y's grotesque double, cannot understand: no mechanical device, and no automatic recording or writing can bring back naked emotion, with all the unseemliness and scandal, all the impolite savour that makes it impossible to assimilate and accept.

'Rails which look quite straight, and aren't!'[20] Because it is truly a style, the emotive style must be indirect if it is to ensure this magic transport. 'Rediscovering the emotion of the spoken word through writing! That's quite something!... It's not much, but it's something.'[21] If we wish to capture the trace of spoken language, it is not enough to preserve the memory of a pure voice that continues to exist beneath the artifices characteristic of the written. It has to be reproduced by a laborious transcription. It has to be so transcribed that the raw statement emerges from the operation transformed, distorted, deformed and perverted. Writing as one speaks is the very opposite of capturing speech, or in other words stopping it; it means the dynamic liberation of its mobile emotivity. 'It's essentially fleeting: evanescent.'[22] Emotion can be captured only by simulating it, and if it is to be simulated it must undergo the process of secondary elaboration that gives it a new authenticity standing in for the authenticity to which it refers fictively; the artificiality of the devices required to capture emotion means that it is careful to keep its distance.[23] Céline the writer does not copy or record spoken language; he writes spoken

---

18 Ibid., p. 31.
19 'Photos are not emotive ... Never!... they are frozen, they are frigid' (ibid., p. 31).
20 Ibid., p. 110. Cf. ibid., p. 121: 'Rails that look straight are not straight.'
21 Ibid., p. 23.   22 Ibid., p. 35.
23 'Translating the spoken word into literature is not a matter of stenography. The sentences and periods have to be imprinted with a certain distortion, using such artifice that when you read the book it seems that someone is speaking in your

language in such a way as to produce the specific effect of 'the spoken', just as he does not capture the natural power of emotion, but recreates it through the 'rendered emotion' which stands in for it in its absence. And Céline is perfectly aware of the fact that the tools he uses to recreate it (the 'three-suspension-point technique') have no value in themselves; if it were reduced to being a mere imitative technique, and were as such imitated in its turn, this stylistic device 'would soon become a chromo',[24] or would lose its dynamic and creative powers.

Things that should not be said

Céline's 'trick' is inimitable because it belongs to him alone: it is inseparable from his personality, and represents his literary commitment. His commitment is that of a writer who is totally carried away by his work and caught up in what he is saying. The magic metro can move only thanks to the expert will-power of its driver, and only under his vigilant surveillance. Céline's style is inevitably a 'spoken' style; the site of its enunciation has to be the position of the individual speaker who espouses it, supports it with his personal presence, and shamelessly exposes himself. It is an obsessional, hallucinatory form of speech, not so much because of what it says as because of the fact that it is saying it: its excesses, paroxysms and frenzy do not require the support of a spokesman, but the actual intervention of a speaker who can take on all its tension and accept full responsibility for it in a mode which can only be that of guilt. This absolute, obscene speech cannot

ear. This is done by transposing every word, which is never quite what you expect, always a little surprise. It is like what is said to happen when you plunge a stick into water; if you want it to look straight, you have to break it a little, if I can put it that way; you have to bend it slightly before you put it in the water. If you plunge a really straight stick into water, it looks bent ...' (letter of 16 April 1947 to Milton Hindus, in the 'Céline' issue of *Cahiers de l'Herne*, reprinted Paris: Livre de poche, 1988, p. 383). Cf. Céline's letter of 15 May 1947 to Hindus (ibid., p. 386). The image of the broken stick reappears in a comic exchange in *Entretiens*, p. 123.

24 'I've tried to make you understand that the inventor of a new style is only the inventor of a technique! A minor technique! ... Does the little technique stand the test? Or doesn't it? That's all there is to it. That's all that matters. It's clear ... My trick is the emotive style. Does the "emotion rendered" style work? Is it valid? ... I say: Yes! Hundreds of writers have copied it, are copying it, doctoring it, plagiarizing it, faking it and doing very well out of it ... so much so ... it's inevitable ... inevitable ... my trick will soon become a chromo' (*Entretiens*, pp. 39–40).

be dissociated from the man who proffers it, from the 'author' who, rather than hiding behind the formal organization of its content, takes the greatest risk of all by inhabiting it and occupying it to the extent that it is possible and tolerable to do so.

Ideally, every sentence written by Céline should be spoken in the first person. That is why he gradually abandoned the techniques of narrative fiction on which he had initially relied in the *Voyage*. Moving away from them with the quasi-autobiographical revelations of *Mort à crédit*, he eventually made the content of his chronicles and pamphlets truly his by 'speaking' them in his own name, and by adopting a completely subjective form of utterance which sticks so closely to the skin of the man who utters it that it becomes impossible for him to dissociate himself from it or escape it. At this point, the author's disconcerting asceticism denies him the poetic licence that might otherwise have allowed him to hide behind his characters. He is totally compromised in his work. Such is Céline's characteristic stance. It is primarily linguistic and only secondarily ideological. He takes his stance within speech and speaks in a frenzy. The logical outcome is the expression of a basic guilt and a reprobation-effect which, paradoxically, confirms its unjustifiable truthfulness.

The words uttered in Céline's name are provocative and disruptive, and they both infringe codes (of utterance, good manners, right-mindedness and polite speech) and undermine any attempt at a codification other than that conferred upon them by their style, their own style. As he reacts against instrumentalist conceptions which in fact neutralize language, Céline gradually perfects a machine for disrupting communication. He takes the natural functions of language to extremes and twists them until they break. The final product is a shattered, irrecuperable and indefensible language. This is why Céline's prime object is language. Language is the only raw material he works as a writer. It is a discordant and disjointed language which is artificially interrupted by the untimely interventions of an enraged speaker who is always in the way, who is impossible, and who is always guilty — disastrously so — of what he has said, of the fact of saying it. Such an 'author' is denied fine words; in order to inhabit language completely and to appropriate it for himself, he has to 'cut loose' from the reality and ideas of his audience. He has to break off contact and disrupt any possible exchange in a permanent act of provocation which compensates for his lack of success, without ever claiming to be heard or understood. 'I don't write for someone.

Stooping to that, that's really degrading! You write for the writing itself.'[25]

We cannot, however, avoid taking into account Céline's 'message', or his attempt to communicate an overall conception of reality and life that resembles a worldview. Writing for the sake of writing inevitably means defending against all comers a cause which is implicitly assumed to be a 'good' cause. Now it is impossible to avoid the disturbing and intolerable character of Céline's 'ideas', which derive the most striking stylistic effects from the rejection they provoke. The magic metro is also a shameful, scandalous and disgusting means of transport. At this point we have to remember Céline's constant declaration: 'I am not a man with a message, I am not a man of ideas, I am a man with a style.'[26] In asserting the preeminence of style, of ways of speaking, over the content it transmits, is not Céline simply avoiding his responsibilities and making a tactical retreat so as to escape the persecutions of which, rightly or wrongly, he believed himself to be the constant victim? Are such assertions primarily attempts to avoid shouldering responsibility and paying the price for the hateful, sordid state of confusion in his 'ideas'? Does he not claim that his discourse, which is indisputably demented, should be listened to as though it were a pure, harmless piece of music which should certainly not be taken literally? Does he not claim that the primary purpose of the text is to enhance the accompaniment?

The answer to these questions has to be that Céline does not ask us to choose between what he is saying and the way he is saying it because, in his view, the two are inseparable, and bear the uniquely indelible mark of his 'tone' and his style as a metro driver. There is no denying that this is anything but an evasion or an escape. We are being asked to choose between what he is saying in the way he says it, and the very fact of his saying it, the fact of saying anything in general, for that is what is at stake — and put to the stake — throughout

25 Interview with Madeleine Chapsal, *L'Express* 312, 14 June 1957.
26 'L.-F. Céline vous parle', Disques Festival. Cf. *Entretiens*, p. 22: 'A minor inventor, quite!... Only invented a little trick!... Just a little trick!... I'm not sending the world any message!... Not me, Monsieur!... I don't clutter up the Ether with words! No, not me, Monsieur!... I don't get drunk on words, or on port, or on being flattered by young people!... I don't cogitate on the planet's behalf!... I'm just a little inventor, and I've only invented one little trick! Of course it won't last! Like everything else! Just like collar studs! I know how unimportant I am! Anything but ideas!... leave ideas to street vendors! All ideas! Leave them to the pimps, to the sewers of confusion.'

his *oeuvre*. If his *oeuvre* does communicate a message, it is this: all speech, whatever it may be, is guilty and cannot, must not, go unpunished.

Céline says out loud what others think quietly to themselves because they are unwilling to take responsibility for it. Indeed, Céline not only says it out loud in the first person; he writes it at great length, displays it and unashamedly reveals it on the printed page he publishes under his own name and in his own name, even though the author's name is not a true patronym — not that that prevents it from functioning as a 'proper' name. This inscription is certainly not designed to make bearable or acceptable the contemplation of certain 'ideas' by watering down their content; on the contrary, it is designed to exacerbate the demented element by taking it to the limit of what can be said. It is always in excess of and inadequate to its manifest content, just like Céline's sentences, with the broken rhythms that always make them sound like invective. 'For my part, I could speak all my hatred. I know. I'll do it later if they don't come back. I'd rather tell stories. I'll tell such stories that they'll come back on purpose to kill me from the four corners of the globe. Then, it will be over and I'll be well pleased.'[27] This is a deadly form of speech. It is content to tell stories that cannot satisfy it, and finds peace only by risking death and destruction: it is caught in a trap of its own making, and there is no remission. It pronounces on the infinitely suspect reality of a world sapped by lies and fear. It spits out the ignominious revelation from which there is no possible escape: 'Can't be talked about'.[28]

Céline is not, however, the only passenger in his vehicle, in his metro; we are his passengers and his readers, and he takes all of us with him. His emotion carries us far beyond where we wanted to go: to the abject scandal of the abyss into which he takes us at full speed. His words, which are proffered in the first person, are not a mechanical, and therefore anonymous, recording of some real and objectively irresponsible speech, nor are they an inner discourse whose only interlocutor is Céline himself. They are not confined to the deceptive intimacy of purely personal convictions. They are an aside which swells and resonates with internal echoes; they solicit, if not the acquiescence of accomplices, at least the horrified presence of a

27 *Mort à crédit*, in *Romans I*, p. 512.
28 Preface to the 1949 edition of *Voyage au bout de la nuit*, *Romans I*, appendix 3, p. 1114.

frightened, transfixed and compromised audience. We are all summoned to hear them, provoked into hearing them. We are called as witnesses, not to justifications for what they state, but to the fact — and it is scandalous in itself — that they have said something, that they have 'spoken'. 'I take everyone in the metro, excuse me ... and off I go, taking everyone with me! Whether they want to go or not! Come with me!'[29] This impossible, grotesque 'I' is both comic and brutal, cynical and lyrical,[30] because of the inner discord that propels it forward. It cannot take any pleasure in the fullness of its subjectivity; it explodes, bursts out of its limits and into the consciousness of the reader, and occupies it completely. In the very resistances it provokes in the reader's consciousness — and Céline's writing calls for resistance and not agreement — it transmits and communicates the only things it possesses: its gaps, its sin. 'The reader who reads me! It seems to me, he could swear it, that someone is reading inside his head! Inside his own head!'[31] All the power of the emotive style is concentrated in this astonishing experience of possession and dispossession, self-control and loss of self. No one boards Céline's metro with impunity. No one can be sure of getting off.

A metro train can come off the rails. Céline's style is in permanent danger of succumbing to its own outrageousness. It is dedicated to the glorification of an absence and a void — this is his 'Pascalian' side — and is in permanent danger of just failing to produce the desired effect. It is the constant risk of failure that gives it its broken rhythms as it continually tries to recover from an inevitable fall. It feeds on that ambiguity, on the insatiable urge to say everything. It therefore cannot stop and is carried still further away — tangentially — from its utterance of the moment. When it bends the stick the wrong way, it is in danger of bending it too far, of bending it further than 'just what it takes' to guarantee the rectitude and success of its undertaking. Bending it too far makes it meaningless. And Céline does constantly come off the rails. He tries to recover his balance, loses it again, and falls still deeper. Hence the very characteristic pulse of his sentences,

29 *Entretiens*, p. 102.
30 Cf. *Entretiens*, p. 66: '"Your technique? ... yes ... Your invention! ... You think a lot of that invention, don't you? ... Very clever! ... The perpetual 'I'. Others are a little more modest". — "Oh!, colonel, Oh! colonel ... I'm modesty personified! There's nothing at all daring about my 'I'. I'm very careful about how I use it. Very, very careful ... I always cover it up, completely, very carefully, with shit."'
31 *Entretiens*, p. 122.

and the ability to bounce back that allows them to go on, to transcend their limits, to go beyond themselves and into us!

Céline is the sole inventor of a literature of disgust, of resentment and sin: his every move is inspired by the spirit that denies. Shame on his imitators! As he never stops telling us, being able to speak like this cost Céline dearly, and it is that which allows him to bear witness, to become the chronicler of a degeneration which he experienced personally and which concerns all of us. He forces us to share that sin, that hatred, with him, and to put aside our finer feelings, at least while we are reading him. That is where his metro goes. His literary technique and the 'style' he forged are designed to project outwards an essential and profound absence that exists in both him and us, to make it visible by exhibiting it and underlining it. The whole of Céline's 'philosophy' lies in that lacunary thought, which is all the more obsessional in that it always returns to an obstacle it cannot get around because this obstacle constitutes its very order: the incoherent coherence of a sinister and sombre logic that secretes its objects in hallucinatory fashion in the course of a corrupt and corrosive speech which is inexpiably distorted by the interplay of its internal elisions. It is self-deluded to the point of martyrdom, or, which from Céline's point of view comes down to the same thing, recognition. In Céline, we are all guilty along with Céline.

PART III

All must pass away

8

❖❖❖

Sade and the order of disorder

❖❖❖

Writing what has never been written, as no one has ever written: the work of Sade is inscribed within a vision of a literature of excess supported by a logic of profanation from which it borrows its destructive principles.[1] What are the objects of this destruction and profanation? Primarily nature. Nature is devastated by the act of writing, which both contests its ends and rejects its everyday and reputedly normal figures; the relationship between Sade's text and reality is an aggressive one. It is negative and criminal from the outset. At the same time, the basic hypotheses behind the act of writing are also called into question: in order to bring about the revelation of an anti-nature, literature has to derange its own order and adopt a new regime. Now this presupposes a speculative stance which is also unprecedented: if Sade does have a philosophy, its interest stems not from its doctrinal content, which is in fact derivative,[2] but from a mutation that affects something more than the destiny of an extremely singular body of work and the fact of reading or writing novels. It also affects certain basic intellectual procedures pertaining to both theoretical issues and practical objectives. In that respect, we might speak of a veritable Copernican revolution which simultaneously creates new objects and a new way of apprehending them.

Sade's work is the product of closure, of carceral or clinical confinement. It begins as a reflection on its own conditions of possibility, centres on the essential question of limits, and of its own limits, and eventually becomes so closely bound up with the situation that was forced upon it and which generated it, that it can do no more

---

1 'It is now, dear reader, that you must incline your heart and your mind to the most impure story that has been told since the world came into existence, no similar book being found amongst either the ancients or the moderns' (Sade, *Les Cent Vingt Journées de Sodome, Oeuvres complètes*, Paris: Jean-Jacques Pauvert, 1986, vol. 1, p. 78).
2 Sade's materialism is midway between that of d'Holbach and that of La Mettrie.

than reproduce its general features. Closure both gives its speculations a concrete content, and its expression a form. Sade's work becomes the history of a closure, and it is also the history of its own enclosure.[3]

Written in prison in Vincennes in 1785, Sade's first great text, *Les Cent Vingt Journées de Sodome*, triggers a process of reflection which calls into question the meaning of reality and the norms of life. This theoretical fiction, which is devoted to the compilation of a systematic encyclopedia of human turpitudes, corresponds to the emergence not of a new body of knowledge, but rather of a new relationship to knowledge and the discourse in which that knowledge is inscribed. Three basic preoccupations merge in this text and provide the main axes for reading it: domination, enjoyment [*jouissance*] and narration. They relate to the issues at stake in a politics, an ethics and a rhetoric. The whole of Sade's 'philosophy', which brought about the closure of an entire system of thought, is contained within the development of these three questions.

Power (What am I permitted to hope for?)

The rigours of a harsh winter, and not the excesses of a torrid summer, provide the framework for the 'one hundred and twenty days'. The snow that cloaks this absolute narrative and turns it in upon itself evokes the whiteness of a blank page on which everything remains to be written, and on which anything can be written.[4] The *Cent Vingt*

---

3 Michel Foucault's radical interpretation sees this closure as being that of an intellectual era. It brings to an end the classical era of representation: 'Sade attains the end of Classical discourse and thought. He holds sway precisely upon their frontier' (*The Order of Things*, London: Tavistock, 1974, p. 211). According to this view, the one purpose of Sade's novel is to recount the limits of representation.

4 'That day, it was noticed that the weather again favoured the vile projects of our libertines and was doing more than their own precautions to conceal them from the eyes of the whole world. A fearful quantity of snow had fallen, filling the surrounding valley and seeming to prevent even animals from approaching the lair of our four villains. As for human beings, there could no longer have existed a single one who would have dared to make his way to it. One cannot imagine how such safeguards encourage voluptuousness, or what one can do when it is possible to say: "I am alone here, I am at the world's end, concealed from all eyes, and it is no longer possible for any creature to reach me; no more restraints, no more barriers." From that moment onwards, desires are given an impetuosity that knows no bounds, and the impunity that stimulates them leads to a delicious increase in their intoxication. One is alone with God and one's conscience: and what power does the former restraint have in the eyes of one who is an atheist

Journées therefore takes the form of a history of a utopia, of a social utopia which has fled to the margins of space and time. It describes the establishment of a society corresponding to literally extraordinary conditions. It exists outside the law, is completely cut off from real societies and their rules, and defies them by the very fact of its existence. This society which challenges norms is, however, anything but a society without norms: whilst it dissociates itself from the normal forms of the social order, it does so by forcing them, or in other words by reduplicating them. It annuls them by adopting the logic of revelatory excess which, thanks to an image which is fictional but truer than nature, reduces them to their essential nature.

This presupposes the fencing off of a perfectly enclosed place. Its enclosure is illustrated by the metaphor, which has often been analysed, of the castle on an impregnable spur of rock. This is the blind spot from whence the law pronounces its truth. Once all the bridges have been cut, the unchained – in every sense of the word – passions establish a new order. 'Let our desires be our only laws.'[5] The requisite precondition for the enunciation of this law of desire is the total isolation that can be achieved within the limits of an inaccessible spot. Total isolation both provokes the explosion of the drives and contains their effusions, rather as though desire can be fully satisfied only if it is circumscribed within the closure of a pure 'in-itself' [*en soi*]. That closure is a besieged citadel protected against the attacks, but also the distractions, that might come from an outside world from which it is radically cut off. It is an inside with no outside, and one can neither leave it nor enter it, for the very idea of communication has been abolished, as has the idea of any exchange with that which escapes its order.[6] This withdrawal is also reminiscent of the monastic isolation

---

by both temperament and conviction? And what influence can conscience have on one who is so accustomed to overcoming his remorse that it has become almost pleasurable? Wretched flock, delivered over to the murderous teeth of such villains, how you would have trembled if the experience you lacked had given you the benefit of these reflections' (*Les Cent Vingt Journées*, p. 225).

5 Ibid., p. 75.

6 'Having examined the premises, the duke resolved that, as all the victuals were inside and as there was no longer any need to go out, all the doors leading into them should be walled up in order to forestall the attacks from without that they feared and the escapes from within that they feared still more. He resolved, I say, that we should shut ourselves up completely, as though in a besieged citadel, without leaving the slightest opening for either enemies or deserters. The suggestion was put into execution: we barricaded ourselves in so well that it was

that results from the decision to renounce the world and to live far away from it, as though in a desert. But its configuration also reproduces the conditions of carceral isolation, with its constraints and enforced renunciations. Now, Sade's visionary text was elaborated in precisely those conditions. An imprisoned story written by an imprisoned man becomes a narrative of confinement.

A besieged citadel, a monastery, a prison: the three references suggest the idea of a social relation whose organization is bound up with a principle of domination which has completely internalized its own workings. The model of power simultaneously evokes an ideal form of knowledge; it corresponds to the establishment of a sort of laboratory where a unique experiment is carried out in artificial and strictly controlled conditions, without any possibility of its being interrupted by unexpected developments. It is not actual or concrete forms of power that are in play here, but rather the idea of power, considered abstractly and in itself. Access to such knowledge requires the icy asceticism of a subterranean story which descends into the 'bowels of the earth' in order to wrest from them their terrible secrets.[7] In the depths of a supremely hidden place, which is isolated even from the narrative that evokes it, an obscure relationship is established between a 'lawless villain', who is, however, ruled by 'the imperious laws of his perfidious pleasures', and his submissive, if not

no longer possible even to tell where the doors had been, and we settled inside in accordance with the arrangements just described' (*Les Cent Vingt Journées*, p. 67).

7 'Depravity, cruelty, disgust, infamy, and the passions we had felt or expected to feel had indeed resulted in the construction of a different place. It is important to give a sketch of it, for laws essential to the interest of this narrative prevent us from painting it in its entirety. A fatal stone was artistically raised beneath the altar of the small Christian church we had established in a gallery; beneath it, a very narrow, very steep spiral staircase of three hundred steps went down into the bowels of the earth through a sort of vaulted dungeon, shut off by three iron doors. Here, one could find all the atrocious devices that the most cruel art and the most refined barbarism could invent, both to horrify the senses and to perform horrors. It was so peaceful there! So reassuring for the villain whom crime brought there together with a victim! He was at home, outside France in a safe country, in the depths of an uninhabitable forest, in a corner of that forest which, thanks to the measures that had been taken, only the birds of the air could reach, and he was in the depths of the bowels of the earth. Woe, a hundred times woe to the unfortunate creature who, abandoned in this way, found himself at the mercy of a lawless, godless villain who enjoyed crime, who had no interests other than his passions, and no restraints to observe but the imperious laws of his perfidious pleasures' (*Les Cent Vingt Journées*, p. 67).

consenting, victims. It establishes the paradoxical figure of a law which overthrows all laws, which is based solely upon the power of the 'passions', and whose disorder proves to be the harbinger of a new order.

This extraordinary order depends upon a precise codification. The 'friends' who control Silling Castle, where pleasure reigns supreme, are bound together by an explicit agreement.[8] For if the masters' undisputed domination over their subjects is to be established, the masters themselves must submit to the self-imposed regulation of their pleasures. There can be no pleasure without rules; although it replaces other laws, the law of pleasure is still a law in the full sense of the term and it imposes a system of obligations and constraints. It might be expected that the latter would apply only to subjects and victims, and that the masters they serve unconditionally would remain free; Sade, however, constantly stresses that in the new order established by their desire, the masters are also bound by rules which constrain their initiatives by subjecting them to the conditions of an ordered and progressive action. True pleasures – and 'true' must retain its full meaning here, 'true pleasure' being the pleasure that allows a truth to be grasped – are therefore not abandoned to the spontaneity of their uncontrolled effusions. Their movement must be willed and directed, the goal being sovereign self-control. This is one of Sade's most constant themes; pleasures [*jouissances*] are authentic only when they are devised by thought – even, or especially, by evil thoughts.[9]

According to Sade, desire does not concern the individual alone, or the individual who is left to his own devices by the removal of the constraints imposed by the two essential figures of alterity, the world and God; it is a matter for a collective administration. The pleasures indulged in by Silling's 'society' are therefore inscribed in advance in a grid which determines when they can be enjoyed on the basis of a

---

8 Sade speaks (ibid., p. 89) of 'rules from which we had sworn never to stray in any way'. Cf. p. 67: 'The four friends worked on a code of laws which was signed by the masters and promulgated to the subjects as soon as it had been drafted.'

9 The imposition of rules implies the possibility of their being broken. Cf. ibid., p. 66: 'Nothing of all that must be apparent in our pleasures. None of it was intended to be. The reason why our self-imposed rules about all this were broken is that nothing can contain libertinage, and because the real way to extend and multiply one's desires is to want to impose limitations upn them.' Constraints stimulate the desire to defy them still further.

complex plan combining a rule of deferral, a rule of repetition and a rule of progression.[10] The communal organization of desire, which also requires desire to be staged as though in a theatre and subjects it, as we shall see, to a principle of narrativity, therefore divorces it from over-facile and immediate satisfactions. From the outset, the mastery it implies takes the form of renunciation. Its satisfaction is always deferred. We have here a politics of desire which relates to the 'social' order whose establishment Sade describes in such detail.

What is new about this order? What distinguishes it from the old order it has overthrown? The new element has nothing to do with the abolition of all laws. On the contrary, no society is better or more strictly ordered than a society ruled by desire. What is new about it is that it establishes a new relationship with the law. When it becomes bound up with desire, the law supports interests that are sufficiently powerful to be defined in their own terms and without reference to external criteria or a hierarchy of necessities. God, who is the prime figure of exteriority or alterity, is not simply absent or excluded from the Sadean universe, since he is constantly called upon as a witness by a discourse of invective which combines disavowal and defiance.[11] God is in a sense still present in this universe, but he is present in the form of an inverted revelation which initially takes the form of a rejection. From that point of view, we can argue that order, as conceived by Sade, comes about through the intermediacy of a system that has been stripped of all reference to transcendence and which has completely internalized its relationship with the other and the law by integrating their most negative aspects. This is the triumph of the idea of power as something which is, because of the perfectly controlled interaction of its agents, completely self-immanent.

This new power could be said to be democratic *avant la lettre*. Sade helps to bring out a concept of law that was unknown in his day. Law is conceived as being centred only upon itself, as coinciding absolutely with the collective order it organizes, and as referring to no external

---

10 Cf. ibid., p. 91: 'They thought for a moment that the bishop was going to come ... but he contained himself, cast far from him the tempting objects that were about to triumph over his senses, and knowing that he still had a task to carry out, at least restrained himself for the end of the day'; and p. 155: 'Everything was forbidden, except what had been done the night before.'

11 It is in this sense that Pierre Klossowski speaks of a negative theology in Sade. See his *Sade my Neighbour*, tr. Alphonso Lingis (Evanston: Northwestern University Press, 1991).

principle. If, however, we describe this system as democratic, are we not flying in the face of the facts and forgetting the indisputably reactionary and despotic aspects of the social utopia imagined by Sade? It brings victims and executioners face to face without any intermediaries, and forces the victims to suffer all the rigours of a power whose complete enjoyment is the preserve of their executioners. And the power of the executioners is all the more arbitrary in that it is supposedly absolute.[12]

Perhaps Sade wanted to make his reader understand that the process of integration that typifies a democratic society also generates a relationship of domination, and that it does so in conditions which make that domination still more overwhelming. Sade uses the resources of literary fiction to trace, in an abstract manner which further underlines its acuity, the figure of a democratic people bound by the law of an unjust society in which the order of the masters reigns. According to this view, man's exploitation of man reaches its most radical extreme when it is based upon a non-reciprocal relation of power which is completely polarized by the confrontation between rulers and ruled. We will be speaking in a moment of Sade's ethics. It is an ethics of pain, of pain inflicted and pain suffered. It gives rise to complaints, but can neither justify nor even imagine resistance. This schema precludes the possibility of a dialectic between torturer and victim, in the sense that it is possible to speak in other contexts of a master-slave dialectic, because the relationship that unites them in opposition is assumed to be non-reversible. This imaginary situation gives the masters a monopoly on both revolt and labour; the 'people' are passive raw material which they mould as they see fit, and as their inspiration takes them. The masters can imprint on the people a perfectly controlled image of the desires through which they assert their will to power. To simplify matters, we might say that the whole of Sade's politics is an answer to the following question: what happens when the people are prevented from rebelling because the law they obey coincides completely with the social order that oppresses them?

A scandalous lesson thus appears to emerge from the thought-processes of the writer-villain: because it is essentially totalitarian, democracy is, insofar as it looks like freedom, the most extreme form

---

12 *Les Cent Vingt Journées*, p. 318: 'In short, we inflict upon the lower orders all the vexations, all the injustices we can imagine, confident of deriving even greater amounts of pleasure because the tyranny will have been inflicted most efficiently.'

of the despotism that flourishes when the principles of interest and desire are given free reign. For, in fiction as in reality, when a duke, a bishop, a magistrate and a financier — the four 'friends' who stage the sinister rituals of the 'one hundred and twenty days' — enter into a free association, they create the conditions for a much more absolute authority, an authority which is shared much less than that available to divine-right monarchs. Their power is unconditional because it derives all its force from within, because its law is, as Pascal would say, self-sufficient — and here Sade comes strangely close to Pascal — and bears no relation to any external law that might restrict it.

In order to argue what appears to be a paradox, Sade has only to turn to nature, which can be reduced to pure power relations. This appeal to nature may seem surprising on the part of an author who is so obsessed with the idea of an anti-nature. The difficulty disappears, however, if we restore to the concept of nature the fullness of its content, namely, that of a reality which, because it exists fully in itself, cannot be limited by anything external to it. What does nature want? Literally nothing, as nature is also, according to Sade, an absence of ends. Yet whilst it wants nothing in particular, it can do everything, in the sense that its general actions do not privilege the production of one exclusive order which it selects at the expense of others. Being permanently in excess of itself, it floods into all the channels available to it and finds its self-realization in the most contradictory forms. This is why the immanent economy of its cycles is governed by a dynamic which is essentially based upon extravagance and destruction: its movements generate a semblance of order only to destroy it. It establishes a permanent exchange between order and disorder, and converts vices into virtues, and virtues into vices. The aggressivity of this power, which is negative at the level of its effects but fully positive in its cause, inevitably turns against it. Its every action gives the lie to the illusion that an absolute norm could contain it within a single order. Those same actions also demonstrate that evil is natural. Being no longer defined with reference to transcendental values, evil can only find its incarnation in relative figures. In Sade's view, radical evil is a possibility which must always remain open-ended — indeed it is the sole 'possibility' left in a system of absolute materialism which has room only for the real — because no event, except an act that attacks nature itself in order to annihilate it, can give it a definite content.

Certain of these themes derive from the naturalist tradition, as handed down from Bruno to Diderot via Spinoza. Yet Sade undoubtedly adds a new chapter to the history of that tradition by injecting a supplementary energy which makes the entire system take on a new meaning. By postulating that nature, which can do everything, can also — and above all — do evil, Sade makes absolute the relationship of domination that links the strong and the weak, and therefore describes it as a relationship between executioners and potential victims. He thus draws the ultimate conclusion from the identification of nature with anti-nature. Not only is nature indifferent to the disorders that result from its incoherent initiatives, it is also indifferent to the differences they generate, since it cannot be stabilized within any system. Nature is always equal to itself to the extent that it asserts its internal inequalities. When it stages its actions, it plays all the roles, and acts the part of both executioner and victim.[13]

It is this that gives the apology for murder its true meaning:

Do conquerors, heroes and tyrants impose on themselves the absurd law of not daring to do unto others what they do not want to be done to us? In truth, my friends, I will not hide it from you, but I shudder when I hear fools say that this is the law of nature. Heavens above! Being greedy for murders and crimes, nature's law inspires us to commit them, and the only law it inscribes in the bottom of our hearts is the law of finding satisfaction at anyone's expense.[14]

In writing these lines, Sade is not saying that conquerors, heroes and tyrants are being unwittingly manipulated by nature, that they are therefore mere agents collaborating on a collective project. The philosophy of nature illustrated by the spectacle of universal devastation, and by the infinitely varied forms it can take, is the complete antithesis of a philosophy of history. In a universally, if not uniformly, murderous world, everything is murder to the extent that nothing is a crime in any absolute sense; when positive and negative, construction and destruction, are inextricably mingled, there is no place for works that are not marked by death.

The apology for murder is therefore anything but a justification for murder insofar as it rejects the principle behind all attempts at

13 The logic of the argument has undoubtedly reactionary implications. Sade puts these words into the mouth of one of the monstrous characters evoked by the storytellers: 'He did not accept that it was possible to outrage nature to such an extent as to upset the hierarchy it had established between different classes of individuals' (*Les Cent Vingt Journées*, p. 281). It is pointless to outrage nature because nature itself is adequate to that task; all its orders are disorders, and no equilibrium can univocally reduce them.

14 *Les Cent Vingt Journées*, p. 332.

justification. Power relations are all that exists, and since it is those relations that give right its real foundations, this right itself is internally riven by potential disputes which corrupt all its values. Laws are necessary because they can be defied and remade in such a way that the best is always combined with the worst, the balance between the two being no more than the result of compromises achieved at the expense of those who are their victims. Left to itself and to the extreme acuity of its contradictions, the social order reveals and rekindles the basic disorder on which it is founded, as though in the crater of the volcano from which it derives its illegitimate legitimacy. No law can wipe the figure of crime from the surface of the earth because laws, which merely give an actual and provisional form to nature's conflicts, bring with them new conflicts, to which they too will eventually succumb. There is no possibility of any final resolution to attenuate the sinister character of this lesson in despair.

That evil is a permanent possibility also means that evil can never be realized in any definitive or absolute form. And perhaps this does mean that there is cause for hope: if one can move from lesser to greater crimes without any solution of continuity because there is no clear dividing line between good and evil, it is not entirely improbable that one might be able to invert the process. It might be possible to make the transition from major manifestations of the criminal tendency, which is in any case present in the heart of every natural existence, to minor manifestations. It might therefore be possible to influence the executioner-victim relationship in the latter's favour. Whereas a gnostic vision of history would reduce history to an open struggle between positive and negative forces, Sade insists on the confused and precarious element in its evolution, which is marked by a purely natural determinism. Nothing is decided once and for all in any sense, since there is never any clear outcome to the debate between Eros and Thanatos.

Good and evil constantly exchange and mingle their effects, and whether individuals pursue good or evil is of little importance: individuals come together only in order to compete and to put their respective pleasures to the test. Being unable to share their pleasures, which belong to individuals as individuals, they share their lack of satisfaction. Sade puts these words into the mouth of the most lucid and villainous character in his novel:

In my view, our happiness is complete but for one essential thing: the pleasure of comparison. That pleasure can arise only from seeing the wretched, and we do not see them here. It is the sight of the man who does not enjoy what I have and who suffers that gives rise to the charms of being able to say: 'I am therefore happier than he is.' Wherever men are equal and wherever those differences do not exist, happiness can never exist. It is the story of a man who knows the value of health only when he has been ill.[15]

Sade might have added, with reference to his own personal history, that no one knows more about freedom than a prisoner. All this is reminiscent of the quasi-social psychology expounded by Spinoza in Part Three of his *Ethics* and of his principle of 'the imitation of emotions'. In both Spinoza and Sade, the establishment of a social bond is articulated with the process of the construction of the individual psyche, as the individual competes with himself in accordance with the same logic that brings him into conflict with others.

This implies that, insofar as it desires anything, nature desires inequality. The loathsome Durcet once again makes the point:

Offering the unfortunate any relief is a real crime against the order of nature. That nature has made individuals unequal proves that this discordance is pleasing to her, as she has established it and wills it in terms of both fortune and strength. And since it is permissible for the weak man to remedy inequality through theft, it is equally permissible for the strong man to reestablish it by refusing the weak his help. The universe would not survive for an instant if all beings resembled one another exactly; it is their dissimilarity that gives rise to the order that preserves and governs all. We must therefore take great care not to disturb it.[16]

When he speaks of what nature 'wills' and of what 'is pleasing to her', Sade seems to restore to it a sort of finality. If, however, there is such a thing as a 'system of nature', to borrow a concept which can be found in both d'Holbach and La Mettrie, in Sade's view its unifying principle is a logic of discordance. This means that the system can never be realized in the form of a stable state. Being in perpetual turmoil and in permanent revolt against itself, nature's only 'system' is a refusal to be confined within any system that could define its good form once and for all and in any uniform way.

Nature, whose choices are always ambiguous, therefore must not grant definitive recognition to any manifestation of individual existence. Hence the long history of the misfortunes of virtue and the prosperities of vice, which demonstrates the extent to which

15 Ibid., p. 181.   16 Ibid., p. 237.

prosperity and misfortune are relative terms: in a world in which everything is a spectacle, in which beings exist only in terms of the spectacles they stage for themselves and for others, there is no absolute good to stand out against the backdrop of misfortune and crime. In one of the passages cited earlier, the bishop asks a deceptively innocent question: 'Would you therefore argue that real pleasure is to be found in the contemplation of the tears of those afflicted by misfortune?' His question triggers the following dialogue:

'Most certainly', said Durcet, 'Perhaps no pleasure is more sensual than the pleasure of which you speak.' 'What, without relieving them?' said the bishop, delighted to hear Durcet on a topic that was so much to the liking of all and which, as they well knew, he was capable of discussing in depth. 'What do you mean by "relieving"?' asked Durcet. 'The pleasure that I derive from comparing their state with mine would not exist if I relieved them. If I improved their wretched state, I would allow them to taste for a moment a happiness which, because it would liken them to me, would remove all the pleasure of comparison.' 'Indeed. In that case', said the duke, 'matters should be so arranged as to establish a difference essential to happiness ... What I am saying, is that we should make their situation worse.' 'There is no doubt about it', said Durcet, 'and that explains the infamies with which I have been reproached throughout my life.'[17]

Since pleasure exists only in comparative terms, a minimal difference — which Sade's didactic fiction transmutes into a maximal difference — must exist to create it. A difference must exist in relation to others, but it must also exist in relation to the self, to the other who exists in everyone, to the other that is the self. Without that difference, comparisons are impossible.[18]

17 Ibid., p. 181.
18 Sade uses the same argument to justify love between individuals of the same sex. In a relationship in which the subject is reflected in the other, individuals of the same sex provide an almost perfect image of one another which reveals their constitutional lack. Since pleasure is bound up with comparison, and therefore exists on the basis of a relationship of domination, the comparison between strength and weakness is heightened when it involves apparently similar beings whose compromised and sullied identity is reduplicated by being confronted with its double. As the bishop puts it: 'In terms of the evil which is almost always the real attraction of pleasure, the crime must seem greater when it involves a being who belongs completely to your species than with one who does not, and at that moment you have twice the pleasure' (ibid., p. 264). By 'possessing' the other, the individual is pursuing the narcissistic ideal of a perfect relationship with himself. The whole of Sade's political speculation is an extension or collective incarnation of this fantasy.

We therefore must not say, as is said too often, that the Sadean hero seeks evil for its own sake or in an absolute sense; or, rather, that he seeks it because he can never find it. He does evil as he might do good, because of the same natural inspiration. In a reality in which reference to the Other, in the sense of transcendence and exteriority, has been erased, communication between values, be they marked negatively or positively, is relative because they differ only in degree; there is no longer any clear-cut difference between vice and virtue. Behaviour that is recognized as 'good' takes its secret inspiration from the same spirit of competition and the same will to domination that is so unbearably obvious in criminal acts. Benevolence and ingratitude are equally hurtful to their victims:

'You will never see a man of wit and learning trying to win gratitude', said Durcet, 'Knowing that he will make enemies, he will never do so.' 'A man who does you a service is not trying to give you pleasure', interrupted the bishop. 'He wishes to feel superior because he is being kind to you. I wonder about the merits of such a project. In doing you a service, he is not saying: "I am doing you a service because I want to do a kindness." He is merely saying: "I am obliging you, in order to humiliate you and to feel superior to you."' 'These reflections prove,' said Durcet, 'that services rendered are abuses and that doing good is absurd. They say, however, that you do good for your own sake. That may be true of those whose souls are so petty as to indulge in those minor pleasures, but those who, like us, find them repugnant would be deceiving ourselves if we procured them.'[19]

Video meliora deterioraque sequor: being a secret vice, virtue is an illusion.

Sade exploits the resources of narrative fiction to adopt the viewpoint of his great villains, and his view of the social bond is so critical precisely because it is so excessive. In these subterranean depths, which are haunted by figures of a demented libertinage, individuals establish new relationships characteristic of a society based upon totally immanent organizational principles. This is an essentially natural society. When Sade has his immoral schoolteacher say that vice is 'better' than virtue, he does so for didactic reasons, to make his reader understand that a system of nature which has integrated all that is excluded from it and which is indifferent to differences, no longer makes any clear distinction between virtue and vice. Everything else is, as he puts it, a matter of organization and temperament. Those who have chosen the path of good have done so because it suited them, not

19 Ibid., p. 241.

in the sense that it was a free choice or the result of a personal initiative, but in the sense that it was an adjustment or orientation determined at the level of the most obscure forms of mental and bodily existence, at a level where the relationship between 'more' and 'less' is measured on an infinitisemal scale. From that point of view, Sade, an exact contemporary of Kant, does seem to be anything but the architect of a doctrine of ethical law. Being the thinker of disrespect, he takes the view that impulses always take precedence over motives, and that the outcome of the debate between the two is a matter of convenience. We can therefore speak of a Sadean immoralism, but it must not be interpreted as the opposite of morality or as a mere absence of morality. According to Sade, the life of the libertine inevitably involves the strict observance of certain rules, without which his pleasures would have no value.

Pleasure (What must I do?)

Sade is reputed to have elaborated a paradoxical ethics of liberation based upon the principle of unbridled licence. But this overlooks the fact that, even in the most excessive figures of his libertinage, Sade increases and classifies the constraints to which human existence must submit if it is to achieve maximum power. At the first level of constraint, there is the law of desire which governs power relations at a truly political level. At the ethical level, which concerns individual aspects of behaviour, there are rules of pleasure, the observance of which is a precondition for what Sade calls felicity. Here, desire loses the sovereignty it enjoys in the political realm; it becomes the object of severe constraints which impose essential limits upon it. Sade's entire ethic could be reduced to this elementary thesis: far from being the fulfilment of desire, pleasure stands in an essentially negative relationship to desire. Hence the prescription: if you wish to enjoy the greatest pleasures, first learn to master your desire.

According to Sade, orgasm [*jouissance*] is simply an organic spasm, or in other words a physiological reaction. When it reaches a certain degree of arousal, the 'machine' suddenly discharges the excess tension.[20] Pleasure wracks the body with its terrible discharges, and

20 '"How can anyone howl and scream as you do when you discharge?", said the duke to Curval ... "Who the devil were you with to make you scream like that? I have never seen discharges of such violence." "Good lord! Who are you to

makes one scream as though in pain; pleasure results simply from the fact of having a body, and of taking it to the extremes of its functional limitations. The happiness sought by the libertine is, then, exclusively physical and material. But does the materiality of pleasure mean that it can be obtained without reflection, unknowingly, and without any effort of will, or that it arises instinctively and irrationally? It is at this point that there intervene the rules that bind its bodily realization to certain rules.

The relationship between pleasure and desire is in fact anything but simple and immediate. The orgasm through which an organism experiences the perfection of its workings is immanent: it is purely a self-to-self relationship. With desire, in contrast, we see the re-appearance of a transcendence which takes the form of a relationship with the other: it requires the mediation of an external object, and is related to a vague awareness that the body is not self-sufficient within the limits that individuate it. From that point of view, desire divides what pleasure brings together. In that sense, nothing could be more alien to authentic pleasure than the order of desire, and that is why we must refuse absolutely to define pleasure as the satisfaction of desire; the spontaneous link between pleasure and desire must be broken. We must learn to play pleasure off against desire. Pleasure implies the complete negation of desire.

Listen to the Duc de Blangis's profession of faith:

There are many, many people who are attracted to evil only when their passion draws them to it; when they have recovered from their aberrations, their tranquil souls peacefully return to the path of virtue and, because their lives are a battleground for lapses and remorse, they end their lives without its being possible to say precisely what role they played on earth. Such beings must be unhappy; always hesitant, always indecisive, they spend every morning of their lives regretting what they did the previous evening. Quite confident that they will repent for the pleasures they are tasting, they tremble as they indulge in them, and so they become both virtuous in crime and

reproach me in this way, you who can be heard a league away? Those cries, my friends, are the result of the extreme sensitivity of the organization; the objects of our passions give such a jolt to the electric fluid that runs in our nerves, and the shock received by the animal spirits that compose that fluid is so great, that the whole machine is shaken by it, and one can no more hold back the cries occasioned by the terrible jolts of pleasure than one can hold back the powerful emotions of pain' (ibid., p. 292). This analysis derives from what J. Deprun calls an 'electrical materialism'; cf. his 'Sade et la philosophie biologique de son temps', *De Descartes au romantisme* (Paris: Vrin, 1987), pp. 133 ff.

criminal in virtue. Being sturdier, my character will never demean itself in that way. I never hesitate in my choices, and as I am always sure to find pleasure in the choice I make, remorse never blunts its attractions. Resolute in my principles because I developed firm principles in my earliest youth, I always act in accordance with them. They have taught me that virtue is an empty void; I hate it, and you will never see me returning to it. My principles have convinced me that vice alone allows man to experience the moral and physical vibration that is the source of the most deliciously sensual pleasures.[21]

To obey one's desires is to enter the path of uncertainty and unhappiness. Libertinage, in contrast, is a system of life which presupposes firm, if not rigid, principles. That is why Sade, in the text cited, describes pleasure as 'physical and moral enjoyment' and thus associates bodily sensations with clearly conceived ideas. Curval puts it more crudely: 'Sperm must never dictate or direct principles; principles must determine the way in which it is spent. And no matter whether one has an erection or not, the philosophy, which is independent of the passions, must always be the same.'[22] The search for pleasure at all cost is therefore the very antithesis of a passive surrender; it is a rigorous conquest, and makes all the power at the disposal of an individual organism serve the essential disorder of nature. True excesses are not the excesses to which one surrenders because it is easy to do so, or as the opportunity arises; they are pursued in cold blood by following the rules of something corresponding to an authentic philosophical ideal, even if it does reject everything that resembles an ideal. It requires one to assert and to perform everything in nature that signals an absence of ends, or in other words to kill God, even if one has to die of pleasure in order to do so.

To kill God is to annihilate desire by removing from the quest for pleasure anything that could be classified under the rubric of the desirable. As la Duclos, who is the woman storyteller for the first thirty days, explains, the logic of abjection corresponds to a deliberate rejection of transcendence:

How is it that there are people in the world whose hearts have been so hardened by libertinage, whose feelings of honour and delicacy have been so deadened that they are seen to take pleasure and enjoyment only from what degrades and demeans them? It is as though they could find their pleasure only in the midst of shame, as though it existed only in what brings them

21   *Les Cent Vingt Journées,* p. 26.   22   Ibid., p. 333.

closer to dishonour and infamy. When you hear what I am about to relate to you, and the different examples I am going to give you to prove my assertion, do not assume that it gives me any physical sensation; I know that physical sensations exist, but you can be quite sure that they exist only because of the powerful support given them by moral sensations, and that if you gave these people the same physical sensations without adding all that they derive from the moral sensations, you would not succeed in moving them.[23]

Desire is facile and weak; pleasure requires strength and implies difficulty because it is also a form of thought (evil thoughts). Precisely because it is useless and not desirable, murder is the exemplary form of a deliberate action that has nothing to do with external attractions. As we can see, a theory of the *acte gratuit* could already be found in Sade.

Pleasure is therefore not simply a given; it too is the fruit of asceticism and work. Sade places enormous emphasis on the fact that there is no such thing as spontaneous immorality, that immorality is bound up with education and with the gradual training that 'immoral schoolteachers' both give their 'pupils' and dispense to themselves.[24] The gradual cycle of depravity and aberrations leads the libertine further and further in his defiance of the divine law, so far that it becomes impossible for him to reverse the process and return to his starting point:

'Once a man has been degraded and demeaned by his excesses, his soul takes on a vicious cast, and nothing can change it. Everything that would have a disagreeable effect on a soul that has been trained differently is meta-morphosed into pleasure and, from that moment onwards, anything that recalls the new stage one has reached.' 'What progress one must have made in vice to reach that point!' said the bishop. 'Indeed', said Curval.[25]

Once he has experienced the practices of a perverse orthopaedics that goes against his own nature, the libertine can enjoy the pure form of his actions, which are now freed from the charms lent them by his desire.

Sade is a *moraliste*, almost in the classical sense of the term, in that, far from attempting to seduce, he underlines the most repulsive aspects of libertinage:

23 Ibid., p. 294.
24 There is therefore no aesthetic without a didactics. The precept is illustrated by Sade's reminder to himself (p. 450): 'On the whole, have morality discussed over supper.'   25 Ibid., p. 298.

One tires of simple pleasures. The imagination becomes frustrated. The pettiness of our resources, the weakness of our faculties and the corruption of our spirit lead us to commit abominations ... It is with the things that nature and crime have dishonoured and blemished, with the dirtiest, most disgusting objects, that our two ecstatic rakes will taste the most delicious pleasures ... Now you tell me what a man is.[26]

The aberrations of pleasure are the conquests of a perverse will, and they push the individual, not beyond himself as though he were in search of an inverted transcendence, but to the very limits of his organism, and once he has reached them, he can deploy the full autonomy of his power. His excesses are a denial of all that is agreeable, and they make him scream with pleasure.

We are now in a position to elucidate the dichotomy between pleasure and desire. Being a spontaneous form of human behaviour, desire is a blind quest for the satisfactions bound up with the possession of objects; seeking and obtaining those objects is a matter of chance encounters. Being something that is systematically conquered and managed, pleasure represents a break with those facile primal interests. That is why it is immanently defined in terms of self-enjoyment and the pursuit of an external object:

The duke attempted to argue at supper that, if happiness lay in the full satisfaction of all the pleasures of the senses, it would be difficult to be happier than they were. 'That is no way for a libertine to argue', said Durcet. 'And how is it that you can be happy, once you can be satisfied at any moment? Happiness does not lie in pleasure, but in desire, in breaking the restrictions placed upon desire. How can I find that here, where I have only to wish in order to be satisfied? I swear', he said, 'that, since I have been here, my sperm has never once flowed for the objects that are here; it has been spilled only for the objects that are not here.'[27]

Torn between pleasure and desire, the libertine, far from trying to reconcile the two, speculates on their division; rather than helping him to satisfy his every desire, his pleasure reveals the elements in desire that must remain perpetually unsatisfied. After listening to Durcet, who is a 'real' criminal because he is a thinking criminal who knows the truth about crime, the Duc de Blangis immediately draws this conclusion: 'I am perfectly sure that it is not the object of libertinage that inspires us, but the idea of evil, and that it is therefore evil alone that gives us erections and not the object; if that object could not make

26 Ibid., pp. 151–2.   27 Ibid., p. 181.

us do evil, it would not give us erections.'[28] The libertine is executioner of his own desire, and his bliss is free of any attachment to useless objects.

True pleasures are, therefore, theoretical. Let us listen for one last time to the terrible Durcet: 'I have always been able to imagine a thousand times more things than I have done, and I have always complained about nature, which, whilst giving me the desire to outrage her, has always denied me the means to do so.'[29] One could not find a better way of saying that pleasure is a form which functions, quite independently of the means of its fulfilment, as an imperative.[30] Ideas precede actions: this rule means that we have to look at a new and final order of constraint, which is neither political nor ethical, but truly rhetorical and bound up with the principle of narrative that allows events to be described in their absence. At this point, speculation about libertinage becomes literature.

Narrative (What can I know?)

The entreaty made by the Marquise de Sade to her husband when he was incarcerated in Vincennes, and when he was embarking upon what was to become a literary career is well known:

Restrain your writing, I beg you, as it does you infinite wrong; and make reparation for it by persevering in the honest way of thinking that is so in keeping with your deepest feelings, and above all do not write and do not tell all the aberrations your mind suggests to you, and by which they want at all cost to judge you.[31]

If Sade had followed this advice and if he had succeeded in restraining his writings, if not in mending his ways, would there be any reason to remember him today? Does he not have the reputation of being a martyr to speech set free? Did he not, in an unbridled narrative, defy and overcome the most powerful taboos? Did he not try to say everything, and above all the things that must not be said at any cost?

Sade's work is of course based upon the hypothesis that it must be possible to say everything. And by expressing the demand for a total

---

28 Ibid., p. 182.   29 Ibid., p. 183.

30 Deprun speaks of Sade's 'categorical imperative to murder' in his 'La Mettrie et l'immoralisme sadien', *De Descartes au romantisme*, p. 129.

31 Letter of 6 August 1782, cited in Gilbert Lely, *Vie du marquis de Sade* (Paris: Gallimard, 1957), vol. 2, p. 214.

revelation which seems to find its ideal locus in literary discourse, Sade seems to have gone to the very limits of that discourse, to the impossible point where the infinite openness of representation gives way to its closure. But when he adopted this discourse of closure, did he not in fact 'restrain' his writing by confining it within an autonomous and exclusive order? Is not his situation – that of a prisoner who is condemned to say the things he can no longer do – a necessary and adequate image of that order? It is at this point that the utopia, or literally the fiction, of an unbridled discourse takes on its most forceful meaning, and it is a rhetorical or poetic meaning. Going beyond the political or ethical interpretations outlined earlier, it exhibits the constraints specific to speech, the finitude which condemns it to evoking things in their absence or even, and this is the Sadean idea *par excellence* that lies at the heart of his conception of literature, to suppressing them, to 'killing' them in order to be able to speak them.

Sade seems to have given a sort of ironic answer to his wife's advice. In the text of the *Cent Vingt Journées* itself, he offers this justification for certain restrictions which he claims to have imposed on his narrative:

Then the bishop stood up, spoke softly to Durcet, who said 'That's it', and the bishop passed it on to Curval who said, 'Yes, indeed', and then to the duke who exclaimed: 'Oh fuck, I would never have thought of that!' As these gentlemen did not explain any further, it was not possible for us to know what they meant. And even if we did know, we think that we would do well to keep it veiled for modesty's sake, for there are many things that should be no more than hinted at; prudent circumspection demands it, and one does encounter chaste ears.[32]

This banter contains, in parodic form, a grain of truth. For if we read Sade's text carefully and attentively, it teaches us a lesson. It is not

32 *Les Cent Vingt Journées* p. 276. To the amusement of the reader who is intrigued by this unexpected eulogy of censorship, the mystification becomes greater: 'Ultimately and, whatever anyone may say, everyone has his soul to save. And what punishment, in this world and in the next, does not befit one who, without any moderation, takes pleasure, for example, in divulging all the caprices, all the tastes and all the secret horrors to which men are subject in the fires of their imaginations? To do so would be to reveal secrets that should be buried for the greater good of humanity ... And God, who sees into the depths of our hearts, the mighty God who created heaven and earth, and who must judge us one day, knows that we do not wish to hear him reproaching us for such crimes' (ibid.). Such was Sade's concern with saving his soul, and ours!

possible – and here the impossible takes the place of the forbidden – to do everything or even to say everything, or at least not directly in the clear form of a naked revelation which refers immediately to the reality of what it is stating. One cannot do everything because, if the disorder of pleasure is to come about, pleasures must be subject to rules which impose a sort of moderation on their immoderation. Nor, as we shall see, can one say everything, in the sense that one cannot describe things as they are, as they might be, or as one does in reality. At this point, the poetic principle of narration intervenes alongside the political law of desire and the ethical rules of pleasure.

In order truly to understand this principle, we must examine Sade's attempt to reconcile pleasure and knowledge. In a sense, he equates the fact of knowing one's pleasure with the fact of being satisfied with knowing it. We can call this the prisoner's equation; although he is unable to realize his pleasures, the prisoner can still know them and make them known by relating them or relating them to himself, and he can thus establish a strict correlation between an aesthetic and a didactics. As a result of this principle, Sade can give his text the character of an experimental narrative, and can attempt to use the resources of fiction to exhaust all possibilities. His project then simultaneously takes on an anthropological significance (knowledge) and an artistic value (pleasure).[33] This explains Sade's attempt to reveal

33 Sade later generalized and commented on this idea in the following terms: 'It was Richardson and Fielding who taught us that only the profound study of the human heart, that veritable labyrinth of nature, can inspire the novelist, whose work must show us man, not only as he is – that is the duty of the historian – but as he can be, as he can be as a result of the modifications of vice and all the tremors of the passions' (*Idées sur les romans*, 1800). One could not hope for a clearer indication that the task of the novelist, unlike that of the historian who sticks to the facts, is to invent imaginary situations or structures that go beyond the domain of experience in order to extend our knowledge. The writer thus uncovers a profound and essential truth which never reveals itself in the bright daylight of reality: the hidden truth of man, that denatured nature which manifests itself in the totality of his aberrations. We find here, reinterpreted in a new context, a distinction which had already been made by Aristotle: 'The difference between the historian and the poet is not that the one writes in prose and the other in verse; the work of Herodotus might be put into verse, and in this metrical form it would be no less a kind of history than it is without metre. The difference is that the one tells of what has happened, the other of the kinds of things that might happen. For this reason poetry is something more philosophical and worthy of serious attention than history; for while poetry is concerned with universal truths, history treats of particular facts' (Aristotle, 'On

everything about man by using the device of a rule-governed narrative to catalogue all the aberrations of which man is capable.[34] For such a project to succeed, he must, and this is a precondition which Sade constantly stresses, 'put some order into these matters', or in other words construct a classificatory exposition which can provide the progressive dynamics required for the realization of this synthesis. Sade's text therefore has to conform to the requirements of a classificatory rhetoric whose forms make it possible to control the gradual expansion of a natural energy so as to maximize its yield. Now the energy in question is also the energy of the narrative, whose unfolding coincides with an increased pleasure. Unlike a flatly objective account, Sade's narrative stimulates pleasure rather than describing pleasure.[35] In a sense, the act of narration becomes an event because it establishes a performative relationship between words and actions.

The combinatory mania, which in Sade's case is associated with numerical obsessions that have often been analysed, is related to the didactic principle that governs his whole undertaking: a methodical analysis of pleasures which can unveil the secrets of the human machine's organization. The *Cent Vingt Journées*, for instance, is systematically articulated so as to move from a description of the 'one hundred and fifty simple passions' to the 'one hundred and fifty composite passions' and finally the 'one hundred and fifty murderous passions' with which the cycle should have ended for lack of combatants, so to speak, and for lack of anything else to recount. Only the first series in this tetralogy was completed by Sade. The project is not unreminiscent of the order recommended by Condillac for a systematic account of the sensations. According to this paradigm, which was dominant throughout the second half of the eighteenth century, the mastery of affect, like that of thought (not that there is any real distinction between the two), depends upon a composite principle and gradually moves from simple to complex. In Sade, this

the Art of Poetry' in Aristotle, Horace, Longinus, *Classical Literary Criticism*, tr. T. S. Dorsch, Harmondsworth: Penguin, 1965, pp. 43–4).

34 This synthetic or totalizing vocation suggests an encyclopedic ideal. The company in Silling Castle are in a sense the Bouvard and Pécuchet of debauchery; like Flaubert's sad characters, they share the same heroic and ludicrous vocation for exhaustiveness. In its way, it is a search for the absolute.

35 Barthes analyses this 'erotic code' very well in his *Sade, Fourier, Loyola* (Paris: Seuil, 1971), pp. 32f and pp. 165–6.

principle structures a systematic narrative in which every element is assigned a place by the set to which it belongs. In other texts such as *La Philosophie dans le boudoir,* Condillac's model seems to be transposed directly: the statue that is endowed with one and then another of the sensations which, when combined, will eventually awaken its intelligence, becomes a pupil, who is assumed to be completely innocent to start with and who is then educated and trained to follow a sort of curriculum in which increasingly complex elements of pleasure and knowledge constantly alternate in an overtly pedagogic manner. The same principle also gives Sade's work a clinical aspect, though this is neither its sole nor its most important aspect; it establishes a reasoned aetiology of human aberrations in order to moderate their immoderation.

This didactic principle is not, however, applied independently of the aesthetic principle; classifying pleasures means increasing their number by heightening the arousal that accompanies their gradual identification. Sade contrasts the immediacy of unregulated desire, which wants everything at once, with the need to graduate pleasure in accordance with the very logic of excess that governs its expansion. 'There is a proverb … which claims that eating whets the appetite. Crude though it may be, the proverb has a very general meaning: it means that by dint of committing horrors, one desires new horror, that the more horrors one commits, the more one desires to commit. That was the story of our insatiable libertines.'[36] The fact that the possible (what one might do) is permanently in excess of the real (what one is doing at the moment) establishes an inextricable relationship between desire and fiction, and it takes the form of an ever-increasing depravity. We constantly do a little more so as to wish to go still further. This gradation cannot, however, be achieved spontaneously. It requires a control mechanism to ensure the deferral function that exacerbates the conflict between desire (the possible) and pleasure (the real). The rules that the partners impose upon themselves in *Les Cent Vingt Journées* play precisely that role; they constantly defer the execution of their projects until they can be formally fitted into the overall configuration that gives them their interest and value by rationalizing them. The formalization of pleasure expresses a specific intentionality: by arranging its manifestations in an infinitely linear series, it both heightens pleasure and makes it last because it keeps

---

36 *Les Cent Vingt Journées,* p. 342.

open the possibility of future manifestations rather than consigning them to the immediacy of an illusory satisfaction. 'We must be sensible. If we wait for our pleasures, we will make them more delicious. Be patient, and you will see that everything comes in time.'[37]

Everything comes in time. 'Everything' means the abyss of destruction and nothingness: the final extermination of the victims of pleasure is the dark side of the human ideal of happiness, and fiction makes it visible or readable. In death, the human essence simultaneously reaches its limits and its truth. This is where the rational catalogue of pleasures leads, and the expectation of this moment governs its deadly organization. The ceremony is basically a narrative; the self-imposed patience of the executioner is also the self-imposed patience of the writer, and he therefore requires it of his reader too. The criminal apotheosis in which pleasure takes the pure form of the destruction of its object should in theory coincide with the end of the narrative. Is not the narrative complete when there is nothing else to tell, when the story is 'finished'? Nothing to say, and nothing to desire: the ritual of narration punctuates the stages leading up to this deadly conclusion. The restraints imposed upon the actions of Sade's characters simultaneously determine the way in which they are recounted; both the facts and the discourse that relates them depend upon the same asceticism.

This explains the crucial role that devolves upon the women storytellers in the dramaturgy of the *Cent Vingt Journées*: its unfolding, which is codified by a diagrammatic calendar corresponding to an analytic table of the perversions, permits abominable acts to be committed. When they are all committed, all human possibilities will have been exhausted, provided that they are committed only when meticulously classified stories have been told. The stories represent the acts even before they can be committed. This arrangement reduces

37 Ibid., p. 308. The draft for Part Three, which was never actually written, illustrates this principle by revealing, thanks to its very schematism, its restrictive aspects: 'On the same evening, Curval deflowers Augustine anally, even though she is the wife of a duke. Sufferings she endures. Afterwards, Curval flies into a rage with her; he plots with the duke to take her down into the cellar that very evening, and they tell Durcet that, if they are permitted to do so, they will allow him to dispatch Adelaide immediately too. But the bishop harangues them and persuades them to wait, in the interest of pleasure. Curval and the duke therefore content themselves with vigorously whipping Augustine in each other's arms' (ibid., p. 402).

torture to the mode of its enunciation: words come before actions and, at least provisionally, take their place. '"Silence, gentlemen, silence," said the duke, "we are here to listen and not to act".'[38] In Sade's view, the 'singular pleasures' that define true libertinage are the pleasures of a well-ordered narrative: we know that the theatre, which collapses pleasure into representation in accordance with the 'as if' principle, was his main lifelong obsession.[39]

The rule of order appears to be reduplicated here: just as it makes the exposition of the composite passions follow that of the simple passions, it ensures that, as the exposition alternates between words and deeds, the passions are represented before they are indulged. Sade's text therefore depicts the storytellers' listeners striving, like attentive pupils, to give an actual content to the scenes that have just been described to them. A cathartic pleasure accompanies the practices of this inverted mimesis in which the real appears to be subordinate to its representation. The real reflects, so to speak, its representation, rather than preceding it and then being projected onto it. It is as though the referent were no more than the shadow cast by its image, as though the image gave it the right to accede to an effective existence in the very special conditions of an 'acting out' that seems to generate reality out of fiction. Sade thus elaborates a whole rhetoric of the simulacrum, and exploits it to the very end. La Duclos, who is the first of the storytellers, is, for example, given the task of recounting

38 Ibid., p. 195.
39 'True libertines are agreed that the sensations communicated by the organ of hearing are the most flattering and create the most vivid impressions. Our four rogues, who wanted their hearts to be as deeply and as fully imbued with voluptuousness as possible, had therefore dreamed up a rather curious arrangement. Having surrounded themselves with all that could best satisfy the other senses with lewdness, they arranged for stories to be told in these circumstances. All the aberrations of debauchery were recounted in the greatest detail and in order: all its branches, all its offshoots, or, to use the language of libertinage, all the passions. One cannot imagine the degree to which man can vary them once his imagination has been stimulated. The differences between them – and they are excessive in all their other manias and all their other tastes – are even greater still in this domain, and anyone who could record those differences in detail might perhaps write one of the finest, and perhaps one of the most interesting, works on morals that one could hope to see. The initial task was therefore to find subjects capable of describing all these excesses, of analysing them, of analysing and expanding them, of graduating them and of using them to add interest to a narrative. Such, then, was the decision that was taken' (ibid., p. 45). Combining instruction with pleasure; once again, aesthetics and didactics merge.

stories about characters who are in the main content to mime, as though on stage, certain criminal deeds. It is only in later stories, told by the last story-tellers, that the same deeds will actually be committed. The powers of literature: the fact of saying things is assumed to trigger a process that will eventually lead to their realization.

The sequence that places speech before action also punctuates, in theory, the rhythm of the 'days'. Each day is divided into periods devoted to speech (the stories), and periods in which theoretical expositions are followed by practical exercises in accordance with a procedure that closely associates pedagogy and libertinage. The same narrative rule governs the organization of Sade's text at the level of its writing. The author of the *Cent Vingt Journées* himself assumes the position of a storyteller who is also the first person to listen to or read his text. He too must therefore be careful to respect the order he has imposed on his narrative; he must follow its sequence and give discourse precedence over the acts it relates. This concern appears quite explicitly in the working notes Sade wrote in the margins of his manuscript. They contain prescriptions that apply to author and characters alike. 'Mistakes I have made. – I have revealed too much about that business in the closets at the beginning; that should not be described until after the stories that talk about it. – Too much talk of active and passive sodomy; cast a veil over it until the stories talk about it.'[40] Insofar as it is the story of the stories, this story eventually coincides with its object; before real acts are recounted, the way in which they are related must be acted out. Before it is acted out, another story is told about telling stories; its subject-matter is the second story. In precisely the same way, the exposition of the simple passions must come before that of the composite passions, and gestures are simulated before they are performed. Hence the author's self-criticisms: 'Tone down the first part greatly; everything is revealed too soon. It cannot be too weak or too veiled. Above all, do not make the four friends say anything that has already been recounted. You have been careless about that.'[41] Literature gives pleasure because it

40   Ibid., p. 363.
41   Ibid., p. 450. It is noteworthy that, in these marginal notes, Sade addresses himself as *vous*, as though he were someone else, whereas, throughout his narration, he constantly addresses his reader as *tu*. The stance he adopts with respect to himself as author is governed by the respective moods of the characters he has created. When Sade criticizes himself for having said too much,

too exists thanks to the retention of its object, because it delays its revelations as long as possible.

There are, however, exceptions to all rules, and the main purpose of a set of rules is to record their non-observance. The author is aware of the danger of being carried away and missing out stages instead of 'casting a veil' over the early parts of his narrative so as to modulate its progression. He is equally attentive to the aberrations which, in similar fashion, disrupt the actions of his characters despite their self-imposed taboos. Not only does Sade's text report these inevitable transgressions; it seems to take pleasure in transgression as often as possible. It constantly finds opportunities to recall and stress its principle of retention, but that principle appears to apply at the level of speech rather than action:

'I want to do so many things.' 'What things?' said Durcet, with Antinoüs shitting in his mouth. 'What things?', said the duke. 'A minor infamy in which I must indulge.' As we went into the far closet with Augustine, Zelamir, Cuidon, Duclos, Desgranges and Hercule, we heard after a moment the screams and oaths that proved that the duke had relieved both his brain and his balls. We do not really know what he did to Augustine but, despite his love for her, we saw her return in tears and with one finger bandaged. To our sorrow, we are still unable to explain all this, but it is clear that these gentlemen were secretly, and without exactly having permission to do so, indulging in things that had not been recounted to them, and that in doing so they were formally breaching the conventions they had established; but when a whole society commits the same sins, it usually forgives itself for them.[42]

In order to make space for these aberrations in, so to speak, the margins of the narrative space, the scenography of the *Cent Vingt Journées* therefore provides closets. The protagonists can repair to them in secret to commit deeds that cannot be talked about and must not be seen, but only on the express condition that nothing explicit is said about them. As the tension rises in the stories told by la Duclos, the duke, the bishop, Curval and Durcet make increasingly frequent

if not having done too much, we can almost hear the bishop scolding one of his accomplices for disrupting the order of the stories in his haste to have done with it. Long before Proust, Sade discovered that the referent of narrativity is not what is being related, but the very fact of relating it. An imprisoned narrator thus becomes an integral part of his narrative – so integral a part that he is completely absorbed into it and ceases to occupy the position of an individual. The apparent objectivity of the narration is therefore undermined and destroyed from within by this mirror construction.   42 Ibid., pp. 308–9.

visits to these mysterious recesses. Only screams and oaths can be heard through the curtains; they are the inarticulate echoes of deeds of which we know nothing and which are completely indefensible.

Sade's narrative is punctuated by feigned interruptions which evoke, in mocking tones, the normal hypocrisy of a society in which one can do anything, or almost anything, provided that nothing is said about it:

'Oh, anything you like', said the duke. 'But I want to add a clause,' said Curval, 'to the effect that everything is permitted.' 'Oh no', replied the duke. 'You know very well that there are things we have promised not to do before they are related to us. Being fucked is one of them; we were to be given a few examples of that passion in the correct order before that happened, and yet, as a result of your urgings, we have ignored the rule. There are many other special pleasures that we should also have forbidden ourselves until they were narrated to us, and which we tolerate, provided that they take place in our bedrooms and closets.'[43]

Forbidden acts are performed, so to speak, outside the text, on the limits of representation, in the semi-clandestinity imposed on them by an ironic litotes, litotes being the figure of discourse that contains and retains actions because it cannot eradicate their factual reality, which now has no importance.

It therefore takes great naivety to write: 'The Sadean monster — who is, let us not forget, a written monster — is presented as a realization of total literality: he is the man who says what he does and does what he says, and nothing else.'[44] In Sade there is, on the contrary, a permanent discrepancy between what is said and what is done: going to the limits of what can be said and to the limits of representation is in fact a way of revealing that discrepancy. Not only is the fact of 'representing' always inadequate to the reality that is its referent because, like the impossible object of desire, reality constantly eludes it; it is also self-inadequate. Its very order is undermined by gaps and symptoms of dysfunctionality that are inseparable from its internal dynamic. And all the disorder of the world erupts into it through these discursive gaps.

Far from illustrating an ideology of liberated speech whose infinite unfolding would ensure it a total mastery of its object, the narrative model perfected by Sade unmasks the constitutional finitude of a

43 Ibid., p. 260.
44 Philippe Sollers, 'Sade dans le texte' in *L'Ecriture et l'expérience des limites* (Paris: Seuil, Collection 'Points', 1971), p. 56.

discourse – our discourse – which can advance only by retreating and which feeds upon the expectations it creates. '"Patience, patience, monsignor", said la Duclos, allow my narrative to proceed in the order that you yourself demanded, and you shall see that we will come in time to the singular libertines of whom you speak."'[45] The whole art of the storyteller lies in her ability simultaneously to awaken and frustrate the listener's curiosity. '"But I will stop now; the limits you have prescribed me prevent me from saying more and la Desgranges will explain all that to you."'[46] Similarly, the task of the writer is to create an interrupted form of speech: 'Curval, whose anger had simply made him still more shameless in his cruelty, did things to his daughter that we cannot talk about yet.'[47] The expectations that are aroused in this way function as so many promises: 'The further we advance, the more we can enlighten the reader about certain facts that we were obliged to keep veiled at the beginning.'[48] But is the veil that was drawn over the beginning of the story ever really removed? '"Come and show me", said the duke. "I am madly fond of seeing traces of the brutality of monsieur my brother." I do not know what Aline showed him, as it has always been impossible for me to discover what went on in those infernal closets.'[49] The author plays at pretending not to know what he certainly does not have the right to say.

The prisoner's equation now comes into its own. Cut off from real pleasure, the prisoner has only simulacra. The equation claims in theory that saying is as good as doing, and can replace it. Yet at the same time it reveals and exhibits the limitations which, because they defer actions, are imposed upon discourses. Thanks to the free play of his literary fantasy, Sade can escape his prison of stone by building a new prison of words in which it is reality itself that is caught in the trap and confined by the limits forced upon it by sovereign speech. Now the relationship between that speech, which is completely self-

45 *Les Cent Vingt Journées*, p. 193.   46 Ibid., p. 220.
47 Ibid., p. 218. Cf. ibid., p. 171: 'We greatly regret that the order of our plan prevents us from painting these lecherous punishments here, but our readers must not hold that against us. Like us, they know that it is impossible for us to satisfy them for the moment; they may be confident that they will not miss anything as a result'; and ibid., p. 286: 'In the meantime, the duke and the bishop had not been wasting their time, but the way in which they had busied themselves being one of those over which circumstances oblige us to cast a veil, we beg our readers to accept that we draw the curtain and move immediately to the four stories that la Duclos still had to tell in order to complete her twenty-first evening.'   48 Ibid., p. 189.   49 Ibid., p. 315.

sufficient, and the reality it designates is essentially negative. It is no longer a mimetic relationship that produces the certainty of the illusion of the full and proximate presence of things. The criminal passion of discourse, which inspires the writer's every action, causes that presence to disappear. It literally kills it by subjecting it to rules.

By the same criterion, anyone who reads Sade's narrative is also put in the position of being a potential prisoner who is condemned to imagine things in their absence. Because of this identification, the narrative's addressee adopts the position of a prisoner telling himself stories and, at the same time, of a libertine who has stories told him. In its solitude, fiction is completely confined within its own order; it evokes possibilities, and at the same time actually makes their evocation subject to fictional constraints. It is this that gives it most of its interest and meaning. The order of discourse is therefore subjected to a carceral rhetoric, which Sade could elaborate only in prison. That rhetoric means that the writer is an eternal prisoner who is confined by the limits that restrict his utterances. Because he accepts the constitutional inadequacy of the form of its expression — which is also its precondition — he is condemned to life imprisonment. His imprisonment establishes a divorce between what is said at the level of fiction and what is done at the level of reality, and it cannot be transcended.

Narrative rhetoric therefore proves to be driven by an essential negativity. The artifices of a composite narrative transform the elements it sets in motion into parts of a mechanism which can only work effectively if it is terrifying. The combinatory is destructive at the level of both its effects and its principle. Ultimately, the asceticism of this deliberate narration reveals merely that things are absent from themselves, and not merely from the discourse that names them or claims to name them. The tactic of the deferred narrative seems to be modelled on *The Arabian Nights* where, in similar fashion, stories lead only to other stories as we wait for the inevitability of death. Telling stories is thus a funerary ritual which prepares us for death. In the text of the *Cent Vingt Journées* that has come down to us, only Part One, which is devoted to the simple passions illustrated by la Duclos's stories, is actually complete, and the three remaining parts exist only in the form of outlines. It is as though the growing abjection demanded by the progress of the narrative discourse as it moves from simple to complex and, as Sade put it, from weak to strong, resulted in an increasing schematism which, as it comes closer to the unspeakable, reduces the reality of its objects to the point where they can be identified by mere traces, before disappearing into abstraction. This is the death of narrative: it exists only because of a dark, blind spot which leads it on until the whole of reality is engulfed and annihilated.

Reading Sade's texts is an ordeal because they reveal, thanks to the resources of a truly literary experience, the final outcome of representation: this experience undoes all the spells of discourse, breaks down its truisms and teaches us there is nothing beyond words. At this extreme point, saying and doing may perhaps be as one, for the nothingness that emerges belongs to words and things alike, and lack of saying coincides with lack of being. No reality emerges unscathed from this ordeal; distanced from itself in a relationship that has ceased to be speculary, reality is no more than an empty stage haunted by ghosts of death, where the great criminals we are ascend to the pleasure of pure and empty speech.

9

Flaubert's non-realism

Flaubert found Spinoza 'staggering' and Comte 'too quaint'. He anticipated Mallarmé's vision of the writer's craft as a real intellectual experience which should simultaneously provide a lesson on literature and a lesson on philosophy which merged into a lesson on style.[1] This twofold lesson can be quite clearly read in the book on which he worked for twenty-five years before giving it what he deemed its definitive form: *The Temptation of Saint Antony*. If we read the various drafts of 1849, 1856 and 1874 in sequence, this reputed failure can now be read as an indefinite work in progress or as a book existing in different states. The first to surrender to 'the temptation' is the writer himself, who is embodied in the saint who serves as his double: both are obsessed by images and exhaust themselves in a vain attempt to capture an object which vanishes before their very eyes. Then what is literature talking about? About an absent object which is almost nothing and which is therefore irreducible to the full presence of a reality that can be accurately represented and reconstructed through a necessary synthesis of its reflections. Style is its only operator. Contrary to the usual interpretations, Flaubert's *oeuvre* is the antithesis of a 'realism'.

The logic of the imaginary

The *Temptation* recounts episodes in the life of a man besieged by images. We know that Flaubert was initially inspired to write his book by a picture: in a sense, Breughel the Younger's *Saint Antony*, which he saw in a gallery in Genoa, supplied the initial vision. The 'temptation' was originally something to be looked at, like the subject

---

1 With the exception of *The Temptation of St Antony*, and *Bouvard and Pécuchet*, Flaubert's texts are cited in the *Oeuvres complètes* (*OC*) (Paris: Club de l'honnête homme, 16 vols., 1971–5).

of a painting, and the book it inspired therefore takes the form of a sequence of visually connected 'pictures'. Flaubert turns Antony into a viewer who is being viewed. How can the fact of looking at images become the subject of a book? In order to understand that, we have to pay particular attention to the specifically bookish nature of the visions Flaubert attributes to his character. St Antony is not a spectator who, from his seat in the theatre, watches in amazement as a frightening series of 'scenes' appears and then disappears. He is, rather, like a reader sitting in a library. He is given a sequence of books, turns their pages, and carefully studies their illustrations, when he is not scribbling his own in the margins – not all the texts that are brought to him have plates which immediately explain the content to him.[2] The world is a book, or rather a collection of books. The images that pass before Antony's eyes are not subjective creations that took shape in the consciousness of a single individual, but a testimony to the accumulated traces of a culture which, in a sense, sums up all humanity's dreams and thoughts. The same encyclopedic project runs through the whole of Flaubert's *oeuvre*, and here it takes the form of an almost complete catalogue of the aberrations of the human mind based upon a comparative catalogue of its myths.[3] To adopt the formula Foucault suggests in this connection, we are dealing with 'a fantastic library'.

What gives these images, these things read and things seen, their disproportionately hallucinatory character? It is not so much the content they outline by giving it more or less definite contours, as the multiplication-effect produced by the very fact of recording them in the way that one entry follows another in a dictionary. The truly fantastic element in Antony's visions is not so much what they seem

2 The point is underlined by Michel Foucault in the study he devotes to Flaubert: 'The text contains evocations which seem to have a great oneiric charge: a great Diana of Ephesus, for example, with lions on her shoulders, fruits, flowers and stars crossed on her bosom, clusters of breasts, a girdle clasping her waist, with gryphons and bulls springing from it. But this "fantasy" can be found word for word and line for line in plate 88 in the last volume of Creuzer: you have only to trace the details of the engraving with your finger faithfully to conjure up Flaubert's very words', 'La Bibliothèque fantastique de Flaubert' in *Travail de Flaubert* (Paris: Seuil, collection 'Points', 1983), p. 105. (This study first appeared in French in *Cahiers Renaud-Barrault* in 1967.)

3 From this point of view, *Bouvard and Pécuchet* is a sequel to *The Temptation*. With the same absurd naivety as poor Antony, Bouvard and Pécuchet will pursue an identical quest for a solution to the insoluble problem of cultural alienation.

to reveal, as the cumulative process that absorbs them into the metamorphoses of a proliferating form. The essential technical problem Flaubert faced in writing his book was therefore not how to select and elaborate the content of each of the visions with which he besieges his character or how to translate it into images, but how to link the images. None of them has any specific value in itself; their meaning derives from their juxtaposition alone, in accordance with the very specific logic that governs their appearance and disappearance. What gives these images their evocative power?[4] It is the visual arrangement which makes them merge immediately into other images in which their apparent content is diffused and dilated as though they were pure illusions.

The visions conjured up change as they move: they are magnified and expand, and then break up and return to the shadows as they complete the cycle of their transformations. We can speak here of an imaginary transformism that simultaneously generates a specifically literary accumulation-effect and delivers a speculative message. The dynamics of these images, which govern a whole system of writing and provoke a specific reading-effect, also convey a doctrine of symbolism applicable to both the raw material worked by the writer and the form he imprints on it. As he revised and reworked his text, Flaubert gave more and more importance to the catalogue of mythologies, which are themselves described in terms of a cycle of incessant transformations. They eventually become the book's main theme. Hence the grand parade of Gods, which is a parodic reduplication of the parade of Christian heresies. Now behind this display, there lies, at an implicit level, a syncretic and comparativist conception of religion which might be briefly summarized as follows: like the images that illustrate them, all religions convey the same content, which they reveal in infinitely varied forms, just as facets mirror and reflect one another to infinity.

---

4 A 'stage direction' at the end of the first tableau brings out this technique particularly clearly: 'Objects are meanwhile transformed. At the edge of the cliff the old palm tree with its tuft of yellow leaves becomes the torso of a woman, leaning over the abyss, her long hair floating ... These images occur swiftly, percussively, showing up against the night like scarlet paint on ebony. They gather speed. They wheel past at a dizzy pace. At other times they halt and gradually fade, or merge; or else they fly away, and others instantly appear' (Gustave Flaubert, *The Temptation of St Antony*, tr. Kitty Mrosovosky, Harmondsworth: Penguin, 1983, p. 72).

In a vital passage of the book, Flaubert goes back to the origins of this cycle by evoking the primitive idols which, because they are premature and incomplete, are primal representations of the very essence of the divine: at the beginning of Part v of the *Temptation*, he conjures up the crumbling and chipped images of the oldest gods as they limp along in procession.[5] The procession is headed by the Barbarians, 'holding their idols in their arms like big paralytic children,'[6] and taking great care not to drop them and break them. These crippled idols provide a surprising transcription of the concept of symbolism on which Hegel based his entire philosophy of religion. According to Hegel, the symbol is a premature and therefore incomplete revelation of a spiritual content which is no more than outlined in an ambiguous form because it is embodied in a tangible content. The symbol is the absolute projected into the order of exteriority, and it is therefore arbitrarily represented.[7] From this point of view, the symbol is inherently clumsy insofar as it functions on the

5 '(Just grazing the ground as they pass, he sees leaves, stones, shells, branches of trees, vague animal figures, and then what look like dropsical dwarfs; these are gods. He bursts out laughing) ... Antony: "How dumb one must be to worship all this!" Hilarion: "Oh, yes! extremely dumb." Now idols of all nations and all ages file past them, made of wood, of granite, of feathers, of sewn skins. The oldest ones, earlier than the Deluge, are hidden under seaweed which hangs down like a mane. A few, too tall for their bases, creak at the joints and break their backs as they walk. Others let sand trickle out through holes in their bellies. Antony and Hilarion are enormously amused. They split their sides laughing. Next follow sheep-shaped idols. They teeter on their knock-kneed legs, half-open their eyes and stammer like mutes: "Bah! bah! bah!" The more they approximate to human form, the more they irritate Antony. He hits out with his fists, kicks them, pitches into them. They become quite frightful – with tall plumes, bulging eye-balls, arms ending in claws, sharks' jaws. And before these gods, men are slaughtered on stone altars; others are mashed in vats, crushed under chariots, nailed up in trees. One in particular, all of red-hot iron and with bulls' horns, devours children. Antony: "The horror!" Hilarion: "But the gods always demand torture. Your own indeed wanted ... "' (ibid., pp. 163–4).
6 Ibid., p. 162.
7 See G. W. F. Hegel, *Introduction to the Lectures on the Philosophy of History*, tr. T. M. Knox and A. V. Miller (Oxford: The Clarendon Press, 1985), p. 151: 'Popular religions and mythologies are products of reason on its way to self-knowledge. Even if they seem still so poor, indeed silly, they nonetheless contain reason as one of their constituents: the instinct of rationality is fundamental in them'; and ibid., p. 158: 'The use of myth is generally an incapacity, an inability to get a grip on the form of thought. Further, we are not to suppose that the mythical form is to conceal the thought, the content; its aim is rather to express the thought, display it, unveil it, but this sort of expression is inadequate.'

basis of a contradiction. The contradiction is one between matter and spirit. The symbol transforms one into the other, spiritualizes matter and materializes spirit, and cannot resolve the tension that produced it.[8] Antony seems to be referring to an analogous conception when Flaubert has him respond to the uncertain image of the idols by saying: 'For matter to have so much power, it must contain a spirit.'[9] Mythologies jostle one another, topple over and collapse on top of one another and into one another, because they cannot achieve a definitively stable equilibrium, and exist on the indefinite edge of reality where inanimate things seem to take on a meaning and where, conversely, meaning becomes so rooted in things that it vanishes into them.

Are we right to read this as at least an indirect reference to Hegel? Yes, if we recall that both Hegel and Flaubert – and they were not alone in doing so – drew on a source which inspired many nineteenth-century writers: Creuzer's *Symbolik*. According to Foucault,[10] Antony spends his time contemplating its plates as he unfolds them in his fantastic library, and the same plates also lay on Flaubert's desk.[11] Now, unlike Hegel, Flaubert does not simply borrow images from

8 This contradiction is illustrated in exemplary fashion by statues of the Greek gods, as interpreted by Hegel in the *Lectures on the Philosophy of History*. At this stage, the activity of mind does not yet contain within itself the matter and the organ it needs to manifest itself. It requires a stimulus, and matter from nature. Mind is not yet the free spirituality that can determine itself; it is nature shaping itself into spirituality, an individuality of an ethical order. The Greek genius is the Greek artist who turns stone into a work of art. During this transformation, the stone does not simply remain stone: it takes on more than a mere external form and, going against its own nature, it becomes an expression of the spiritual. The artist, conversely, needs stone, colours and sensible forms in order to express his idea; without that element he can neither become conscious of the idea nor objectify it for others, because it cannot become an object in his thought. The same theme is developed at length in the *Aesthetics*.

9 *The Temptation of St Antony*, p. 163.   10 See note 2 above.

11 Georg Friedrich Creuzer's *Symbolik und Mythologie der alten Völker* was published in Leipzig in 1810–12. Creuzer taught philology at the University of Leipzig. Hegel also taught at the University and came to know Creuzer there; Creuzer's book was one of the main sources for his studies of art and religion. The Hellenist Guigniaut, the director of the Ecole Normale Supérieure, published a French adaptation of Creuzer's book under the title *Religions de l'antiquité considérées principalement dans leurs formes symboliques et mythologiques*. This version, which is a heavily reworked version of the original, and the plates depicting all the divinities in the history of the world, were a major source of inspiration for Nerval, Hugo and Lecomte de Lisle, as well as for Quinet and Flaubert.

Creuzer; he finds in his work an outline theory of religious symbolism and uses it as a model for his literary work. This theory is articulated around three main ideas: the affective revelation of the immanent meaning of things is shared by all peoples, and constitutes a sort of primitive pantheism that lies at the origin of all religious feeling. That revelation finds spontaneous expression in the form of the symbol, which combines the tangible and the intelligible, the finite and the infinite. Polytheism is merely a later reworking of this primal content, which is now dispersed through a series of diversified mythologies.[12] Different forms of religious thought, and the cycle of their transformations, are, in other words, either derived or abstracted from a common source. It is therefore legitimate to compare them. This also means that the symbolic function, which is based upon the primitive failure to distinguish between matter and spirit, is the first manifestation of human thought. It is present in the most archaic mythologies, and it subsequently gives a sort of meaning, or at least a necessity, to what appear to be their most irrational figures.

12 These three ideas figure in a passage from the introduction to Creuzer's book, which is cited here in Guigniaut's version (*Religions de l'antiquité*, Paris, 1825, vol. 1, p. 8): 'For people who worship the elements, natural phenomena are so many signs which nature uses to speak indistinctly to men in a language which only the educated can understand. This is not of course the philosophical dogma which sees the world as a great animal, still less the sublime doctrine of the world-spírit, but it is perhaps the seed that is planted deep in the human heart, and it will inevitably grow there. Hence the popular opinion that everything in the material world is alive, that everything is animate, that stone itself is not dead and lives in its own way. Soon, the imagination seizes hold of this crude pantheism, sorts it out, determines it and peoples the world with its gods; to be more accurate, every body, every phenomenon and every agent in the physical world becomes a god. And the philosophical doctrine of pantheism which, having become more abstract, comes down to the Greeks in the form of the axiom: "Everything is made in the image of the Divinity", is in principle resolved into their most ancient belief, of which polytheism was the first expression. And when metaphysical speculation attains its loftiest expression at the end of Antiquity, it posits a further axiom: "Nature uses symbols to produce invisible conceptions in visible forms, and the divinity sees fit to make manifest the truth of ideas in tangible images." Many centuries earlier, this great idea was already germinating in the imagination, which was both childish and creative, of the works of the old world.' Auguste Comte was probably not unaware of the work of Creuzer who, in his own way, had elaborated his own theory that fetichism, or primitive pantheism, is the basis of all religious philosophy. One could also make a study of the possible influence of Creuzer on Renan. If we pursued this line of descent still further, we would encounter Durkheim and Mauss, with their theory of symbolic man, which was mentioned in chapter 6 above.

Hegel and Flaubert do, however, draw very different, even contradictory, lessons from Creuzer's syncretic comparativism. Given that all religions express the same spiritual content but give it different outward forms, it must, according to Hegel, be possible to reduce them to the intrinsically rational principle around which they are organized, and to reconstruct a logic of the religious spirit which coincides with its evolution towards an increasingly intellectualized expression of that content. In the vision expounded by Flaubert, all religions merge, so to speak, into one another because they share and reciprocally exchange the same irrationality, the same age-old bestiality and stupidity, the same impotent aspiration towards the final reconciliation of spirit and things. Nothing positive can therefore emerge from their comparison but, unlike the progressive theory, the pessimism professed by Flaubert leads him to use the resources of art to unveil the inanity of the universal idolatry that is embodied in the senseless cult of images, the first and last temptation to beset the human spirit.[13]

13 Renan read Flaubert's *Temptation* with enthusiasm. Witness his letter of 8 September 1874 to Flaubert (initially published in the *Journal des débats* and then in *Feuilles détachées, Oeuvres complètes*, Paris: Calmann-Lévy, 1948, vol. 2, p. 1134ff). In his letter Renan writes: 'The fact that the sequence of humanity's dreams sometimes looks like a masquerade is no reason not to depict it. Poor humanity! The older I become, the more I love and admire it. The work it has done! For something that started out so low, it has produced so many great and charming things from its bosom. Man is such a wonderful animal! There is not one of his holy follies that does not have its touching side, which does not reveal our race and the minds it produces ... And it is not a vain attempt. The imagination has its philosophy. Ask Goethe and Darwin. Morphology is all, and all will be reduced to morphology.' We know that Renan initially came into contact with Hegelianism by reading Cousin's philosophy, and he seems to have expanded the visions described by Flaubert in *Caliban* (1878), the first of his philosophical dramas. At the end of Act 2, the magician Prospero uses spells to conjure up processions of religious illusions: 'The heavens split asunder. A vast aurora borealis shines from the zenith; a prodigious heap of gods, genies, nymphs and demi-gods rises and falls in rays of light. Then a storm sweeps all these divine beings away in an immense, swirling dance. Order is imperceptibly restored and eventually the gods appear sitting around a festive table' (*Oeuvres complètes*, Paris: Calmann-Lévy, 1949, vol. 3, p. 402). The dance which both reveals the divinities and then carries them off is the evolution of history, outside which they have no reality; today's gods take over from those of the past, before being supplanted by the gods of tomorrow. Prospero's vision ends with the gods of the future: 'To the left, there appear giants with enormous legs and arms made entirely of polished steel. Their joints move thanks to powerful eccentric articulations. On each joint, a can of oil, so placed that it will never spill, lubricates

A journey to the centre of matter

The repetitive character of Flaubert's book and the monotonous effect produced by the systematic accumulation of its successive tableaux have often been denounced. Those who criticize it on these grounds fail to see that the monotony is not empty repetition, but supplies a lesson which records a trajectory: the trajectory which traces all humanity's visions back to their effective content. Their content is a void. It is empty. It is nothing. The apparent outline of these multiple images therefore reveals a contingent determination which finds its truth in the moment of its abolition. From that point of view, we can say that the *Temptation* which, like an encyclopedia, is a book about everything, is also, like *Madame Bovary*, a book about nothing; it pronounces the discourse of the nothingness to which all things are reduced once the screen has been pierced, once the glittering and ludicrous mask of their visible form has been removed. At this level, literature plays the role of a veritable critique of representation.

The *Temptation* is constructed like a *Bildungsroman*. It tells the story of a naive man — for Antony believes that reality lies in what he sees, just as Bouvard and Pécuchet believe that the truth lies in books — who learns, as he reviews all his illusions, that his convictions have only the strength of his belief in them. In the final resort, blind faith is his only escape from the despair to which that revelation reduces him. We will look only at the final two stages in this itinerary in the definitive version of 1874: the exploration of infinity by science, which is implicitly described as the religion of modern times (Part VI) and the fantastic evocation of living matter (Part VII).

The journey of exploration which takes Antony through the

---

the articulation. Beneath them, there is an incandescent tube, which is their soul. They appear to eat coal. — These gods of steel hurl themselves upon the gods of flesh, break everything, kill and crush everything. Frightful disorder. ... The voice of mortals. "We thought that science meant peace, and that when the sun had no more gods and the earth had no kings, there would be no more fighting" — great outburst of laughter. Cold blast of wind. Darkness, chaos' (ibid., pp. 403–4). When the scientific spirit strays into a world of machines and is ruled by purely material interests, it inevitably gives birth to new mythologies which are even more barbaric than the old: the twilight of the gods is a prelude to the night of the spirit, rather than to the great day of its final realization. This means — and this is what Renan is really getting at, and here he is once more in agreement with Flaubert — that reason will never finally come to terms with its origins, with the primitive images from which it emerged and which it will always reflect.

immensity of worlds begins like an extraordinary voyage in the style of Jules Verne (*Five Weeks in a Balloon* was published in 1863, *From the Earth to the Moon* in 1865), but, as its object constantly recedes, it takes on the dimensions of a veritable metaphysical quest, the basic inspiration for which appears to have been borrowed from Spinoza. At the end of the quest, it is the vision of *Deus sive natura* that fills Antony's mind:

Antony: 'Ah! higher! higher still!... What is the purpose of all this?' The Devil: 'There is no purpose! How should God have a purpose? By what experience could he be taught, by what reflections determined? Before the beginning he would not have acted, and now he would be useless.'... Antony: 'Might matter... then... be part of God?' The Devil: 'Why not? How can you know where he ends?' Antony: 'On the contrary, I bow, I fall prostrate before his power!' The Devil: 'And you claim to move him! You speak to him, you even grace him with virtues — goodness, justice, mercy — instead of recognizing that he possesses every perfection. To conceive of something beyond, is to conceive of God beyond God, of Being beyond Being. Therefore he is the one Being, the one substance. If Substance could be divided, it would lose its nature, it would not be itself, God would no longer exist. He is therefore indivisible as well as infinite.'[14]

Just now, we saw Antony turning the pages of Creuzer's *Symbolik*; he is now consulting Spinoza's *Ethics* with even greater stupefaction, even though it has no illustrated plates for him to admire and copy.

Now, Antony is reading Spinoza over Hegel's shoulder. It was Hegel who supplied the despairing interpretation of 'substance' as *Abgrund*, the undetermined foundation which gives all things the absolute origin in which they merge. The Spinoza described in *The Science of Logic* and the *Lectures on the Philosophy of History* is the radical thinker of origins who seems to encapsulate all the philosophies of the East. Part VI of the *Temptation* ends in similar fashion. Antony's mind expands to such an extent that it becomes one with the whole.[15] The content of the revelation he is vouchsafed is, ultimately, negative,[16] and it is echoed by the Devil's suggestion that '"Perhaps there is

14 *The Temptation*, pp. 208–10.
15 Conversely, the simple Félicité (*Three Tales*) restricts her absolute to such an extent that it can be contained within the stuffed parrot into which she compresses all her dreams of a mystical beyond.
16 'Antony cannot see a thing. He feels faint. "An icy cold grips my very soul. I'm past the point of pain! It's like a death deeper than death. I'm spinning in vast darkness. It's inside me. My conscious self shatters under this dilating void"' (*The Temptation*, p. 212).

nothing".'[17] If the absolute is always and everywhere identical to itself, it must be nowhere, in the sense that it is nowhere in particular. When a finite reality is reintroduced into the absolute that supplies its principle it therefore loses its determinate character. In that sense, Hegel, following Kant, interprets Spinoza's thought as an 'acosmicism' that denies the worldly reality of things any consistency of their own and makes substantiality a property of the absolute alone. Being pure substance, the absolute, or the totality of things, exists beyond, or perhaps prior to, all determination. Hence the lesson: perhaps nothing exists, at least in any particular form.[18]

In the final version of the *Temptation*, this perception of the infinite world as an empty immensity results in a further vision, which is expounded in the seventh part of the book. It describes the fermentation of the primal matter which produced all forms of existence. It now seems that the movement of absorption, which

17 Ibid. Bouvard and Pécuchet, who are also in search of the absolute, will refer in their own way to this experience of the infinite: 'The sky was very high, and covered with stars; some shone in clusters, others in lines, or alone at long intervals. An area of luminous dust, going from north to south, split into two above their heads. Between these bright patches were great empty spaces, and the firmament looked like an azure sea, with archipelagoes and islands. "What a quantity!" cried Bouvard. "We can't see everything!" replied Pécuchet. "Behind the Milky Way are the nebulae; beyond the nebulae, still more stars; the nearest is 300 billion myriameters from us." He had often looked through the telescope in the Place Vendôme, and remembered the figures. "The sun is a million times bigger than the earth, Sirius twelve times bigger than the sun, comets are 34,000,000 leagues long!" "It's enough to drive one mad', said Bouvard"' (*Bouvard and Pécuchet*, tr. A. J. Krailsheimer, Harmondsworth: Penguin, 1976, p. 84). When they study Spinoza's philosophy, using a volume inherited from a member of the University who was exiled under the Empire and skipping the proofs, they experience the same anxiety, which is expressed in almost the same terms: 'Thus our world is only a point in the totality of things, and the universe is impenetrable to our knowledge, one portion of an infinity of universes giving out infinite modifications besides ours. Expansion envelops our universe, but is enveloped by God, who contains in his thought all possible universes, and his thought itself is enveloped in his substance. They felt as though they were in a balloon, at night, in icy cold, borne away in endless flight to a bottomless abyss, with nothing around them but the incomprehensible, the immobile, the eternal. It was too much for them. They gave up' (ibid., p. 205).
18 In 1861, or in other words at a time when Hegel was becoming unfashionable and when it was *de rigueur* everywhere to refer to him as a 'dead dog', as Marx puts it, Edmond Schérer published a long article on Hegel and Hegelianism in the *Revue des deux mondes* (subsequently reprinted in the collection *Mélanges d'histoire religieuse* published by Michel Lévy in 1864). This text represents a particularly important moment in the history of Hegelian studies in France. In this long study,

in which Schérer attempts to recapture the whole spirit of Hegelian philosophy, he draws a new parallel between Hegel and Spinoza, displacing Hegel's interpretation of Spinoza onto Spinoza himself. Schérer writes: 'Hegel states quite expressly that the absolute is stasis in movement; it is a movement which is stasis itself. Just as the ocean has no existence distinct from the waves that emerge from its bosom and then sink back into it, and just as time consists of a succession of moments which have already ceased to exist when their turn comes, so it is with the absolute. If we are to discover the final truth about things, we must contemplate them within the eternal current from which they emerge only when they have made way for other things; our gaze must fall on all the millions of individual existences in each of which the species is particularized; we must work backwards from law to law, to one supreme law, to the final word of what exists; what is revealed by this incessant production and destruction, from this succession, this sequence, is the rule governing all movement, the reason for those transformations, the link that connects them, the whole that they make up, the idea that is manifested in it ... that is the essence of things, that is the only reality, that is the absolute' (*Mélanges d'histoire religieuse*, pp. 323–4). The coincidence between absolute movement and absolute stasis results in a sort of nihilism. Schérer concludes his study thus: 'Hegel ... did not simply establish the law of contradiction; the contradiction of which he speaks is the principle behind a movement, and that movement is not merely the evolution of things; it is their content. In other words, nothing exists, or existence is mere becoming. Things or facts have only a fleeting reality, a reality which consists in their disappearance as well as their appearance, a reality which is produced only to be negated as soon as it has been asserted' (ibid., pp. 373–4). Hegel would obviously have rejected this interpretation of his thought, for it completely inverts the process by taking it back to its starting point and turning it into a doctrine of absolute foundations.

Schérer's text found a passionate, speechless and transfixed reader in Mallarmé, who was teaching in Tournon at this time. Perceiving this web of nothingness in a sort of mystical trance, he saw it as the fabric that constitutes the basis of all things, in which they renounce their limited identity and are destroyed by the very movement that realizes them. He made it the founding element of a literary experience: it then became clear that writing was the one gesture that restores to the world its shadowy nature, in which all beings must renounce their artificial existence in order to become once more that which they have never ceased to be: the nothingness from which they emerged and which constitutes their entire truth. Flaubert's prose and Mallarmé's poetry, which were written within a few years of each other, develop the same 'acosmicist' discourse, and both authors regard the aesthetic renunciation of the world and its illusions as the artistic gesture *par excellence*. The most surprising thing of all is the sight of a writer who is classified as 'realist' entering into this theoretical alliance with the most incisive doctrinaire 'symbolism' which is assumed to reduce all literature to a discourse on the meagre reality of things.

But Schérer found many other readers, notably Bouvard and Pécuchet, who no doubt take their inspiration from him when, to the great dismay of Chavignolle's parish priest, they expound the basic principles of Hegel's philosophy: '"We consider death in the individual, where it certainly is an evil, but relative to all things it is different. Do not separate mind and matter." "Yet, sir, before creation ..." "There was no creation. It always existed. Otherwise it would be a new

purified reality by emptying it of its determinate content, gives way to the opposite movement of a positive genesis which restores to things the fullness and intensity of their own life. As we shall see, however, the plasticity of the images of living matter and their ability to reproduce and to be constantly modified also bears witness to the facticity of the process of becoming, to the incessant flux of things that is the authentic form of their permanence.[19]

We can now understand why Flaubert opens Part VII with the duet between Death and Lust: these contrasting but inseparable figures express the flight into the abyss that is the movement of existence and life.[20] On reading these pages, one might think that Antony is contemplating and dreaming about a new volume that has been delivered to him, namely Schopenhauer's *The World as Will and Idea*, and that he is commenting on the famous appendices to Volume Two, which are devoted to the metaphysics of love and death.[21] The

being added to the divine thought, which is absurd." The priest rose, business called him elsewhere. "I flatter myself, I put him in his place!" said Pécuchet. "One word more! Since the existence of the world is only a continual passage from life to death, and from death to life, far from everything being, nothing is. But everything is becoming, do you understand?" "Yes, I understand, or rather no!" In the end idealism annoyed Bouvard' (*Bouvard and Pécuchet*, p. 214).

19 A preparatory 'scenario' for the *Temptation* (*OC*, vol. 12, appendix 12, p. 318) clearly shows that this vitalist and transformist discourse, which, as has already been indicated, derives from both Darwin and Haeckel, also derives directly from the acosmicism expounded in Part VI: 'The divine substance (God, the very essence), of which nature is one form, radiates in its extension and develops everything. Everything will be born of that, of relations of sympathy between the parts (through which the parts strive to be reunited). Just like the blood in our veins, the canals of the universal body irrigate one another and strive to unite. There are therefore no degrees, no difference (between good and evil), as the absolute is everywhere identical to itself.' Indifferent nature: the proliferation of existences expresses the uniformity of the substantial absolute which is both embodied in every existence and which simultaneously dissolves and disperses existences into an incessant flow of appearances.

20 'Death sniggers, Lust roars. They take each other by the waist and together sing: "I hasten the decay of matter!" "I help to scatter seeds." "You destroy, for my renewing!" "Make me more potent!" "Impregnate me where I rot!" Antony comments: "Death is then a mere illusion, a veil, masking in places the continuity of life" (*The Temptation*, p. 220). The same point is made in another preparatory scenario in which the echoes of Sade are obvious: 'Death and orgasm: it is all one. Nothingness and life, illusion and reality are identical' (recto of folio 99, *OC*, vol. 4, p. 315).

21 A French translation of these texts was published in the *Revue Germanique* in 1861, but it is true that it was accessible only to a limited audience of specialists. Was Flaubert aware of its existence?

inclusion of Buddha in the gallery of Gods in the final version of the *Temptation* can certainly be explained in terms of Schopenhauer's growing influence in France in the 1870s.[22] We know, however, from other sources that it was only after the publication of the *Temptation* that Flaubert became interested in Schopenhauer's philosophy, and that his reading of Schopenhauer, whose texts did not become widely available in French translation until after 1880, cannot have been a direct source of inspiration. A comparison of the two is not, however, totally devoid of interest. It allows us to understand the development of a would-be literary 'naturalism' – primarily in Zola and Maupassant, who saw themselves as Flaubert's heirs and who were also influenced by Schopenhauer. This naturalism, which goes against the very idea of a return to the 'real', as defined in its living, concrete fullness, would signal the same fascination with the formless and nothingness, and the philosophy of will did, in very simple (not to say simplistic) terms, supply its general themes. This approach was, in a word, designed to replace a literature of presence with a literature of absence. Whilst it claimed to perceive things and beings in terms of the contours that seemingly establish their identity, its real aim was to reveal the facticity of their content by disintegrating it.

Flaubert himself remained on the fringe of the decadent drift that was to mark intellectual developments in the 1880s. Whilst he had in a sense paved the way for it by establishing its framework of reference, he in fact saw his own undertaking in a different light. His *oeuvre*, which was elaborated as an act of protest against the cultural illusions that had developed out of the attempted political and social revolution

22 Flaubert published the *Temptation* in 1874, which also saw the publication of Th. Ribot's *La Philosophie de Schopenhauer* (Paris: Baillière), which reproduced numerous extracts from Schopenhauer, including (p. 83) this from 'The Metaphysics of Death' (Arthur Schopenhauer, *The World as Will and Idea*, tr. R. B. Haldane and J. Kemp, London: Kegan, Paul, Trench Trübner and Co, 1906, 5th edn, vol. 3, pp. 260–1): '"What!" it will be said, "the permanence of the mere dust, of the crude matter, is to be regarded as a continuance of our being?" "Oh! do you know this dust, then? Do you know what it is and what it can do? Learn to know it before you despise it. This matter which now lies there as dust and ashes will soon, dissolved in water, form itself as a crystal, will shine as metal, will then emit electric sparks, will by means of its galvanic intensity manifest a force which, decomposing the closest combinations, reduces earths to metals; nay, it will, of its own accord, form itself into plants and animals, and from its mysterious womb develops that life for the loss of which you, in your narrowness, are so painfully anxious.' Birth therefore always means rebirth, and the certainty of another death.

of the mid-century, was still dependent on the modes of thought it challenged, and its reaction against them presupposed, if not collusion and complicity, at least the possibility of an exchange or dialogue. Flaubert may look like an obsessional enemy of the spirit of 1848, but that is primarily because he supported it wholeheartedly and continued to identify with it even as he tried to shrug off its spell. From that point of view, the analogy between certain passages in the *Temptation* and Schopenhauer's ideas is more apparent than real. When Flaubert asserts that the absolute remains self-identical throughout all its natural expressions, he is thinking of something very different from Schopenhauer, in whose view the same 'will' manifests itself in all beings and explains the cycle of their appearance and disappearance. Schopenhauer depicts nature as a circle so as to indicate the repetitive character of its elements and its events, and to deny the possibility of progress and development. In his system, and it is this that makes it so fundamentally different from Hegel's, there is no mediation between the moments of the process to ensure the transformation and the transition from one to the next. For Schopenhauer, neither moment nor process exists. Defined in itself, will is made shapeless by the genres that make it aesthetically recognizable. It denies individual existences and relations between them any identity; they are merely artificial appearances with no content of their own. The revelation vouchsafed to Antony at the end of his journey of initiation is very different: he sees a flux of things that are worn out by their movement. All definitive forms are dissolved into a continuous cycle of metamorphoses and exchanges. This is why we find no trace of a doctrine of the eternal return in Flaubert, but only an assertion of pure becoming. Becoming is absolute because it does not relate to any *en soi* that could serve as an ultimate term of reference, as both its truth and its negation.

It would therefore no doubt be more profitable to compare the texts by Flaubert that we are discussing here with the theses of the German materialists who reformulated the materialist tradition on a completely new basis after 1850.[23] Like that of his successor Büchner, Moleschott's materialism is anything but a mechanical materialism, since it is based

23 Jacob Moleschott's *Der Kreislauf des Lebens* was published in 1852. Dr Cazelle's translation was published as *La Circulation de la vie* by Ballière in 1866. The translator's preface to the book, which was to have considerable impact in both Germany and France, spelled out (p. xv) what was at stake: 'It would be a grave mistake to take literally the expression *German* materialism because of the

upon the idea that matter was originally set in motion by the dynamic of the forces that shape it, multiplying its forms and preventing them from ever reaching a definitive state. This perpetually incomplete matter in motion is not merely a substantial support for those forces; it prefigures the vitalism which was to be the great scientific ideology of the final years of the nineteenth century. Matter itself is force, to borrow the title of Büchner's great book *Kraft und Stoff*, which was first published in 1856, and then translated into French in 1865.[24] More specifically, this materialism has nothing to do with an elemental materialism, and there is no room in it for the notion of the atom.[25]

It is quite understandable that Moleschott should have used the term *Kreislauf* (circulation) in the title of his book, which gave this materialist revival its initial impetus. In the system of unrestricted communication in which everything is interchangeable and exchangeable with everything else, apparently stable forms of existence have an effective value only because they are caught up in and swept along by an incessant movement. Through its intermediacy, they can 'trade' with one another; this is why they survive only because they are in permanent danger of becoming something else.[26] One might have

adjective. It was born of the breakdown of Hegel's syntheses, and its formulations still bear the mark of that great thinker's genius. It is still a pantheism in which the one substance that is the content of the world is known as Matter; it never perishes, and natural forces are no more than the modalities of its transformations. If we look at the almost religious respect with which the author of the *Kreislauf des Lebens* speaks of this "eternal" substance, which alone enjoys indestructibility in the midst of the destruction of all forms, of the source of all beings in which all beings are dissolved so that their elements can undertake new activities in new forms, it is clear that we are not dealing with La Mettrie's materialism.'

24   The date is that of the second edition, the first to be listed in the catalogue of the Bibliothèque Nationale.
25   In his *Le Matérialisme contemporain en Allemagne* (Paris: Ballière, 1864), the academic Paul Janet defends spiritualism by denouncing this materialism without matter, which he likens to a phenomenalism. He regards it as an attempt to reduce the world to its representation: 'What weakness and what ignorance to limit the real being of things to the fleeting appearances grasped by our senses, to make our imagination the measure of all things, to worship, as do these new materialists, not even the atom, which had at least a semblance of solidity, but some unknown quantity which has no name in any language and which we might term infinite dust' (p. ix). Hence the conclusion which, according to Janet, 'is repugnant to the mind': 'Matter vanishes and is dispersed' (ibid., p. 42).
26   In the third of the letters that make up his book, which is devoted to 'The Indestructibility of Matter', Moleschott writes (p. 26): 'Not even the smallest particle of matter is lost. Man's excretions feed plants. Plants transform air into immediate solid principles, and feed animals. Carnivores feed on herbivores; they

expected Moleschott's book to have been entitled 'The Circulation of Matter'. In choosing the formula 'The Circulation of Life', he was stressing the point that there is no clear distinction between matter, movement and life. Life is no more than the movement of matter, and matter is inseparable from the life which constantly carries it beyond its momentary realizations and never allows it to stabilize in any definitive way. Matter circulates, and it is in that sense that it is alive. Hence the images, which border on the hallucinatory, of a universe in perpetual effervescence, of a universe in which nothing is anything in particular because everything is becoming everything else.[27]

In Flaubert's text, this exchange, which has already been evoked by the dialogue between Death and Lust, also finds expression in the encounters with the Sphinx, an enigmatic and massive incarnation of the Unknown, and with the Chimera, an evanescent manifestation of Fantasy. And they in turn make way for the parade of monsters. Their composite and incomplete forms provide a sort of fearful and grotesque counterpart to the procession of heresies with which the text began: Astomi, Nisnas, the Blemmyes, the Pigmies, Sciapodes, Cyncephales, the Sadhazag, the Mantichoras, the Catoblepas, the Basilisk and the Griffin. These purely imaginary creatures, which seem to have been drawn by the hand of a Breughel or a Callot, in their turn make way for the appearance of various figures of natural existence. First come the beasts of the sea, 'round as wineskins, flat as blades, jagged as saws'. The dumbfounded Antony then sees the birth of living things which, as the genera and kingdoms of nature merge, seem to be extensions of one another. They seem to transmit the impetus that brings them into being:

> themselves fall prey to death and scatter new elements of life throughout the vegetable kingdom. This is what we call the exchange of matter. That is the right word, and we do not pronounce it without a feeling of respect. For just as trade is the soul of relations between men, so the eternal circulation of matter is the soul of the world.' 'Destruction provides a basis for construction; the movement will therefore not be interrupted, and it guarantees life. The immutability of matter, of its mass and its properties, and the reciprocal affinity between the elements, or in other words their tendency to combine because of their contrary properties, are the foundations on which the eternity of circulation rests' (p. 29).

27 Moleschott supports this theory with arguments borrowed from the specific domain of chemistry. Even though it gives an insight into the universal movement of things, his theory therefore inevitably reintroduces a rigid, and ultimately fixist, conception of materiality because of the chemical 'elements' that supply the final units of his analysis. Hence the limitations, and perhaps the internal contradictions, of his analysis.

Mosses and sea-wrack have sprouted. And all sorts of plants extend into branches, twist into gimlets, elongate into points, curve round into fans. Gourds look like breasts, lianas are interlaced like snakes ... Vegetable and animal can now no longer be distinguished. Polyparies looking like sycamores have arms on their boughs. Antony thinks he sees a caterpillar between two leaves; but a butterfly takes off. He is about to step on a pebble; a grey grasshopper leaps up. Insects resembling rose-petals adorn a bush; the remains of may-flies form a snowy layer on the ground. And then the plants become confused with the rocks. Stones are similar to brains, stalactites to nipples, iron flowers to tapestries ornate with figures. In fragments of ice he perceives efflorescences, imprints of shrubs and shells − so that he hardly knows whether these are the imprints of the things, or the things themselves. Diamonds gleam like eyes, minerals pulsate.[28]

Nature is like a single being which is constantly undergoing metamorphoses, and it is through that movement that it achieves its multiple unity.

Ernst Haeckel's *Naturlich Schöpfungeschichte* (1868) appeared in French translation (*Histoire de la création des êtres organisés d'après les lois naturelles*) in the same year as the definitive version of the *Temptation* (1874). It is prefaced by a famous text written by Goethe in 1780 which prefigures similar visions.[29] Haeckel's monism itself derives from a naturalistic and transformist reinterpretation of Darwin's doctrine which removes all scientificity from the idea of evolution, or at least so extends it as to make it a general interpretative schema midway between science and poetry, dream and reality. Haeckel's book is illustrated with sumptuous plates reproducing fantastically detailed engravings of rudimentary organic forms which, just like the monstrous figures of a mythology, look like the products of the imagination of a hallucinating God. It is conceivable that Flaubert's saint, who is an indefatigable reader, had now been shown this work and had begun to fantasize about its illustrations.

Haeckel's guiding principle is that all living beings are descended from common ancestors and can therefore be included in a single

---

28 *The Temptation of St Antony*, p. 231.
29 Goethe describes nature as surrounding us, as pressing in on us from all sides. We can neither escape her embrace nor penetrate her bosom. Without consulting us or warning us, nature sweeps us into her eternal dance, pursues her course and abandons us only when we are collapsing with fatigue. Nature is constantly creating new forms; what exists has never existed before. What once existed will exist no longer. Everything is new, but that does not prevent its being old.

genealogical tree in which all organic groups, from the simplest to the most complex, are related to one another.[30] Their genesis did not require any supernatural intervention, since it resulted from its intrinsic development and integrated into the realm of nature what seemed to be the most extraordinary productions. Hence the implicit lesson: it is nature itself that is the permanent miracle. The stupefying operations of archigony, ontogeny and plasmogeny, which were, according to Haeckel, the three forms of spontaneous generation, created *monere*, or in other words the simplest organisms imaginable. *Monere* are 'organisms without organs',[31] undifferentiated particles of living matter, and all the figures of 'natural creation' originated from them. Flaubert may later have become fascinated by Haeckel's book, which reproduces, in scientific terms and with the authority of science, the final vision of the *Temptation*, and may, so to speak, have been inspired by his own character. Flaubert did not, however, follow Haeckel. He preceded him, and it is as though he had, with the resources of his own culture, discovered his own equivalent to Haeckel's transformism, whose visionary power seemed boundless.

On the basis of the above references, it is possible to ascribe a meaning to Antony's final orison, with which the *Temptation* ends because, after this, there is nothing left to say:

'O happiness! happiness! I have seen the birth of life, I have seen the beginning of movement. The blood in my veins is beating so hard that it will burst them. I feel like flying, swimming, yelping, bellowing, howling. I'd like to have wings, a carapace, a rind, to breathe out smoke, wave my trunk, twist my body, divide myself up, to be inside everything, to drift away with odours, develop as plants do, flow like water, vibrate like sound, gleam like light, to curl myself up into every shape, to penetrate each atom, to get down to the depth of matter – to be matter.'[32]

It is at this point that the author's identification with his character produces its principal effect: the 'materialism' that is evoked here is primarily a literary materialism, a dematerialized materialism, or at

---

30 See Haeckel, *Histoire de la création des êtres organisés*, tr. Letourneau (Paris: Reinwald, 1874), p. 4: 'This doctrine claims that, despite their diversity, all organisms and all the species of plants and animals that have ever lived on earth and which still do so, are descended from a single ancestral form or a very small number of extremely simple ancestral forms and that, from that starting point, they evolved through a gradual metamorphosis.'
31 Ibid, 13 leçon, p. 303.   32 *The Temptation of St Antony*, p. 232.

least a materialism that has become unreal. For this materialism, matter can be seen only when it disperses and vanishes. By adhering to the multiple aspects of existence and by becoming matter, Flaubert's saint unveils the principle that creates them, the substance which circulates between them and through whose intermediacy they commune with one another. When read in Hegelian terms, Spinoza thus reveals the truth of Darwinism: the apparent reality of beings masks the one thing that is permanent: an elusive force which cannot be confined by any form.

To be matter: that boundless dream, that desperate wish for an absolute identification with a world apprehended in its self-immanence, is exhausted in the moment of its enunciation. To state the truth about nature and life by slipping into their visible forms so as to bring them back to life with words, is also to destroy them. Is it not in fact tantamount to suggesting that their reality can be captured in the moment of that recognition, or that it can no longer be dissociated from fiction? Once one has reached this point, one is forced to admit that the world exists only as will and idea. It survives only through the will to representation, which gives it a kind of eternity. This is the triumph of an aesthetic vision of the real, according to which the real is reducible to images and discourses. But the assertion that, in order to reach the heart of things, one must first empty them of their own content and replace them with simulacra, contains a glorious admission of failure rather than an apotheosis. Everything is literature because, behind appearances, there lies only the nothingness into which they merge and fuse. Literature announces the vacuous reign of images.

This is why Flaubert, no doubt ironically, gratifies Antony with one last vision which strikes him dumb; it also restores, *in extremis*, his faith in the world and in himself:

Day at last dawns; and like the raised curtains of a tabernacle, golden clouds furling into large scrolls uncover the sky. There in the middle, inside the very disc of the sun, radiates the face of Jesus Christ. Antony makes the sign of the cross and returns to his prayers.[33]

This heavenly apparition completes the cycle of images, and it is as though the cycle closed just as the author is completing his book. This is obviously not a definitive closure, and the miraculous possibility of salvation it offers is as uncertain as it is unexpected. We can wager that

33 Ibid., p. 232.

Antony will always be exposed to 'temptations', just as our nagging doubts about the reality of the world and the objectivity of our representations are far from having been exorcised.

Gold from the dungheap

In the first (1849) and most elaborate version of the *Temptation*, Flaubert gives a major role to an emblematic animal which seems to be a concentrate of appetites and temptations: the pig. The pig accompanies Antony on his various wanderings, commenting on them as they go in its own way, and speaking the harsh truth about them. For this double, who is no saint, is equally obsessed with visions. Because they are so elementary, its visions are both a crude demonstration of the laws of the circulation of images and an explanation of their fascination.

The description of the pig at the beginning of Part I of the text serves as a self-portrait:

I delight in wallowing in my own filth all day; then, when it has dried on my body, it gives me armour against midges; I admire my robust face in the water of pools, I like to see myself. I devour everything ... I sleep and excrete as I please, I digest everything ... [34]

This is an evocation of the writer's self-image: he too wallows in the filth of things, devours everything and digests everything. For him, the world is not merely a spectacle, but also a store-house of raw materials and foodstuffs on which he can draw indefinitely in order to satisfy his voracity. Because of its bestiality, the boundless appetite of the pig achieves a sort of absolute: it eventually embraces the whole of the real, encyclopedically.[35] The wish to be matter, which is the

34 *OC*, vol. 9, p. 33.
35 'I will look for a tree with a hard trunk; if I bite it long enough, my teeth will grow. I want to have tusks like a boar, but still longer, still more pointed. I will run and gallop over the dry leaves of the forest, and as I run I will swallow sleeping grass snakes, little birds that have fallen from the nest, and cowering hares; I will bowl over the furrows, trample the young corn into the mud, crush fruits, olives, melons and pomegranates; and I will cross the water, reach the bank, and break the shells of great eggs on the sands so that the yolk flows. I will terrify the towns, devour children on the doorsteps, go into houses, trot between the tables and knock over the dishes. By dint of scratching at the walls, I will demolish temples, dig up graves so as to eat rotting monarchs in their coffins, and their liquid flesh will run down my chops. I will grow, I will swell and I will feel things swarming in my belly' (*OC*, vol. 9, p. 46).

writer's ultimate project, now takes on an exaggerated form: to be matter is also to be in all things and to have all things in one, to be absorbed into them and to absorb them.[36]

In this first version of the *Temptation* the devil explains to Antony the mechanism of this act of possession:

The Devil: 'You have often stopped and stood still with staring eyes, your heart open at the sight of something banal – a drop of water, a shell, a hair. The object you were contemplating seemed to encroach on you as you bent over it, and bonds were forged; you clung to one another, and countless subtle bonds made you huddle together; then, you looked so long that you could no longer see anything. You listened so long that you could no longer hear anything, and your mind eventually lost the notion of individuality that had kept it alert. It was as though an immense harmony had engulfed your soul with its wonderful abundance, and you felt in its fullness an ineffable understanding of a whole that had not been revealed to you; the gap between you and the object narrowed more and more, as though the edges of an abyss were coming together, and eventually there was no more difference between you and it because you were both bathed in the infinite. You penetrated one another, and a subtle current ran from you into matter, whilst the life of the elements slowly flowed into you like rising sap; a little more, and you would have become nature, or nature would have become you.' Antony: 'It is true; I often felt that something greater than me was merging with my being; I was gradually becoming part of the green fields and the flowing rivers, and my soul became so diffused, so universal and so expansive that I no longer knew where it was.'[37]

The assimilation, the osmosis, and the exchanges of energy and substance are so equal and so perfect that, in this moment of boundless communication, one no longer knows what is what.

36 In 1857, the year in which his father published *Les Misérables*, Victor Hugo's son Charles published a sort of baroque fantasy entitled *St Antony's Pig*. He ascribes to that filthy animal the brutal wisdom that speaks 'the language of things'. He also has the pig say: 'When man has rejected all forms of wisdom, I come along and pick up all the sweat of doubt, all the poisons of hatred and all the saliva of envy, or in a word, all the liquid waste of the earth that gradually fills the human sewer; I drink truths from them' (Victor Hugo, *Oeuvres*, Paris: Club français du livre, vol. 9, pp. 1806, 1825).

37 *OC* vol. 11, p. 220. This text, with its obvious echoes of Spinoza, describes relations between what, thanks to the influence of Victor Cousin, everyone in the nineteenth century called the ego [*moi*] and the non-ego [*non-moi*]. This was the 'pantheism' that the bishops of France denounced in so many pastoral letters between 1835 and 1850, when the famous quarrel was raging in France. In his *Dictionary of Received Ideas*, Flaubert inscribes this ironic entry under the heading 'Pantheism': 'Ridiculous. Thunder against it.'

When the pig dreams, it develops the hideous aspects of the same vision:

The rottenness of an entire world lay around me in order to satisfy my appetite. In the smoke, I could see clots of blood, blue intestines and the excrement of every animal, the vomit from orgies and the greenish pus that flows from wounds, like pools of oil; closer to me, it became thicker, so thick that when I walked on all four trotters I almost sank into that sticky mud, and a hot, sugary, fetid rain constantly poured on to my back. But I kept swallowing, because it was good.[38]

This passage is a concentrate of the most astounding visions to be found in *Salammbô*. The writer is invaded, satiated *ad nauseam* by the temptation to appropriate all things so as to be at one with them, even in what would seem to be their most unacceptable, inassimilable manifestations.

But if literature absorbs the real, it does so in order to reconstruct it. On returning from the journey he made to Africa in 1858 in order to carry out research for *Salammbô*, Flaubert wrote this artist's prayer:

May all the energies of nature that I have inhaled penetrate me, and may they be exhaled in my book. Oh power of plastic emotion, be mine! Resurrection of the past, be mine! Mine! Mine! Despite it all, the living and the true must be created out of the Beautiful. Have pity on my will, God of souls. Give me strength and hope. —midnight, night of Saturday 12–Sunday 13 June.[39]

Literary work is therefore a combination of two operations which would appear to be very different: inhalation and exhalation. To write is to assimilate the real in order to metamorphose it through a complex relation of exchange which alternates between attraction and repulsion. In order to penetrate its depths, the writer must keep close to the real, all the real, and must in a sense merge with it. But he must also use his boar's tusks to dig in the mud for food if he is to impose upon it the aggressive mark of his style, which reveals or 'exhales' its ideal meaning. His relationship with the world is therefore fundamentally ambivalent. It is both positive and negative, passive and active, and based upon both desire and hatred.

In a letter to Louise Colet, Flaubert expresses this ambivalence by using a metaphoric formula that is both directly reminiscent of the pig's daydream and parallel to Antony's dream: 'The artist is like a pump. He has within him a great tube which goes down into the bowels of things, into deep strata. It sucks up what was lying flat on

38 *OC*, vol. 9, pp. 179.   39 *OC*, vol. 2, p. 208.

the ground, what no one could see, and then squirts it out into the bright light of day in great jets'.[40] Two images are being associated here: that of the workings of a shit pump, and that of a monstrous, mystical ejaculation whose outpourings have an irresistible power to evoke, since it makes the invisible visible, and thus turns reality upside down. The writer plunges into the world, just as the pig plunges into the fetid pond that is the setting for its dreams, but he does so in order to wrest from it its subtle quintessence, which he produces by virtue of his efforts. This poetics is truly excremental, as is indicated by another admission made to Louise Colet, with whom Flaubert readily shared his artistic effusions:

But ultimately, don't we have to know every apartment in the heart and the social body, from cellar to attic, not forgetting the latrines. Above all, don't forget the latrines. A wonderful chemistry goes on there, a fertilizing process of decomposition. Who knows the excremental juices to which we owe the smell of roses and the taste of melons? Has anyone counted the number of abysses that have to be contemplated for a soul to become great? Who knows how many sickening miasmas have to be swallowed, how much suffering and torture has to be endured to write one good page? That is why we writers are emptiers of cesspools. From mankind's putrefactions, we derive humanity's delights; we grow baskets of flowers on displays of misery. Fact is distilled into Form and rises, just as the pure incense of the Spirit rises up to the Eternal, the Immutable, the Absolute, the Ideal.[41]

Emptier of cesspools and gardener, the artist 'expresses' the abject matter of things so as to extract their ideal essence which, without his intervention, would remain unused and unnoticed.

Flaubert also projects this aesthetic speculation onto the activities of Bouvard and Pécuchet, who provide an ironic mirror-image of his own project:

Pécuchet had a large hole dug in front of the kitchen, and divided it into three compartments, for making composts which would make a lot of things grow, whose waste matter would bring along other crops, supplying further fertilizer, and so on indefinitely. He went into a reverie at the side of the pit, visualizing future mountains of fruit, floods of flowers, avalanches of vegetables. But he lacked the horse manure so useful for hotbeds. The farmers did not sell it, the innkeepers refused. At last, after much searching, despite Bouvard's pleas, and casting shame to the winds, he decided to go out himself 'on the dung-hunt'.[42]

40 Letter of 25 June 1853, *OC* vol. 13, p. 365. In his letter of 8 May 1852 to Louise Colet, Flaubert writes (ibid., p. 190): 'I have been sniffing at unknown dungheaps.'
41 Letter of 23 December 1853, ibid., 442.   42 *Bouvard and Pécuchet*, p. 40.

In his correspondence, Flaubert never ceases to recall that the writer too must go on the dung-hunt in the hope of finally creating a dream world out of the store of filth he has stubbornly collected and accumulated.

Aroused by Pécuchet, [Bouvard] went into a frenzy about fertilizer. In the compost pit were heaped up branches, blood, intestines, feathers, anything he could find. He used Belgian liqueur, Swiss 'lizier', washing soda, smoked herrings, seaweed, rags, had guano sent, tried to make it – and, carrying his principles to the limit, did not tolerate any waste of urine; he did away with the lavatories. Dead animals were brought into his yard, and used to fertilize his land. Their disembowelled carrion was strewn all over the countryside. Bouvard smiled amid all this infection. A pump fixed up in a farm cart spread out liquid manure over the crops. If people looked disgusted, he would say: 'but it is gold! gold!' And he was sorry not to have still more dungheaps. How fortunate are those countries with natural caves full of bird droppings![43]

The compilation of an encyclopedia of excrement in which smoked herrings rot and merge with branches and rags, is, like Antony's attempt to produce an exhaustive catalogue of human aberrations, a way of pursuing the salvational project of an ideal transmutation: the treasure that Bouvard and Pécuchet are looking for in the depths of the rubbish tip is both the substance of the world and its essential truth.

Like Antony's visions, Bouvard and Pécuchet's efforts alternate between two extremes. Disappointment gives way to hope and a new outburst of enthusiasm that takes them in a new direction. The noisome pit from which they dredge the stuff of their dreams – human stupidity – is also the receptacle into which they throw the material frame in which their aspirations were briefly incarnated once they lost interest in them because they no longer believed in them. Thus, the statue of St Peter, an unlikely object which was for a while the most beautiful ornament in their museum,[44] will be sacrificed in a

43 Ibid., p. 48.
44 'But the best of all was in the window embrasure, a statue of St Peter! His gloved hand clutched the key to Paradise, coloured apple-green. His chasuble, decorated with fleurs-de-lis, was sky-blue, and his bright yellow tiara was pointed like a pagoda. His cheeks were rouged, he had great round eyes, gaping mouth and a crooked, turned-up nose. Above hung a canopy made of an old carpet on which two cupids could be made out, and at his feet, like a column, stood a butter jar, with these words in white letters on a chocolate backgound: "Executed before H.R.H. the Duc d'Angoulême, at Noron, the 3rd October 1817"' (ibid., p. 104). This masterpiece, whose gaudy and ludicrous image reduplicates that of Félicité's parrot, also evokes, by putting it into perspective, the literary ideal pursued by

moment of spiritual depression, and ends up in the abyss where all images perish:

One evening, in the middle of a dispute about the monad, Bouvard stubbed his toe on St Peter's thumb, and, venting his annoyance against him: 'He gets on my nerve, that clown; let's sling him out.' This was difficult to do by the stairs. They opened the window and leaned him gently over the edge. Pécuchet, on his knees, tried to raise the statue's heels, while Bouvard pushed down on the shoulders. The stone effigy did not budge; they had to resort to the halberd as a lever, and finally managed to get him out full length. Then, after tipping up and down, he dived into the void, tiara first, a dull thud resounded, and the next day they found him, broken into a dozen pieces, in the old compost pit.[45]

Shortly afterwards, newly converted to the simulacra of the Christian religion and having begun to collect devotional articles, Bouvard and Pécuchet can only contemplate the pieces in the vague hope of bringing them back to life:

What a pity that the St Peter was smashed, and how well he would have looked in the vestibule! Pécuchet sometimes stopped in front of the old compost pit, where one could recognize the tiara, a sandal, a bit of ear, and heaved a sigh or two, then went on gardening, for he now combined manual labour with religious exercises and dug the ground, dressed in his monk's habit, comparing himself to St Bruno. Dressing up like this might be sacrilege; he gave it up.[46]

Everything ends up in the same pit, which is also, because it is perpetually changing, the source of new possibilities for speculation and dreams.[47]

Flaubert, who ironically projects himself on to the characters of Bouvard and Pécuchet, and makes them his doubles.   45 Ibid., p. 211.

46 Ibid., p. 226.

47 Maupassant's war-story 'Saint-Antoine' (1883) was no doubt written as a tribute to Flaubert. The story centres on a Norman peasant, dubbed 'St Antony' by his neighbours, who, at the time of the Prussian invasion, has a Prussian soldier billetted on him. Much to the delight of his neighbours, and in a spirit of derision, he feeds him as though he were fattening up a pig (St Antony's pig). Farce turns to tragedy one evening when the two men get drunk and fight to the death: St Antony fells the soldier with a whip and buries his corpse in a dungheap. The next morning, when he has sobered up, he is drawn back to the dungheap by the barking of his dog: 'Then he saw a shape, the shape of a man sitting on his dungheap! He stared at it, transfixed in horror and panting for breath. It was his Prussian. Covered in mud, he had scrambled out of the heap of manure, which had kept him warm and brought him back to life. He automatically sat down, with the snow falling on him like powder, still fuddled with drink, stunned by the

The permanent circulation that is established between above and below is a combination of assimilation and expansion – which would seem to be operations with quite different meanings – and it contains a direct reference to the theory of the '*circulus*' which brought Pierre Leroux such fame in the mid-nineteenth century. The theory, which claimed to bring about the complete reconciliation of production and consumption at the level of the individual, was an attempt to create, by rather unexpected means, a human world, in the absolute sense of that expression, or in other words a world produced by man himself:

Nature has established a *circulus* between production and consumption. We create nothing and we destroy nothing; we bring about changes. We use seeds, the air, the earth, water and fertilizer to produce foodstuff to feed ourselves. When we feed ourselves, we convert them into gases and fertilizers which produce more foodstuff; that is what we call consumption. Consumption is the goal of production, but it is also its cause.[48]

Man will overcome destiny. How? Through his own creation of the fields that reproduce his subsistence, by becoming his own land, by artificially creating human land.[49]

Man absorbs things by consuming them and passing them through his body. He incorporates them into himself, and makes them his. When he returns them after having appropriated them in this way, it is as though he had remade them in his image in an act of creation, or rather recreation, whose absolute character is inseparable from the vile

blow, exhausted by his wounds.' St Antony finishes off his victim with a pitchfork, and then buries him again: 'He dug a hole in the ground, dug deeper still, working with all his strength in disorganized fashion, his arms and legs working furiously. When the ditch was deep enough, he rolled the corpse into it and smiled when he saw the heavy snow finishing the job for him and covering up his traces with a white veil.' See Guy de Maupassant, 'Saint-Antoine' in *Contes et nouvelles*, ed. A. M. Schmidt (Paris: Albin Michel, 1957), pp. 194–201. The ignominies can be covered by the shroud of a blank page that has yet to be written!

Maupassant's short story refers to the literary paradigm established by Flaubert: the cycle of derision and horror, of humours and words, incarnated in the grotesque pair of 'saint' and 'beast', is the same. Here, the values of above and below commune and are inverted so as to bring out the fantastically absurd character of the 'realities' of the war: writing is merely a means of depicting their carnivalesque communication.

48 Pierre Leroux, 'L'Humanité et le capital', *Revue sociale* 6 (March 1846), reproduced in Alexandrian, *Le Socialisme romantique* (Paris: Seuil, 1979), pp. 266–7.

49 Pierre Leroux, 'Aux Etats de Jersey, sur un moyen de quintupler, pour ne pas dire plus, la production agricole du pays' (London, 1853), cited, ibid.

conditions in which it is carried out. Leroux turned this parody of the divine gesture into the basis for a new religion: the religion of Humanity.

One can imagine what Homais would have had to say about the *circulus*, which is a perfect weapon against the machinations of the clergy. But it is because it is so ludicrous that this elementary and radical theory is so profoundly interesting. It is both an imaginary economy of substances and commodities, and an outline for an economics of the imaginary. That much is obvious from the way it was exploited by Hugo, who was close to Leroux during their shared exile in the Channel Islands: his poetic vision of a luminous transfiguration of the world of shadows is symmetrical with Leroux's dream of recuperating the filth that will regenerate nature and humanity by plunging them into the same nauseating pit.[50] For Flaubert, the doctrine of the *circulus* becomes the basis of a pure aesthetics: 'Beauty

50 In the description of 'The Entrails of the Monster' in *Les Misérables*, Hugo writes (p. 873): 'Do you know what all this is — the heaps of muck piled up beside the milestones, the scavengers' carts that jolt through the streets at night, the dreadful barrels in the rubbish dump, and the foetid flow of sludge that the pavement hides from you? It is the flowering meadow, green grass, marjoram and thyme and sage, game, cattle, the contented lowing of great bulls in the evening, the scented hay and the golden wheat, the bread on your table and the warm blood in your veins — health and joy and life. Such is the mysterious creation that is transformation on earth and transfiguration in Heaven; it is like the wind. Return all that to the great crucible and you will reap abundance. The feeding of the fields becomes the feeding of men.' A single schema can explain the transformation of matter and the transfigurations of spirit, and it thus establishes an analogical correspondence between them. Material things can be metamorphosed into spiritual things. In its highest form, poetic activity consists in recapturing, on the dazzling surface of the written page, something that was slowly elaborated in the dark depths of the substance of the people. The writer is a thinker in the shadows, the master of secret gestations, and he drains the waste-products of life, the detritus of the social body, in order to recycle them in the vast process he calls progress. That is why Hugo makes the sewer — intestine and labyrinth — the setting for a journey of initiation leading to an absolute revelation: 'A sewer is a cynic. It says everything. This sincerity of filth pleases us and soothes the spirit ... Philosophy is thought's microscope. Everything seeks to flee it, but nothing escapes it. To compromise is useless: what side of oneself does one show by compromises? The shameful side. Philosophy pursues evil with its unflinching gaze and does not allow it to escape into nothingness. Amid the vanishing and the shrinking, it detects all things. It reconstructs the purple from the shred of rag and the woman from the wisp. With the cloaca, it reconstructs the city; from the mire it recreates its customs' (ibid., p. 877). His aim is to make the Beautiful emerge from the depths of the People: poetics is also politics.

and morality are, in my view, the only things that matter. Poetry, like the sun, gilds the dungheap. Too bad for those who cannot see it.'[51] The writer wallows in the mud like a pig because mud alone can provide the revelation from which literature derives its essential significance.[52]

A lesson in style

'Let us absorb the objective, and let it circulate within us. Let it reproduce externally, even though we can understand nothing of its marvellous chemistry. Our hearts cannot be good unless they feel the hearts of others. Let us be mirrors that magnify the external truth.'[53] The literary act is therefore subject to a twofold rule. On the one hand, it presupposes that the author allows himself to be completely eclipsed by the external reality of things, which he simply 'records' or 'renders' as it is; on the other hand, his ability to render it depends upon his prior absorption of reality and is therefore subject to the transmutations of a mysterious internal chemistry. This is a clear

---

51 Letter of 19 February 1880 to Guy de Maupassant, *OC*, vol. 16, p. 327.
52 In his *L'Eau de jouvence*, which is the second of his philosophical dramas and the sequel to *Caliban* (see note 3 above), Renan (*Oeuvres complètes*, Paris: Calmann-Lévy, 1949, vol. 3, pp. 518–19) gives his openly political version of the theory of the *circulus*. Confronted with the problem of the democratic republic, he rejects its basic premise because, in his view, the true source of power lies in the knowledge of the elite, but he still accepts its inevitable necessity. 'There can be no history without Caliban. Caliban's grunts and the bitter hatred that leads him to supplant his master are the principle behind humanity's evolution. There is nothing pure or impure in nature. The world is an immense circle, in which decay emerges from life and life from decay. The flower is born of the dungheap; exquisite fruits swell with the juices of manure. As it goes through its transformations, the beautiful is alternately exquisite and hideous. There is a purpose to all this, and even though we have no proof that a clear consciousness presides over the government of the universe, definite indices reveal the existence of a dim consciousness, of a profound tendency in pursuit of a goal set in infinity.' In order to exorcise the fear of the popular pig that had haunted him since 1848, Renan falls back upon a Hegelianism which has been reinterpreted in terms of the categories of Cousin's philosophy. The people are a grunting pig which no culture can ever control; but their dim consciousness also represents, in the form of its spontaneity, the primal moment which spirit needs if it is to reflect upon itself as it develops. Let us tolerate democracy, despite its constitutional stupidity, until such time as the evolution of the world, or the improvisation of a new Greek miracle, allows other spiritual figures that are closer to a rational ideal to prevail.
53 Letter of 6 November 1853 to Louise Colet, *OC*, vol. 13, p. 428.

indication of the ambiguity of Flaubert's 'realism', which is the product of a cycle that combines two operations with very different meanings because there are two possible relations between inside and outside.

The former aspect is embodied in the fantasy of the writer's impersonality, which Flaubert erects into an absolute rule. 'One of my principles is that one should not write about oneself.'[54] When he wrote up the notes he made during his travels in the Orient, Flaubert tried to pare them down, and to reduce them to the status of mere 'impressions' by deleting anything that might indicate his personal involvement in what he had transcribed. 'You will observe that I have not written a single reflection. I merely formulated the indispensable as briefly as possible, namely the sensation, and neither the dream nor the thought.'[55] Sensation has the value of objectivity because it is quite spontaneous and non-reflexive; things seem to describe themselves, without any intermediaries, in a sequence of pure images. Similarly, the *Dictionary of Received Ideas*, that universal encyclopedia of human credulity, is intended to be a catalogue of credulity, a collection of snapshots which are so recognizable as to require no commentary. 'There must not be a single word of my own devising in the entire book, and once one has read it, one should not dare to speak again for fear of naturally using one of the expressions in it.'[56] Perhaps anyone who has read the *Voyage en Orient* should be afraid to travel, as all possibilities have been exhausted and negated by a collection of impressions which is supposed to sum up every possible experience offered by travel. And perhaps anyone who has read *Madame Bovary* should be afraid to live, since the book stands for so many lives and identifies or abstracts the purely artistic interest to be found in any life.

The conquest of impersonality certainly does not mean passive abstention: it coincides with an active intervention 'in' the reality of

54 Letter of 18 March 1857 to Mlle Leroyer de Chantepie, *OC*, vol. 12, p. 567.
55 Letter of 27 March 1857 to Louise Colet, *OC*, vol. 12, p. 312. The same letter also contains (ibid., p. 314) the following suggestion: 'So let us try to see things as they are, and try not to be wiser than God. It used to be believed that sugar cane was the only source of sugar. We can now make sugar from virtually anything; and the same is true of poetry. Let us extract it from everything, for it lies everywhere and in everything. There is not an atom of matter than does not contain thought; let us accustom ourselves to considering the world to be like a work of art whose devices have to be reproduced in our works.'
56 Letter of 27 March 1853 to Louise Colet, *OC*, vol. 13, p. 312.

things which necessarily alters their immediate manifestations. In the naive self-portrait he drew in 1834 when he was writing the first version of *L'Education sentimentale*, in which he appears as 'Jules', Flaubert expresses his fantasy-image of the writer in these terms: 'He refused to respect anything. He plunged his whole arm into things, turning the lining of fine feelings inside out, testing empty words, seeking for hidden passions in facial features, taking off every mask, tearing away veils, undressing every woman, going into alcoves, sounding all wounds, looking closely at all joys.'[57] Undressing women, so as to be able to tell them all; that could be one of St Antony's temptations. And that is precisely what Flaubert tries to do with Emma Bovary in another book about nothing: describing a typical woman means reconstructing the whole of her existence with the help of a set of imaginary features which have been recorded and arranged in stylized fashion, and substituting them for her real existence so as to reveal her secret, or in other words her essential nothingness. Undressing a woman means groping beneath her skirts and her dreams to uncover the vacuity or the absence, and not the fullness of flesh or meaning, that they hide. There is something sadistic about Flaubert's literary fantasy of undressing women – and it will be recalled that Flaubert was an enthusiastic reader of Sade – because it is bound up with a desire to destroy and annihilate; the artist's attitude to the object that awakens his curiosity is essentially negative because he strives to use mockery to break it down and annihilate it. Remember the *Dictionary of Received Ideas*; anyone who has read it cannot say anything 'naturally' or innocently. It is as though the point

---

57   *OC*, vol. 8, p. 145. The same demiurgical impulse appears, in almost identical terms, in the *Voyage en Orient* of 1850 (*OC*, vol. 10, p. 443): 'An invincible curiosity makes me wonder despite myself about the life of every passerby I meet. I would like to know his trade, his country, his name, his preoccupations of the moment, his regrets, his hopes, his forgotten loves, what he is dreaming of, everything – down to the hem of his flannel waistcoat and the expression on his face when he takes a purge. And if the passerby is a woman (especially a middle-aged woman), the longing becomes unbearable. Admit it, how you would like at once to see her naked, naked to her very heart. How you try to guess where she has come from, where she is going, why she is here and not there. As you let your eyes run over her, you imagine her having an affair. You assume she must have certain feelings. You think of the bedroom she must have, of a thousand other things, ... I don't know ... the broken-down slippers into which she slips her feet when she gets out of bed.' This is a complaisant description of the ritual of erotic possession; when Flaubert speaks of 'penetrating' reality, it is not difficult to grasp his meaning!

of getting to reality were to render it absent unto itself rather than to remain true to it in the positive sense of the term: in the novel, Emma eventually 'disappears'.

Being impersonal therefore means being careful not to add any consistency to a reality which has so little consistency; poetic asceticism means becoming completely absorbed in a world which is nothing in itself, and making the reader understand its emptiness. That is why the artist's absorption is also a detachment which allows him to escape the spells and temptations of the immediate appearance of things. 'We must do all we can to be souls; thanks to that detachment, the immense sympathy of things will be ours in greater abundance.'[58] The writer's sexual bulimia and the excremental power of his style, which allows him to spit out what he has sucked in in a truer form, make him a disembodied being. 'Personally, I would like to be an angel.'[59] It is because it is in search of its ideal that literature dredges the latrines of reality. 'Above life, above happiness, there is something blue and incandescent, a great sky, immutable and subtle, and the rays that come to us from it are enough to give life to worlds. The splendour of genius is no more than a pale reflection of that hidden Word.'[60] The obverse of Flaubert's realism — symbolized in his dream of 'being matter' — is a basic idealism which culminates in an attempt to rid the world of all reality.

There have been many commentaries on Flaubert's project of writing a 'book about nothing, a book with no external supports that can stand by itself thanks to the internal strengths of its style, just as the earth exists in the air without being supported, a book which has almost no subject, or in which the subject is at least almost invisible, if that is possible'.[61] As nothing has any value in itself, other than the value of what can be written about it, the world exists for the writer only to the extent that he can express it. Provided that it is expressed well, anything can be brought into the timeless presence of the Beautiful, which is infinitely more interesting than any contingent appearance. In the fiction that brings it back to life in its absence, Carthage is truer than nature; it is as though the image of a world which was, in every sense of the word, lost, had risen again from the

58 Letter of 27 August 1853 to Louise Colet, *OC*, vol. 13, p. 402.
59 Letter of 19 September 1852 to Louise Colet, *OC*, vol. 13, p. 238.
60 Letter of 29 November 1853 to Louise Colet, *OC*, vol. 12, p. 433.
61 Letter of 16 January 1852, *OC*, vol. 13, p. 158.

ruins. Ultimately, anything that can be enunciated can stand in for reality, provided that it is enunciated with terrifying inflexibility. It is not that it depicts reality in the naive sense by using the edifying and frozen permanence of a perfect image to capture its unstable features; by penetrating reality completely, it exhausts the whole of its content. That is why, when all things have been reduced to the pure lines of their expression, which describe them well, literature can speak of the most insignificant realities because it can describe them in ideal terms. At this point, everything becomes literature: St Antony's pig, Homais's bottles, Hamilcar's elephants, and Félicité's parrot are symptoms of all the failures, all the defeats of life. They are the fantastic and grotesque remains of a reality that has been emptied of its living content.

It is at this point that the theme of stupidity finds its constitutive and truly foundational function within Flaubert's aesthetic. According to Flaubert, the objective of all literary work lies in this simple observation: reality is so stupid, and it is so fine to be stupid and to be recognized as such! In this perspective, the apparently formal search for a stylized expression coincides with the didactic intention of revealing the hidden essence of things, the 'nothing' on which they are based. Writing then functions as a real disenchantment machine. Flaubert's books belong to quite incomparable genres and deal with the most disparate subjects, and yet their tone is always the same, for they are all narratives of failure and disillusionment. This thematic of failure delivers a message whose basic orientation is that of a nihilology: ultimately, reality is only one more obsession, a 'temptation'. The stylized transcription of the real causes a whole fountain of bitterness to spring forth: feelings, ideas, things and beings emerge from it emptied of their substantial content, just like the stories we tell and the stories we tell ourselves:

No limits; for you humanity is no more than a puppet wearing a bell. You make the bell ring at the end of every sentence, just as the puppet-master makes it ring by pulling the string (I have often avenged myself on life in this way; I have treated myself to all sorts of luxuries with my pen; I have given myself women, money, travel); just like the contented Soul that moves through the azure that ends only on the frontiers of the True. Where form is lacking, ideas no longer exist. Looking for one means looking for the other. They are as inseparable as substance and colour, and that is why Art is truth itself.[62]

62   Letter of 15 May 1852 to Louise Colet, *OC*, vol. 13, p. 194.

All must pass away

The art of writing is thus a response to the disappointment experienced by the writer when reality betrays him. He can triumph over it only by stylizing it. 'Humanity hates us; we do not serve it and we hate it because it wounds us. Let us therefore love one another in Art, as mystics love one another in God, and let all pale into nothing in the face of that love. Let all the other candles of life (which all stink) disappear in the light of that great sun.'[63] In the broad light of day and in the light of derision, it is as though the things of this world became strangers to themselves and were returned to that non-essential essence which destroys their appearance from within. How true I am; I the 'realist' who shows you the extent to which they are unreal and false!

63 Letter of 14 August 1853 to Louise Colet, *OC*, vol. 13, p. 384.

10

Foucault reads Roussel: literature as philosophy

The title of Foucault's *Les Mots et les choses* [literally 'Words and Things'] makes a direct allusion to the problems of literature and is an indication of the special status he grants throughout his work to literature, which is seen as revealing something about theory. Foucault does more than reflect *on* literature. He works *with* literature; he is preoccupied with making theoretical use of it rather than with elaborating a theory *of* literature. The book on Raymond Roussel which he published together with *Birth of the Clinic* in 1963, that is two years after *Madness and Civilization*,[1] is an expression of this basic preoccupation and represents an important stage in Foucault's research. Michel Leiris speaks of Roussel's writings being bound up with 'that attempt to prospect the virgin lands of the mind'.[2] Taking what seems to be a similar view, Foucault regards the word games to which Roussel devoted his life as having the value of an intellectual experience and attempts to bring out its significance. The reading he undertakes on the basis of that hypothesis provides a veritable lesson in philosophy.

The Roussel case and the sickness of language

Why does Foucault choose to devote a whole book to Raymond Roussel, a determined and marginal *littérateur* who would have been remembered mainly as a wealthy eccentric,[3] had not the surrealists and then Leiris rescued from oblivion an *oeuvre* which was greeted with indifference or scorn during its author's lifetime? The answer seems

---

1 Michel Foucault, *Death and the Labyrinth: The World of Raymond Roussel*, tr. Charles Ruas (London: Athlone Press, 1987).
2 Michel Leiris, 'Documents sur Raymond Roussel', *Nouvelle Revue Française* 259 (April 1935), reprinted in *Roussel l'ingénu* (Montpellier: Fata Morgana, 1987), p. 20.
3 These adventures are related in F. Caradec's fabulous *Vie de Raymond Roussel* (Paris: Pauvert, 1972).

obvious: Foucault's interest must have been awakened not so much by the books, as by the man himself, who seems to have stepped right out of the pages of *Madness and Civilization*. Raymond Roussel was, by his own admission, 'mentally ill' and should, one might have thought, be placed under the generic heading of 'literary madmen'.

Indeed, in *Comment j'ai écrit certains de mes livres*, which stands as a posthumous confession, Roussel reproduces the passage devoted to him by his doctor, the psychiatrist Pierre Janet, in his book *De l'angoisse à l'extase*, which was published in 1926. He figures there as 'Martial', which is the name of a character in one of his stories. For Janet, Roussel's literary works were, because of their obsessional character, the prime symptom of his illness. The implicit assumption behind that diagnosis defined literature itself as a pathological product or a delusion. In that sense, Roussel was mad because he wanted to play at being a writer and was fictively mimicking literary activity to compensate for other forms of satisfaction of which he was incapable.[4]

Janet explained this simulation in terms of the unhealthy fixation on a mental state which Martial first experienced when he was nineteen years old. He was then writing *La Doublure* in a state of rapture which would lead him to a kind of ecstasy. His literary activity thus corresponded to a search for a substitute satisfaction that could compensate for his rejection of reality. Janet's account of the 'case' concludes thus:

4   Here is Janet's account of the Roussel 'case': 'With great effort, and often great fatigue, he regularly works a set number of hours every day, permitting himself no irregularity, on constructing great literary edifices. "I sweat blood over every sentence" he says. These literary works, and it is not my task to study their value, have until now had no success; they are not read and they are considered insignificant, except by a few initiates who take an interest in them. But the author still has a curious attitude towards them. Not only does he continue his work with tireless perseverance; he has an absolute and unshakeable conviction as to their matchless artistic value. That an author should be convinced of the value of his works and should appeal to posterity to remedy the injustice of his contemporaries, is natural and to a certain extent legitimate, but it seems, however, that Martial's conviction takes an abnormal form. He accords his works an exaggerated importance; he is never disturbed by their obvious lack of success, he will not accept for a moment that their lack of success is justified by certain imperfections, he never accepts the slightest criticism or advice, and has an absolute faith in the destiny that awaits him: "I will reach the greatest heights, and I was born for dazzling fame. It may take a long time, but I will achieve greater fame than Victor Hugo or Napoleon ..."' (cited in Raymond Roussel, *Comment j'ai écrit certains de mes livres*, Paris: Lemerre, 1935, pp. 175–6). Poor Martial!

Martial has a very interesting conception of literary beauty; the work must contain nothing real, and no observation of the world or of minds; nothing but totally imaginary combinations; they are ideas from an extra-human world. True ecstasy, which involves immobility and complete disinterestedness, and a life and a happiness that are quite outside human existence, must necessarily take a more religious form and will lead to a divine life, a life in God, a life as God.[5]

This last comment relates to Janet's central thesis: ecstasy is a response to anxiety. Anxiety is the truth behind ecstasy, and ecstasy is therefore a flight from reality. This could be seen as an outline theory of sublimation, but there is no reference to the category of the unconscious in the Freudian sense, for Janet replaces it with the notion of a subconscious.[6] The broad outlines of this analysis are easily identified: for Roussel, literature is no more than a mask, and once the mask is removed, we find the man with all the 'problems' he is trying to forget by choosing to live in the artificial world of fiction which allows him to escape the constraints of reality.

This is precisely the type of interpretation that Foucault rejects. He adopts the opposite approach and, rather than using the work to explain the man, and therefore devaluing it, gives the work its full weight. This means that Roussel's works are to be regarded as the site for the emergence of a truth. It is not a psychological truth about the man and his 'illness', but a truly literary truth which belongs to literature as such, and which may perhaps define literature.[7] Roussel was obsessed with literature, possessed by a need to write to which he sacrificed his fortune and even his life, and he turned his existence into an *oeuvre* which reproduced techniques he had developed in order to write his books and not in order to satisfy some personal inclination

5 Ibid., p. 183. The beginning of this passage is also reproduced by André Breton, who appears to take it quite seriously, in his introduction to Roussel in his *Anthologie de l'humour noir* (Paris: Jean-Jacques Pauvert, 1966).

6 See Elisabeth Roudinesco, *La Bataille de cent ans. Histoire de la psychanalyse en France* (Paris: Ramsay, 1982), pp. 244 ff.

7 Particular consideration is given to this point in the final chapter of Foucault's book, which is entitled 'The Enclosed Sun', a formula not unreminiscent of the story and the works of President Schreber. Foucault's text, which is written in the form of a dialogue, starts with a discussion of the expression: '"He's a poor little patient", said Dr. Pierre Janet' (*Death and the Labyrinth*, p. 155) and proceeds to challenge it. Foucault sees in this expression the characteristic approach of the psychologist, for whom 'the work and the illnesses are entangled and incomprehensible one without the other' (ibid., p. 160). The relationship between the two is precisely what Foucault is attempting to disentangle.

which could be described in terms of frustrations or anxiety. He did so because his *oeuvre*, and to a certain extent his life, was the site of what Foucault calls an 'experience', and it was not specific to Roussel alone.[8] It is the experience of literature itself insofar as it expresses a basic relationship with language.[9] This is why the fault-line that undeniably runs through the whole of Roussel's work, and the fact that it is in a perpetual state of self-inadequacy, cannot be explained in terms of the constitutional inadequacies of the individual known as 'Roussel', even if those inadequacies are real, which is a different problem altogether. Leaving aside Roussel's personality, his work states the very constitution of language: the dividing line that lies at the heart of language and turns it into an 'enclosed sun', or in other words the site of an attempt, which is at once necessary and impossible, to speak things as a totality.

If we follow Foucault, we cannot accept the psychiatric diagnosis or say that language is sick in Roussel because Roussel uses it for personal ends in order to find an imaginary compensation for the lack that haunts him. It is, rather, Roussel who is sick in language, who is suffering from the sickness of language itself, from a sickness of which literature exhibits the exemplary marks. 'This solar void is neither the psychological background of the work (a meaningless idea) nor a theme that coincides with his illness. It *is* Roussel's linguistic space, the void from which he speaks, the absence which binds and mutually includes his work and his madness.'[10] We are therefore not dealing with anxiety about things or words, but with anxiety about language itself. 'Roussel's "unreason", his derogatory play on words, his obsessive application, his absurd inventions, communicate doubtlessly with the reasoning of our world.'[11] It is the reasoning of our world that makes us recognize the world as reasonable by virtue of the fact that we speak about it and that, when we speak about it, we speak about it as it is. Now the 'unreason' that is systematically professed by

8 The term recalls the title of the final part of Maurice Blanchot's *L'Espace littéraire*: 'La littérature et l'expérience originelle'. It also evokes Bataille and the theme of 'inner experience'.

9 'In the context of the work, and fundamental to Roussel's experience of language, there seems to be a place where birth is hidden ... This labyrinth is not a visible result of his illness (a defence mechanism against sexuality), any more than it is the veiled expression of esoteric knowledge (hiding the way in which bodies can give birth to one another); it is a radical experience of language which proclaims that it is never quite contemporary with its solar experience' (*Death and the Labyrinth*, p. 162).   10 Ibid., pp. 164–5.   11 Ibid., p. 166.

Roussel — and no madness was less deranged than his — reveals to us the other side of that reasoning. By inverting our relationship with language, and therefore with the world, it reveals its other side, displays the unreason of our reasoning by indicating the price that has to be paid if we are to speak 'reasonably' about things.[12]

We can now understand why the study Foucault devotes to Roussel, which has not in general been well understood and which has been seen as a marginal part of his work, allows us to grasp its overall economy. It is this study which marks the transition from *Madness and Civilization* to *The Order of Things*. The former asked the question: 'what could have given form and meaning to the institution of mental illness?' and related it to the general problems of a history of reason. The latter considers the fact of reason in its own right, relates it to its historical conditions of possibility, and therefore asks the question: 'what could have led us to consider and regard the world as reasonable?' Roussel's 'madness' thus has an exemplary character insofar as it allows Foucault to move from the problem of a history of unreason to that of a history of reason, and to flush out the monstrous, irrational(?) figures that inhabit our reason.[13]

A lesson in ontology: the work of words

How does Foucault read the work of Roussel, which is analysed in detail in his book? He begins with the median moment of its development, with the central kernel of the *Impressions d'Afrique* of

12 'If Roussel's work is separated from this space (which is ours), then it can only be seen as the haphazard marvels of the absurd, or the baroque play of an esoteric language which means "something else". If on the contrary his work is placed there, Roussel appears as he defined himself: as the inventor of a language which only speaks about itself, a language absolutely simple in its duplicated being, a language about language, enclosing its own sun in its sovereign and central flaw ... No doubt it was necessary that from all sides of our culture be articulated this experience before all language which is anxious and animated, is extinguished and then brought back to life by the marvellous void of the signifiers. The anguish of the signifier is what has made Roussel's suffering the solitary discovery of what is closest to us in our language. It makes his illness our problem' (ibid., pp. 166–7).

13 Gilles Deleuze is one of the few to have recognized the true importance of Foucault's book on Roussel. Its importance relates not only to specific questions about literature, but also to Foucault's other theoretical preoccupations. See Gilles Deleuze, *Foucault* (Paris: Minuit, 1986), p. 105. See also the contributions of Raymond Bellour and Denis Hollier in *Foucault philosophe* (Paris: Seuil 1989).

1910, and relies upon the clarifications about how the text was elaborated by the posthumous revelations of *Comment j'ai écrit certains de mes livres*, in which Roussel reveals the 'procedure' he developed to write his fictional texts.

At its most elementary, the procedure consists of using transformational sentences which play, like mere puns, on verbal assonances, to elaborate narrative texts which formally imitate certain of the stories of Jules Verne, for whom Roussel professed great admiration. Take, for example, the two utterances:

Les lettres du blanc sur les bandes du vieux billard
('The white letters on the cushions of an old billiard table')
Les lettres du blanc sur les bandes du vieux pillard
('The white man's letters about the hordes of the old plunderer')

In the first of these utterances, the formula '*les lettres du blanc*' evokes typographical characters traced in chalk on the edge of the baze of a dilapidated billiard table. In the second, it designates a missive from a white man about an ageless adventurer and the expeditions he leads with his companions. Thanks to a punctual, apparently tiny and 'insignificant' (as they say) modification of the context in which it is inserted – the 'b' in '*billard*' becomes the 'p' in '*pillard*' – an identical signifier produces divergent meaning-effects out of all proportion to the 'things' in question. Roussel's work of writing consists in using narration to fill in the void that has been created – a hole in discourse resulting from the sliding of the signified over the signifier – and in telling a whole story which begins with the first utterance and ends with the second. He repeats the process in the interval that separates the two, or in other words plays on the meaning-effects that can be induced by purely verbal variations. As a result of imperceptible variations, words begin to move, to be displaced as they move away from the things they are supposed to represent. In this way, verbal incidents eventually produce all the details of a real plot, real settings, and real characters. In a word, they produce what we call a 'story' in which words seem to talk about things.[14]

14 Michel Leiris brilliantly characterizes Roussel's method in the following terms: 'It is a magical nominalism in which the word conjures up the thing, and the dislocation of a random sequence of sentences ("rather as though puzzle-pictures were being extracted from them") leads to the re-creation of the universe, the construction of a special world that replaces the ordinary world. As the final outcome is the description, or the story, of imaginary objects or events –

When we reduce it to its basic principles, the first thing that strikes one about Roussel's 'Work' is the childish character of the deliberate stringing together of puns that gives rise to these crackpot and unlikely narratives. We find here the symptoms of a ludic and maniacal activity, which it would be only too easy to explain in terms of Roussel's 'illness'. But at the same time – and this is the serious side to the game – these operations, which produce compositions of extraordinary precision, correspond to what Foucault calls an 'experience of language'. By making words begin to move, Roussel finally disturbs the use we make of language in such a way as to challenge the very fact of speaking and writing. Plato did the same with the equally extraordinary, and almost surrealist *avant la lettre*, puns of the *Cratylus*. So did Saussure, an exact contemporary of Roussel's, when he 'played' with anagrams at the time when he was refounding on a new basis a linguistics quite distinct from the traditional 'science of language' which defines language as the direct expression of a meaning.

If we read him carefully, we realize that what Roussel is doing is inverting the spontaneous conception that we form of language without thinking about it because we are its users. According to this conception, a language expresses reality by reproducing it, by representing it, by stating it, so to speak, word by word, as though there were a term for term equivalence between the world of things and the world of words, as though the invisible thread of discourse traced the order of the real as it unfolded, as though things were the way words say they are and as though words could say things the way they are. By shifting the order of discourse away from itself through an operation that makes the series of the signifier and the series of the signified slide over one another, Roussel makes it necessary to rethink the relationship between words and things completely. It then transpires that words are not the other side of things, that they are in themselves a two-faced reality and that their two faces do not automatically match. By taking the use of language to its limits in such a way as to give the relationship between sign and sense an apparently aberrant form, Roussel reveals that language is not at all designed to

basically, a series of mythical inventions replacing word games – this suggests that Roussel has rediscovered one of the human genius's oldest and most widespread mental habits: using words to form myths, or transposing what starts out as a mere fact of language into a dramatic action' (review of *Comment j'ai écrit certains de mes livres*, NRF 268, January 1936, reprinted in *Roussel l'ingénu*, p. 38).

say things, or rather that the things it says are not necessarily the things we think. The thread of discourse is not parallel to the reality of things and does not represent it. The thread of discourse – and discourse does hang by a thread – is in permanent danger of being broken and may be interrupted by unexpected connections. It is therefore both in excess of and inadequate to the reality it is supposed to be stating.[15] This is why Roussel can tell stories, or quite simply generate meaning-effects and conjure up the marvellous visions of *Impressions d'Afrique* and *Locus solus* by merely 'playing' with the sonic contours of words. This of course is the speculative function of the pun: it makes it possible to flush out the logic of the signifier by showing that, far from being mere noise, that logic is perfectly capable of switching into a signified content without there being any need to make that content correspond to the actual existence of anything.

Because it is disconcerting, exceptional and marginal, Roussel's endeavour raises the question: what if it were always like that? What if we always spoke in order to say 'nothing'? Or rather, what if 'saying something' were an operation that is not reducible to the reproduction of a signification that is pre-given in reality? What if the things we say were not, as we are all too willing to believe, mere things? What if they were not banal things that lent themselves of their own accord to the discourse which speaks of them or says them? What if the things we talk about, and on which we have a grip because we talk about them, were something other than objects to be represented, something other than elements of reality or figures of existence to which the signs of language adapt term by term when they designate them?

Roussel's approach is exemplary because, thanks to his rigorous work on the forms of language, it results in a questioning of the order of things. We can speak here of an ontological question. What is a thing? What, for example, is a *billard*? Could it be a *pillard*, with the 'p' removed and replaced by a 'b'? Could there be more to the world of things than the reality which we ascribe to them and which seems to give them their meaning? Could there be secret groupings and kinships which, because they make things rhyme, turn one thing into another? If words are also things, why should they not be significant? The second chapter of *The Order of Things* ('The Prose of the World')

15 It is in this sense that Leiris (*Roussel l'ingénu*, p. 57) speaks, with reference to *Nouvelles Impressions d'Afrique*, of 'an internal proliferation of text'.

expounds this very specific form of speculation, which was destroyed by the representative conception of language established in the seventeenth century. Now this representative conception, which posits a relationship of strict equivalence between the order of words and the order of things, and therefore defines language as a rational system of meanings, or as a system subordinate to a demand for meanings, is by no means self-evident. The prejudices that support it have a reductive function to the extent that they retain only the meaningful – or apparently meaningful – elements in language and eliminate anything that overflows or lacerates its representative network.

When language is put into perspective like this, a series of radical philosophical questions arises, since we have to ask why we speak about something rather than nothing. And that in turn evokes another, and more familiar, question: why is there something rather than nothing? Perhaps the sickness of language, to which Roussel's experience of language bears witness, reveals that things themselves are sick, or in other words not quite as we see them. Foucault's study of the work of Roussel is therefore concerned with the field of a primal philosophy rather than with the field of a poetics.

The illusions of meaning

Is Roussel's approach, with all its philosophical implications, truly original? We inevitably have to compare it with other approaches which apparently lead in the same direction and raise similar questions. In his book, Foucault does not even mention one of them, namely Freud's theory of slips of the tongue, but that is because he can evaluate it indirectly by seeing it as an extension of the approach taken by Breton and the surrealists, which he subjects to a categorical critique.

Freud was extremely interested in aberrant phenomena of language, and constantly refers to them in *The Interpretation of Dreams, The Psychopathology of Everyday Life* and *Jokes and Their Relation to the Unconscious*; he regards them as gaps in the representative discourse that gives rise to the conscious mind, and attempts to work backwards from these cases of dysfunctionality to the other discourse of the unconscious, to which consciousness has access only though its lacunae and gaps. This analysis presumes the existence of a latent content, or a meaning which has been both repressed, displaced and distorted. And its goal is the 'liberation' of that meaning though the removal of the taboo that prevents it from being expressed and communicated. The very notion of interpretation implies that words 'must' speak of something else. They do not, however, do so because of some ontological determination, due to which they are constitutionally obliged to speak of something else, as though the very function of words were to speak of something else, and as though it were in the nature of things to be always 'other', to be permanently out of step with what we say. If they do speak of something else, it must be because the things of which they speak have been held back or distorted by circumstantial factors. Putting things back in their place or restoring their identity should therefore be enough to restore order. Even though Freud's reasoning is much more complex than this, the fact remains that the spirit of psychoanalysis, as revealed by a more or less pertinent reading of his texts, does frequently refer to the schemas of taboo and liberation which Foucault always refuses to accept.

At the beginnings of the history of surrealism, André Breton used a reference to Freud as a theoretical basis for his own projects. And when the works of Roussel caught his interest or, as he puts it, 'filled him with wonder', he interpreted them in the light of that reference by exploiting a schema which was formally analogous to that of liberation. Because they removed the controls imposed upon the use of language by conscious reason, new linguistic practices like automatic writing would, he believed, open up the road that led to a wonderful and occult world, namely the world of imagination and dreams described in the first *Surrealist Manifesto* of 1924.[16] The founder of surrealism saw Roussel as an initiator and a guide because he defied the supposedly normal use of language and led his readers

16 See Breton on Roussel in the *Anthologie de l'humour noir* (Paris: Pauvert, 1966, pp. 382–3): 'The wonderful thing is that this automaton can, potentially, be set free in any man: he has only to reconquer, like Rimbaud, the feeling of his absolute innocence and power. We know that "pure psychic automatism", in the sense in which those words are understood today, is intended only to designate a limit-state state which requires man to lose logical and moral control over his acts. Whilst he may not agree to go so far, or rather to remain in that state, he may, once he has reached a certain point, sense that he is being driven by a motor with an unsuspected power, that he is mathematically obeying an apparently cosmic cause which escapes him. The question that arises in connection with these and other automata is whether or not a conscious being is concealed within them. And, one asks oneself in the presence of the work of Roussel, to what extent is it conscious?'

towards the magical universe of a 'surreality' by conjuring up, for instance, the extraordinary visions of *Impressions d'Afrique* or *Locus solus*.

But there is something about Roussel which is an obvious obstacle to this type of interpretation, namely the fact that his approach was anything but that of a dreamer, or even a day-dreamer. His efforts may well have given rise to automatisms, but they were controlled automatisms based upon what might be called the scientific discovery of certain mechanisms specific to language. From that point of view, his approach is closer to Saussure, who was of no interest to Breton because of his apparent formalism, than to Freud. Far from being an unexpected or inspired revelation from another world of wonders, Roussel's discovery allowed him to do something much more important. It allowed him to elaborate new language-practices relating to a very rigid and deliberate conception of literary work which was incompatible with the uncertain adventures of free or 'liberated' investigation. Like Queneau and Leiris, who broke with or departed from the surrealist tradition over this very point, Roussel replaced the romantic doctrine of inspiration, which tacitly informed all surrealist research, with the rigorous and theoretically grounded perspective of an anonymous production in which the desire · of the author or 'director' has no role, or no central role.[17] In order to recuperate Roussel, surrealism, like the psychiatrists, therefore had to explain everything in terms of madness because madness made it possible to regard his diurnal and waking existence as a hallucinatory nocturnal life which was subject to the same necessities as a dream.

This recuperation was, however, obviously based upon a misunderstanding. For surrealism, the poetic act *par excellence* was an act which freed verbal expression from all formal rules so as to permit the emergence of an original and authentic content that could be grasped in a primal or wild state. Roussel, in contrast, was trying, in precisely the opposite sense, to reinforce the constraints that govern the

---

17 The point did not escape Leiris. 'Certain aspects of Roussel's work notwithstanding (the important role played by techniques of divination, the frequent appeals to wonders and legends), this work without chiaroscuro has an essentially positivist coloration and nothing we know about the life of this brilliant writer – not even the phase in which he was inspired by a sensation of "universal glory" – suggests that he should be credited with having any mystical intentions' ('Conception et réalité chez Raymond Roussel', *Critique 89*, October 1954, reprinted in *Roussel l'ingénu*, p. 80).

workings of language. In order to do so, he elaborated new rules based upon the elision of any primordial relation with a content or meaning. When he made deliberate use of non-meaning, he was therfore not trying to get at a different or hidden meaning that lay behind the apparent meaning of words and awaited an interpretation; he was trying to reach something that existed prior to all meaning, to reach the point where things and words communicate independently of the mediation of meaning.

In a crucial passage in his book, Foucault takes a stance on this point, and describes Roussel's approach in these terms:

What I see there is not automatic writing as such but the most conscious writing of all; it has mastered all the imperceptible and fragmentary play of chance ... It sets up a verbal world whose elements stand tightly packed together against the unforeseen; it has turned to stone a language which refuses sleep, dreams, *events* in general, and can hurl a fundamental challenge toward time. But this is accomplished by totally removing all that is random at the origin of everything that has speech, on that silent axis where the possibilities of language take shape.[18]

It is language as such, the fact that words exist and can be 'used', that belongs to the order of the pure event; far from surrendering to the random element in language, Roussel relates language back to the essentially aleatory nature of the order it constitutes.

If we go back to its source, the flow of words reveals its authentic nature:

It's not a night atwinkle with stars, an illuminated sleep, nor a drowsy vigil. It is the very edge of consciousness. It shows that at the moment of speaking the words are already there, while before speaking there was nothing. Short of awakening, there is no consciousness. But at daybreak the night lies before us, shattered into obstinate fragments through which we must make our way.[19]

Before speaking, there is nothing, no other world into which we could enter, giving ourselves up to the free figures of a nocturnal language. Nor is there any longer another language, a language before language, setting the ultimate limit to the movement of interpretation. Before language, there is only this nothing which is the absence of meaning. But if, before speaking, there is nothing, that is perhaps because language has 'nothing' other to say than the 'nothing' to which it responds. This is the pure language whose secret Roussel discovered.

18   *Death and the Labyrinth*, pp. 38–9.   19   Ibid., p. 39.

It speaks only about itself because it is not the expression of any preexisting reality to which it has been miraculously matched. And the plenitude of this language is, perhaps, the obverse of the emptiness of things. What it has to say is essentially that the fact of speaking has to do with the existence of a world which is not full of things and full of being, but with a world in which there is nothing.

A lesson in ethics: structures and death

Roussel turns literature into the singular experience of an ordeal, of an investigation into language's conditions of possibility. 'The only serious element of chance in language does not occur in its internal encounters, but in those at the source. These occurrences, both within language and external to it, form its first limitation. This is demonstrated not by the fact that language is what it is, but that there is language at all.'[20]

Yet in its most current usage, language does not seem to pose any problem at all. It functions as a system of indicators and constraints, and makes implicit reference to certain normative practices according to which things are both what they must be and what they are called. A spade is a spade. And so, over and beyond the particular significations it orders, language conjures up the representation, which is probably fictive, of a solid and flawless world which constitutes the horizon of all that is said. By relating language to itself and demonstrating that, ultimately, it says nothing but what it is, and by reconstructing the inner space within which it moves, literature introduces a freeplay into the system of significations. It therefore distorts or jams the system. As we have just said, in doing so it does not 'free' access to another, equally solid and colourful world that lends itself to representation; it undoes the apparently natural link between what seems naturally to connect words and things, and it thus reveals that it is not natural. This break comes about because the normal working of language has been rigorously disrupted; it stems from an elision of meaning which reveals the basic structures of language. We then understand that although language functions, it does not do so because of some preestablished harmony between sign and meaning expressing the substantial reality of a consistent world whose elements it designates. Its roots and origins lie in the freeplay

20   Ibid., p. 39.

indicated by the failures of representation that occur when the network of the signified slides over that of the signifier, when *billard* is transformed into *pillard*. By speaking of things in their absence, language, ultimately, says nothing but the absence of things.

The whole question is, then, whether this absence is relative, with things being absent only from language, or absolute, with things being absent from themselves, as language reveals them to be when its operations are traced back to its origins. Foucault speaks in this connection of 'the non-being that is activated when one speaks'.[21] In that sense, language's condition of possibility appears to be the existence of a world made up not of being, but of non-being. Rather than manifesting or 'reflecting' a reality that is the true property of things, the work of literature sets in motion a whole process of shattering and fragmentation. It creates 'a void towards which ... language rushes'.[22] Language seems to fill that void in such a way as to mask its emptiness, but if, like Roussel, we invert the movement, we see that language does nothing but talk about that void. It says things as they are, that is, as they are not.

Hence the idea that recurs throughout Foucault's book on Roussel: there is an essential relation which binds language up with death. 'It's everyday language ravaged by destruction and death.'[23] 'An internal dimension of language which [is] his own sentencing of that language to death.'[24] This sentencing to death of language is also a sentencing to death by language: it reveals not only the nothingness of language, but also the nothingness of which language speaks. That is Roussel's real discovery. 'Roussel invented language games that have no other secret outside of the process than the visible and profound relationship that all language maintains with, disengages itself from, takes up, and repeats indefinitely with death.'[25] 'The sovereign process which binds together with its blinding crystal, in its endless weaving, and in the depth of the mine, both fire and water, language and death.'[26] Roussel lived, so to speak, language's essential relationship with death: he experienced the deadly element in language. In that respect, his suicide was a literary act, and was inseparable from the link he had personally established with language. The act 'said' the same thing as his works.

There appears, then, to be a sort of unthought element [*impensé*] in language, and literature reveals it: it is because of that unthought

21   Ibid., p. 390.   22   Ibid., p. 53.   23   Ibid., p. 45.
24   Ibid., p. 45.   25   Ibid., p. 54.   26   Ibid., p. 73.

element that 'it' speaks [*ça parle*] from the depths of language, from beneath words. But what does it talk about? About that nihilating experience, of course; about death, which is the secret of any true language. Far from recentring the system of language on itself by restoring a meaning to it, the revelation of the unthought displaces it and unbalances it a little more. It makes it slide towards infinity and literally get lost in the sense that it loses its way, rushes to its destruction and eventually disappears. 'This subsurface language ... The language hidden in the revelation only reveals that beyond it there is no more language and what silently speaks within it is already silence: death is the leveller in this last language ... '[27] Language, all language, the whole of language, states the absence and emptiness of language, the void and the absence of which language is built: ' ... language moving towards infinity in the labyrinth of things, but whose marvellous and essential poverty forces it back on itself by giving it the power of metamorphosis; to say other things with the same words, to give to the same words another meaning.'[28] Literature exploits language's defining ability to absorb itself into its own absence, to abolish itself.

This is precisely the same thing that Mallarmé discovered in the ordeal he experienced during his nights in Tournon in 1863: poetry is the limit-form of language in which language says nothing; and it takes us to the frontiers of language and things, to the point where they become, or become once more, 'nothing', because they are nothing more than being said, or what is said of them. They are that nothingness. As a text included in Mallarmé's *Divagations* puts it: 'I say a flower ... the one flower that is absent from any bouquet.' Saying a flower means not only saying it in its absence, but saying it absent; it is to say its absence, that is, not only to declare its absence, but to say that it 'is' this absence, making it 'appear'.

Language, as ordered by nature when it breaks its rules, or, perhaps as ordered by nature when it introduces rules by disordering it, is an irreplaceable source of revelation because it gives access, not to the living reality of things, but to the emptiness of their death. It is out of kilter with a world that has lost its stability and its solidity because it has been emptied of its content and its meaning. The absolute experience of language is an asceticism which allows us to take stock of the facticity of the 'things' of which we speak. There is nothing

27 Ibid., pp. 66–7.   28 Ibid., p. 96.

beyond the things of which we speak and which, to the extent to which we speak them, are nothing because, ultimately, to speak is to state the emptiness or nothingness of all things. What literature does is to introduce us into the presence of that nothingness.

This is why the lesson in ontology taught by literature results in a lesson in ethics. For the figure of death that reappears on every page of Foucault's book is not the nauseating figure of a death that is undergone or suffered; it is that of a death which is at once known, recognized and mastered because it has been understood and deliberately controlled. It is a death which is not heavy, but light, which treads lightly on the surface of things and illuminates their reality with its singular light. In *Birth of the Clinic*, which was written and published at the same time as *Death and the Labyrinth*, Foucault derives the same lesson from the work of Bichat:

Instead of being what it had so long been, the night in which life disappeared, in which even the disease becomes blurred, [death] is now endowed with that great power of elucidation that dominates and reveals both the space of the organism and the time of the disease ... Death is the great analyst that shows the connexions by unfolding them, and bursts open the wonders of genesis in the rigour of decomposition: and the word *decomposition* must be allowed to stagger under the weight of its meaning. Analysis, the philosophy of elements and their laws, meets its death in what it had vainly sought in mathematics, chemistry and even language: an unsupersedable model, prescribed by nature; it is on this great example that the medical gaze will now rest. It is no longer that of a living eye, but the gaze of an eye that has seen death – a great white eye that unties the knot of life.[29]

The eye also belongs to Roussel, who 'opens up' language as though he were dealing with a corpse. Roussel's poetic gaze does for the space of words what the anatomical gaze of Bichat does for the space of the body.

It does the same thing for the space of things. It explodes it by emptying language and reality of their living substance because it regards them from the viewpoint of that 'great white eye that unties the knot of life'. This is the priceless lesson about things given by a gaze which has seen death:[30]

29 *The Birth of the Clinic*, tr. A. M. Sheridan (London: Tavistock, 1976), p. 144.
30 At the intersection between the history of the sciences and literary history, Foucault thus rediscovers certain of Georges Bataille's political intuitions, as we can see from this posthumous text: 'He who gazes on death and rejoices in that fact is already something more than an individual whose body is destined for corruption, as death's entry into the game has already projected him out of

From the Renaissance to the end of the eighteenth century, the knowledge of life was caught up in the circle of life folded back upon itself and observing itself; from Bichat onwards, it is 'staggered' in relation to life, and separated from it by the uncrossable boundary of death, in the mirror of which it observes itself.[31]

As practised by Roussel, literature too holds out to us that deathly mirror in which the network of things and events is dissolved: it teaches us to see things from the point of view of their death and, in doing so, it teaches us how to die.

himself, and into the glorious, laughing community of his fellows in total misery; as each instant drives off and annihilates the preceding instant, the triumph of time seems to him to be bound up with the conquest of his fellows. Not that he imagines that he can escape his fate through the substitution of a community that lasts longer than himself. Quite the contrary; he needs the community in order to become aware of the glory bound up with the instant that will see him torn from being ...' ('La Joie devant la mort', manuscript dated 1934, *Oeuvres complètes* vol. 2, Paris: Gallimard, 1970, p. 240). Foucault was probably not acquainted with this text, but he seems almost to be referring to it or echoing it in 'Préface à la transgression', which he wrote in tribute to Bataille in 1963, a year after Bataille's death. It contains a variation on the eye, which is a central figure in Bataille's literary thought: 'For the eye, death is not a constantly high horizon, but the point at which death is located in the hollow of all possible gazes, the limit it never ceases to transgress, which is raised up as the absolute limit in the movement of ecstasy that allows it to leap to the other side. The upturned eye uncovers the link between language and death at the moment when it represents the interplay between limit and being' (*Critique* 195–6, August–September 1963, p. 764).   31   *The Birth of the Clinic*, pp. 145–6.

II

❖❖

Towards a literary philosophy

❖❖

When we consider the poetic monument Foucault erected to the glory of Roussel in a text which is neither literary nor philosophical because it is located at a point midway between the two genres, we cannot but think of the work Heidegger achieved with Hölderlin, who was his constant companion on his philosophical journey from 1934 onwards. Both projects appear to be defined by the same speculative experience: listening to a madman speaking, listening to a man whose way of speaking escapes the conformist norms of 'speaking properly' and calls into question the normal, and which therefore also calls ways of thinking into question. Could the writer be the philosopher's madman? And could literature's position with regard to philosophy assign it the ambiguous position of a limit which is neither completely inside nor completely outside?

If, however, we restrict ourselves to such formulations, are we not in danger of reactivating an essentialist conception of Literature and Philosophy which attempts to establish once and for all the relation between the two? For there is madness and madness, and not all limits are of the same kind. Although Foucault appears to follow, using Roussel as an example, the approach taken by Heidegger, he does so by displacing it onto a different terrain, where it accedes to a new dimension: Roussel's gentle madness, with the derisory character that gives it its obviously critical function, is innocent of the reference to lofty, heroic and icy grandeur that characterizes Heidegger's Hölderlin. And we would try in vain to find in the reading undertaken by Foucault an equivalent to the essential 'Germanity' which Heidegger, rightly or wrongly, bestows upon his poet, for the inconsistent and gratuitous 'Frenchness' that seems to emanate from Roussel's puns is no more than a mask. The removal of the mask would reveal, in the absence of another mask, the void of an absence. In other words, the Roussel Foucault talks about cannot be recuperated by a hermeneutic interpretation. With their childish word-play and their formal research into the essence of language, Roussel's texts speak of death, and of nothing else: they say that all must pass away.

By ending our cycle of philosophical readings of literary texts with a study of the Roussel 'case', we seem to have completed a sort of theoretical journey leading from speculations about evolution ('roads to history') to variations on the theme of immanence ('into the depths') and then to a reflection on death ('all must pass away'). Evolution, immanence and death: if we link these notions, we seem to see the emergence of something resembling a message. It is as though these works of Literature, in the historic sense of that term as it has been defined and established over the last two hundred years, each gave their own version of a single discourse, which they share and which constitutes their 'philosophy'. That discourse might be summed up as follows: if we follow roads to history, we, go down into the depths, down to the point where all things must pass away.

If, however, we adopt this way of deciphering the philosophical lesson of literature, we come up against an enormous difficulty. In claiming to avoid it, we seem finally to have come back to the basic premises of a hermeneutic approach: the revelation of a hidden meaning. To profess a literary philosophy, and to assume that literature as such 'thinks', leads us to assert that it thinks something and therefore exposes us to the temptation to isolate that something from its texts in the form of a separable body of statements — *what* it is thinking — because it is a theoretical content which has a value and a meaning in itself. We thus succumb to the illusion of a literature that is full of philosophy in the sense that a form encloses a content which it holds and clothes, and which also gives it its essential truth. Precisely what role does truth play in literature? Does this truth result from a philosophical determination? And if that is the case, to what extent does that determination constitute the literary order as such?

A philosophy without philosophers

Why should philosophy take an interest in literature, and what forms should that interest take? Does this interest result solely from the universalist ambitions of philosophy which, having no particular object of knowledge, seems to have a natural vocation to look indiscriminately at all objects? That would imply that literature, like right or philosophy, is amenable to a philosophical recuperation designed to reveal its essential meaning, to give it rational foundations, and to determine the limits that restrict its endeavours. We could then speak of a philosophy of literature in the sense that we speak of a philosophy of right or religion: a philosophy of literature would give literature the status of a philosophical thought-object to be analysed alongside other objects, so as to make it state the forms of speculation that dwell silently within it, perhaps without its knowing it.

Such an approach looks very much like an attempt at recuperation or annexation which brings literature into the field of philosophical reflection in order to absorb it and, once the process of inclusion is complete, to make literature as such disappear, either by defining it completely in terms of a thought that remains external to philosophy, or by devaluing it by passing judgement on it from a transcendental viewpoint. This approach is unsatisfactory because it reduces the question of the relationship between philosophy and literature to a problem of positions: according to this view, our object is to assess the respective importance of spheres of influence or intervention, with a view either to integrating them (which is what happens when we rethink literary works in philosophical terms), or to establishing a relationship of exclusion between them (which is what happens when we trace more or less distinct lines of demarcation between what is and what is not philosophical in literature). We thus adopt either an extensive or intensive representation of the powers of 'literature' and 'philosophy' and reduce them to spatial determination, as though they were territories to be delineated, annexed, protected or defended.

To speak of a literary philosophy is to attempt to adopt a very different perspective to that corresponding to a philosophy of literature, and to pose the problem of relations between philosophy and literature in terms of production and not localization (delineation of sites). It is to make an investigation into the modalities, which are of necessity diversified, of how philosophy can 'do' literature and literature can 'do' philosophy. It means foregrounding the operational aspect which produces real works, which makes concrete the network within which literature and philosophy merge and mutually transform one another. It is within the work of literature itself that we will find indices of an intellectual productivity that should be of great interest to philosophy insofar as it can be seen as an on-going process of work, of production. And taking into consideration this essentially working aspect of thought is the way to look for the forms of an effective link between literature and philosophy.

What kind of thought is produced in literary texts? At first sight, we might identify it as a blind or mute thought whose uncontrolled emergence breaks the apparently continuous thread of their discourse, and opens up a new, transversal dimension within the texts. That dimension would correspond to what they think without realizing it, and therefore without saying it, or at least without saying it to themselves. Literary philosophy would then be the spontaneous philosophy of writers, in the sense in which we can speak of the spontaneous philosophy of scientists: it would be an effect of the theoretical ruminations which, beneath the manipulations of writing, replace writing within the space of a preconceived and therefore completely objectified 'knowledge'. As a result, we would have to speak of a sort of ideology of literature rather than of a literary philosophy; that ideology would be a body of statements, latent and anonymous, preceding the intervention of the poetic and narrative forms, and establishing the conditions for their every realization. Such an ideology would represent, in a necessarily allusive form, the non-reflexive – and, strictly speaking, non-philosophical – residue of the literary act. The only way that we could authentically philosophize about literature would therefore be to take a stance against the ideology that haunts it with its chimerical figures: in order to exorcise those figures, we would deny literature any right to think for itself, so as to protect its innocent beauty.

But philosophy is not literature's unconscious, and we do not gain access to it thanks to a theoretical analysis. Textual writing is not an analysand caught up in the great game of the other who helps it recover its lost or forgotten identity. For the thought that accompanies all literary works is not reducible to an external consciousness through whose intermediacy literature gives up its secrets and simultaneously admits that it is possessed by its secrets rather than in possession of them. It coincides with the constant self-reflection undertaken by literature as it produces its texts. In Sade, Flaubert, Roussel and Queneau, writing generates meaning, and that meaning is anything but latent, even if does take a careful and informed reading to see it. As it works on language as though it were a raw material with which it can elaborate its own forms, this writing reveals, with a view to their explicit theorization, the conditions of possibility and the limits that define the very order of language.

We therefore have to seek literary philosophy within literary forms, and not beneath what they seem to be saying; literary philosophy is thought which is produced by literature and not a form of thought that more or less unwittingly produces literature. It follows that it is not something to be extracted from those forms as though it were a foreign body which would be reconstructed through the intermediacy of a system of discrete statements. If we follow the roads to history into the depths, we reach the point where all must pass away: the formula with which we summed up the spirit common to the literary corpus we subjected to a philosophical reading has no value and no meaning in itself or independently of the works and texts which elevate it to a sort of veracity or veridicity. Content is nothing outside the figures of its manifestations: it coincides with those figures, as reflected in the movement that generates them. The 'message' could be described as being part and parcel of the vehicle of its transmission.

Literary writings exude thought in the same way that the liver produces bile; it is like an oozing secretion, a flow, or an emanation. All these terms evoke a continuous and gradual process which takes place insidiously at the level of a microscopic chemistry within the subtle parts of the textual organization and the cellular network that makes it up. The slowly accumulated, speculative sap is stored and concentrated in inaccessible reservoirs of signification and therefore remains unnoticed for long periods; it is then disgorged, overflowing with intentions and surplus thoughts which make its manifestations excessive, even abusive. The alternating pattern of retention and discharge means that literary philosophy is always either in excess of or inadequate to its expression, which never adopts the regular form of a measured and reasoned argument whose effusions are tightly controlled.

The same thing could be said without using metaphors: insofar as it is inseparable from the forms of writing which actually produce it, literary philosophy is a form of thought without concepts that is not communicated through the construction of speculative systems which liken the search for truth to a form of proof. Literary texts are the home of a form of thought which speaks its name without displaying the marks of its legitimacy, because its exposition is a form of theatricality. This form of thought tells its own story casually, with an ironic gratuitousness that is anything but naive or lacking in self-awareness or awareness of the limitations placed upon its obviousness. By producing such speculative effects, the work of literary writing opens up new prospects for philosophy, new fields of investigation that escape the strictly codified competence of professional philosophers. It reintroduces into the exercise of thought an element of play which, far from weakening its speculative content, encourages it, on the contrary, to follow unknown paths. At this point, we begin to see the truly philosophical effect of literature, which breaks up all systems of thought. No matter how exclusive they may seem to be to start with, literature introduces into them a collective and shared polyphonic reflection stemming from the free circulation of images and schemas of narration and enunciation, rather than from a strictly ordered deductive organization.

This breaking down of barriers has its effects on literature itself. Seen in the light of the speculative thought that circulates within it, the fabric of the text looks like a single network which transcends the individual intentions of 'authors'. Their ideological ambitions are absorbed and metamorphosed by the process of this subtle elaboration. When they write, they therefore think both less and more than they know, or would like to know, for this philosophy is a philosophy without philosophers, and it is irreducible to any particular project bound up with the initiative of its scribe. From this point of view, it is strictly meaningless to speak of the 'philosophy of Hugo', 'the philosophy of Flaubert' or 'the philosophy of Céline'. Literary philosophy is not even a common core that is shared by all these 'thoughts', or that can be identified with the specific relationship they have with the individual who gives them a voice; it is a philosophy that runs through all literary texts to the extent that they form a disparate and conflictual whole whose theoretical vocation is precisely to explain a shattered and differentiated multiplicity of thoughts which are grasped in their independent movement and which therefore exist independently of authors and systems. When authors speak and write, it is literature as such which is speculating as it establishes itself in the element of the philosophical, which exists prior to all individual philosophies.

The task of literature is, it would seem, to state the philosophical element in philosophy. What does this mean? It means that literature's specific relationship with the truth, which stems from the free play of its forms and the various modalities of its enunciations and which is characteristically ludic and gratuitous, is essentially critical: it coincides with the production of a sort of *Verfremdungseffekt* which, at the very moment when literature is reflecting upon its own discourses, introduces into its reflections an internal distance. That distancing makes it impossible to identify them with definitively closed and self-contained systems of thought. Literature is, so to speak, philosophy's *Threepenny Opera*.

In the final instance, all literary texts have as their object – and this seems to be their real 'philosophy' – the non-adhesion of language to language, the gap that constantly divides what we say from what we say about it and what we think about it. They reveal the void, the basic lacuna on which all speculation is based, and it relativizes individual manifestations of speculation. This ironic relationship with truth, which demands above all else a disabused interpretation, means that literary philosophy is an essentially problematical intellectual experience: it consists in revealing philosophical problems, expounding them and 'staging' them in the theatrical sense of the term, and eschewing any definitive, or supposedly definitive, attempt to resolve them, put an end to them and suppress them with arguments.

In this way, literary philosophy – and this would appear to be its essential lesson – also reveals the inseparable link between truth and history. The problematical thought which runs through all literary texts is rather like the philosophical consciousness of a historical period. The role of literature is to say what a period thinks of itself. The age of literature, from Sade to Céline, does not project an ideological message which demands to be believed on the basis of the actual evidence. If taken literally, the message seems to be patently inconsistent and incoherent. It projects an outline sketch of its own limits, and that sketch is inseparable from the introduction of a relativist perspective. What, from this point of view, is the philosophical contribution of literature? It makes it possible to relocate all the discourses of philosophy, in its accredited forms, within the historical element which makes them the results of chance and circumstances, the products of a pathetic and magnificent throw of the dice.

Ideas in letters

Philosophy and literature are like two sides of the same discourse. Their high and low points are inverted images of one another: what appears in one as plenitude and continuity appears in the other as a lack or an elision. When it is filtered through the modes of narrativity specific to literature, the attempt to rationalize that characterizes philosophical speculation and gives it homogeneity and logic is transformed into a lacunary, jerky and irregular exposition. Which is why the truth-effects produced by the movement of ideas emerge in an inverted form: they appear in the form of unfinished, incomplete and fragmented allusions which seem to be quite devoid of the logic of coherent arguments. And when philosophical expression itself borrows these rituals and speaks as history – one thinks of the astonishing fables told by Kojève or Nietzsche – or to sound like music – as in Wittgenstein's posthumous texts – it comes so close to the aesthetic phenomenon as to merge with it.

The philosophy of philosophers almost always presents itself as a discourse of legitimation: it is as though it professed that 'everything must become apparent', and as though it had to be understood as such. Literary philosophy, described here as the philosophical consciousness of a period extending from approximately 1800 to the present day, echoes this basic thesis with a ragged refrain: all must pass away. We find the same digestive fantasy in both Flaubert and Céline, and it supports a whole poetics: the writer 'swallows' everything. He digests the whole of reality, and everything that occurs or does not occur in it, in order to bring it up in a completely dematerialized form after an almost alchemical operation. That is the precondition for the transmutation of things into words. A dark light gleams from within literature. It traces the outline of a nocturnal and despairing thought which is terribly disquieting even – especially? – when it takes on banal, amusing or reassuring forms. From that point of view, it is Sade's texts that allow us to give Queneau's texts their full meaning; for all these texts speak, in narratives that are interrupted or suspended, of the end of history. Similarly, Bataille and Céline lead us to reread Hugo and Flaubert: a carnivalesque fascination plunges them into the same sewers.

Let us go back to the intellectual schema around which the presentation of the 'exercises in literary philosophy' proposed here is organized, in order to show, without adopting once and for all a reasoned exposition which would turn them into elements of a theory, how they are part of what we have termed a shared network. Literature as such has now been in existence for almost two hundred years, and it has always centred on a certain number of themes or obsessional figures around which it organizes its theoretical ruminations: excess and limit, when it is centred on a general rhetoric (illustrated here by the texts by Sade, Flaubert and Foucault); depth, when it is centred on a negative ontology resulting from the inversion of the values of above and below (as in Hugo, Bataille and Céline); and evolution, when it centres on a historical anthropology (as developed by Mme de Staël, George Sand and Queneau). Now a correlation is almost automatically established between these three perspectives, thanks to a system of references which has more in common with the poetic devices of rhyme, and with the specific effects of rhythm, anticipation and repetition they induce, than with a gradually constructed argument. It is thanks to this schema literature succeeds in thinking the basic problems of a historical world in a form which is not that of a reasoned doctrine.

The destruction of Spiridion's monastery in Sand's novel prefigures, for instance, the fire that destroys the Luna Park in *Pierrot mon ami*; when both history and the story are coming to an end, how can a literary book end, if not with a catastrophe, if not with an evocation of a world that has been destroyed or undermined by the circulation of the images which haunt it and condemn it to death? At a much more abstract level, the problem of communication between cultures, which gives *Corinne* its fictional fabric, is discussed at length in Sand's reflections about the themes of tradition and heresy in a fable which, like that elaborated by Mme de Staël, has an initiatory significance; and that same reflection seems to be continued in the various versions of *The Temptation of St Antony*, whose theoretical schema could well traverse the simultaneously historical and fantastic world constructed by Sand, even though it seems to unfold in a far-off time and place. It is not impossible to imagine certain episodes in Sade's *Cent Vingt Journées* taking place before the horrified gaze of Flaubert's 'hero'; couldn't they also take place in the slums of *Les Misérables*, on the edge of the City where characters who emerge from the shadows also set off on the perilous 'journey' that takes them 'to the end of night'?

We appear to find in Sade, Mme de Staël, Sand, Hugo and Queneau elements of a historico-social thought which, even though it appears in fragmentary form, directly governs the establishment of narrative structures; it is this which founds the economy of the 'one hundred and twenty days', in which knowledge and power are subordinated to the law of a narrative that takes the form of an organized progression; it also makes it possible to sketch the character of Corinne, who seems to be the concrete embodiment of the notion of cultural relations; it gives a content to Spiridion's secret, the revelation of which ultimately concerns the whole of humanity; it sends Jean Valjean off to explore the world of the abyss, where the customs and values of society will be both challenged and regenerated; it gives a dialectical dimension to the terrain that provides the setting for the adventures of Queneau's character Pierrot, who experiences the tensions provoked by the clash between a terrestrial and a celestial world. The alternation between the two is itself in a sense explained by the images discussed in Bataille's early writings, where the contradictory logic of above and below becomes the support for a poetics through which all the forces of the universe communicate as they are dispersed.

None of these ideas, which are embodied in images and represented by the movement of the letters which evoke them, can be reduced to the communication of some speculative message with a purely ideological content. Provided that it is rigorous, literary rhetoric relates to the ideology of an era only insofar as it brings it into conflict with itself, divorces it from itself, brings out its internal conflicts, and therefore makes a critique of it. Ultimately, we might say that rhetoric absorbs ideology and then exudes it in an unrecognizable form, in a form in which it ceases to inspire, or even require, open support. From that point of view, Roussel and Céline do as much as Mallarmé to illustrate the absolute nature of the act of writing, which both dematerializes reality and gives the thought suggested by a world devastated by words and events a phantasmagorical, incredible, unbearable appearance which is at once powerful and ludicrous, insensate and guilty.

From Sade to Céline, literature seems to have devoted itself to the exposition of all that should not be said. The images it sends back to us from the historical world in which we live are distorted and deformed, completely indecent and corrupt. It is as though the images had taken shape in a broken mirror in which the world is reborn larger than life in the pitilessly cruel and cynical light projected on it by the truth of a style. For the world would not be as true as it is if it did not also speak its name through books.

Index

Index